Kelly Sheridan
Central Washington Bouldering
Leavenworth & Gold Bar

Sharp End Publishing
Authentic Guides From Core Climbers

INTRODUCTION

CENTRAL WASHINGTON BOULDERING:
LEAVENWORTH & GOLDBAR by Kelly Sheridan

©2007 Sharp End Publishing LLC. All rights reserved. This book or any part thereof may not be reproduced in any form without written permission from the publisher.

Published and distributed by:
Sharp End Publishing LLC
PO Box 1613
Boulder, CO 80306
p. 303.444.2698
www.sharpendbooks.com

ISBN: 978-1-892540-48-5

Cover Photo Credits: Joel Zerr on the immaculate arête of Pretty Hate Machine (V8)
Photo: Max Hasson

Opening Page Photo Credit: Jessica Campbell on The Rubik's Cube V9
Photo: Brian Sweeney

All unlabeled photos throughout the book are credited to Kelly Sheridan

READ THIS BEFORE USING THIS BOOK
WARNING:

Climbing is a very dangerous activity. Take all precautions and evaluate your ability carefully. Use judgment rather than the opinions represented in this book. The publisher and author assume no responsibility for injury or death resulting from the use of this book. This book is based on opinions. Do not rely on information, descriptions, or difficulty ratings as these are entirely subjective. If you are unwilling to assume complete responsibility for your safety, do not use this guidebook.

THE AUTHOR AND PUBLISHER EXPRESSLY DISCLAIM ALL REPRESENTATIONS AND WARRANTIES REGARDING THIS GUIDE, THE ACCURACY OF THE INFORMATION HEREIN, AND THE RESULTS OF YOUR USE HEREOF, INCLUDING WITHOUT LIMITATION, IMPLIED WARRANTIES OF MERCHANTABILITY AND FITNESS FOR A PARTICULAR PURPOSE. THE USER ASSUMES ALL RISK ASSOCIATED WITH THE USE OF THIS GUIDE.

It is your responsibility to take care of yourself while climbing. Seek a professional instructor or guide if you are unsure of your ability to handle any circumstances that may arise. This guide is not intended as an instructional manual.

INTRODUCTION

Acknowledgements

I'd like to thank:

My family, Kelly, Connie, and Kara. None of this would have been possible without your love and support.

The O'Meara Family, Ralph, Donna, Kyle, and Kaylan. Thank you so much for opening your home to me, and accepting me as a member of your family. Kyle, you're my best friend and favorite person to go climbing with. I wish you the very best in life, wherever it takes you.

And Erin, for showing me true strength, and for following your passion.

I'd like to give an additional thanks to the following people, who were all helpful in the creation of this guide in some capacity, be it technical, informational or inspirational:

Joe Treftz, Joel Campbell, Cole Allen, Brian Sweeney, Joel Zerr, Max Hasson, Jens Holsten, Jessica Campbell, Drew Schick, Brian Behle, Scott and Susan Mitchell, Anita Snyder, Lisa Graham, Jeff Hashimoto, Ryan Hopkins, Viktor Kramer, Jeff Smoot, Dave Thompson, Gabriel Cisneros, Bob Buckley, Dick Cilley, Fred Beckey, Jason Duckowitz, Chris Kirschbaum, John Peak, Erik Lambert, John Joline, John Gill, John Sherman, Bobby Hardage, Todd Mannherz, Jackie Hueftle, Herman Feissner, Kristie Lonczak, Nico Muhly, Alexis C. Jolly, James Lucas, Coach, Dave Pegg, Cheryl Bogardus, Squamish Warm-Ups, Nathaniel, Jerry Moffatt, Ben Moon, Earl, Valerie, Coffee, Jerry Garcia, and Etna. Thank you all!

And of course, Fred and Heidi Knapp. Thank you both so much for giving this guide a chance, and for working with me throughout the entire process. I am so glad that we met and I wish you both nothing but joy and success for your family and company. Cheers!

> "The earth does **not withhold**, it is generous enough,
> The truths of the earth continually wait,
> they are not so conceal'd either,
> They are **calm, subtle, untransmissible** by print,
> They are imbued through all things conveying
> themselves willingly,
> Conveying a sentiment and invitation,
> I utter and utter,
> I speak not, yet if you hear me not
> of what avail am I to you?
> To bear, to better, lacking these of **what avail am I?**"
>
> -*Walt Whitman, from A Song of the Rolling Earth*

TABLE OF CONTENTS

0 INTRODUCTION ... 6
Author's Note 6, How to Use This Guide 8, Problem Names and Problem Grades 10, A Bit of History 12, Ethics 16, Climate 18

1 LEAVENWORTH ... 21
Introduction 22, Lay of the Land Map 23, Leavenworth Amenities 24

Icicle Canyon ... 29
Introduction 30, The Fridge 32, Starfox 34, YFAW 36, The Sleeping Lady 38, Mad Meadows 40, Clam Shell Cave 50, Barney's Rubble 54, Forestland 58, The Lonely Fish 66, Hook Creek Boulder 70, Straightaway Boulders 72, Rat Creek Boulders 78, JY Boulders 80, Carnival Boulders 84, Pretty Boulders 88, Twisted Tree 92, Little Bridge Creek Wall 96, The Machine Gun 97, The Sword 100, Egg Rock 106, Fuzz Wall 109, Tin Man 112

Tumwater Canyon ... 115
Introduction 116, The Torture Chamber 118, The Labyrinth 120, The Range Boulders 124, Beach Parking 126, The Beach 128, Pitless Avocado 135, The Driftwood Boulder 138, Jenny Craig 140, That Demon 142, Swiftwater 144

Mountain Home Road ... 153
Introduction 154, The Star Wars Boulder 156, The Pasture 159, The South Seas 162

2 GOLD BAR ... 167
Introduction 168, Lay of the Land Map 169 & 171, Gold Bar Amenities 170, The Camp Serene Boulder 173, The Beach Boulder 175, The Five Star Boulder 178, The Clearcut 182, The Forest 192, The Sanctuary 200

3 INDEX ... 209
Introduction 210, Lower Town Wall 211, The River Boulders 214

4 OTHER AREAS ... 215
Lake Serene 216, Steven's Pass 216, Alpine Lakes 216, About the Author 218, Index 219

INTRODUCTION

AUTHOR'S NOTE

Just before beginning work on this guide, I found myself sleepless at the Hueco Rock Ranch. Lying in my mummy bag in the midst of the nightly mayhem, I couldn't sleep, pondering my impending decision to share these areas with anyone I could. This was my second trip to Hueco, and it was giving me second thoughts about writing a guide.

The climbing that day had been, well… annoying. True, after the south-of-the-border-style bureaucracy, the problems were wonderful. But each wonderful hold was coated in a revolting paste of chalk-sweat. The landings were trampled and littered with tape and butts, and the abundance of tick marks made the beautiful formations look like walls in a gym. And every time I tried to rock climb, some sinewy chimp would hop up and bark beta at me, only to walk away spraying something like "yeah it's a cool problem, bra, but the original sequence is like six grades harder…" As I lay in my tent, I watched to one side as a group of college kids from Colorado blasted techno and gave each other high fives. On the other side, the standard misfits and bro-bros took turns leaping over the fire and asking each other "so whaddya wanna get on, dude?" I had even seen a guy that afternoon with gelled hair and gold chains, hauling around a boombox as he asked for a spot "on this easy V12 I'm gonna do." I mean… bouldering and hair gel? This was too much.

"Why on earth would I want to risk this happening to Leavenworth and Gold Bar," I wondered? It took me a few worried weeks to believe it, but the truth is, it won't happen. Both of these gorgeous areas are extremely spread-out, and can accomodate the small amount of people who'll even believe that boulders this good could possibly be found in central Washington. Sure, Squamish is just a few hours away, but that's the kicker: nobody's going to believe that these areas are even better. Furthermore, with Leavenworth's areas so scattered and diverse, a *real* guide will help get people on the good stuff and freed from overused areas like Forestland and Swiftwater. And a bigger, more-defined rock climbing user group may just be what preserves the bouldering in Gold Bar. In a way, Washington has come to embody this spirit of sharing for me. There have been so many moments when I've found myself just glowing about a problem, ripe with the desire to show it to others and share in their joy. And if it weren't for the altruistic friends who coaxed me to the area to begin with, showed me the fantastic boulders, and encouraged me as I thrutched my way up some of them, I would never have seen Washington for the bouldering paradise it is.

So welcome to Central Washington Bouldering, and the bounty of raw granite contained herein. If you wish there were more chalk, more spray, and more grades, then you may be lost – go ahead and return this book. If you've liked other bouldering areas but wished there were less people, less grime on the stone, and more, more, more boulders, then central Washington may be the place for you. Happy Climbing!

Kelly Sheridan
October 31, 2006

Johnny Goicoechea flashing the sit-start to Tin Man (V7)

INTRODUCTION

HOW TO USE THIS GUIDE

So you've got this book, you've traveled to Leavenworth or Gold Bar, and you're psyched. But how do you get to the boulders? I've tried to ensure that any practical climber can find each and every area in this guide despite such common limitations as the utter lack of compatic orientation, daylight, and even literacy. Regardless, I'm confident that numerous members of our noble clan will venture beyond the conceptual continuity of the text, finding themselves hopelessly lost.

The Bird's Eye View

For each area covered in this guide, I've provided an overview map along with a verbal description of the approach. I've aimed for total simplicity when creating the overview maps, which is probably why they're totally cluttered. The maps are 'overviews' both in presenting an overhead or "bird's eye" view of the area, as well as in the sense that they show other aspects of the overall area on the same map as the topos themselves. Parking areas are marked with mileage information, and approaches are noted in detail. In the maps, trees near boulders are precisely placed, while those along trails or at the edges of areas are not. Photographs of an area or useful landmark are occasionally also included in the chapter introductions. Be sure to check out both the map and the description before you're driving to the boulders.

Once you make it to the rocks themselves, you're in pretty good shape… You're just one step away from tracking down that "savagely heinous testpiece" you've been reading about. Fortunately, the fine areas in this guide tend to have independent, obvious lines (striking, even?), and you won't be spending much time figuring out which feet are and aren't allowed for the B-H-Z variation to "Rufus's Eliminate." Problems are indicated with a number on the overview maps, each with a corresponding description in the text. You know the deal. For less obvious climbs, or just to highlight neat features, photographic 'topos' of certain problems have also been included. A picture's worth a thousand words, yes, but many of the bouldering areas in this guide are constantly changing, especially in Leavenworth. Holds break, moss returns quickly, and seasonal change, fires, and floods all impact the landscape of Washington's bouldering areas. So bring your sense of adventure!

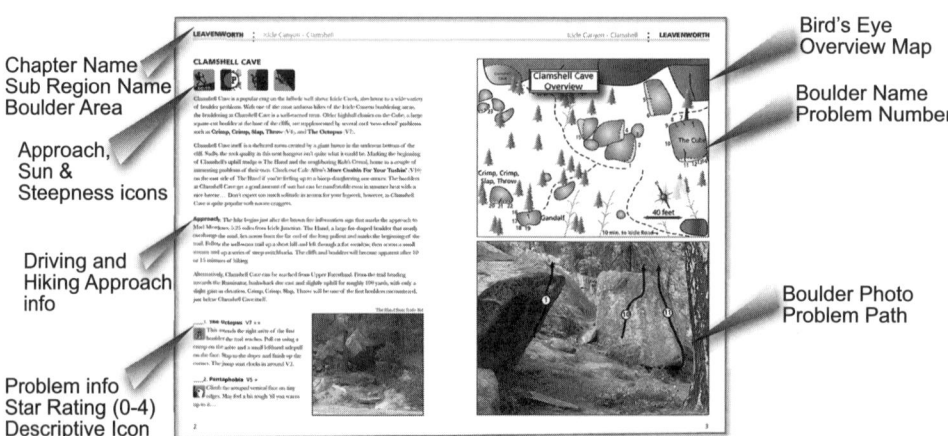

INTRODUCTION

Icons

Icons are used at the beginning of each bouldering area to familiarize you with the essential information at a glance.

Approach Information and Time

Easy   Moderate   Difficult

Sun Exposure

all-day sun   all-day shade   AM sun   PM sun

Rock Steepness

Slab   Vertical   Steep   Roof

Nature of the Climbng

Crimpy   Powerful   Pumpy   Technical

Bouldering Icons

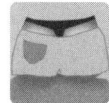   
Sit Start   Bad Landing   High Ball   Odd Ball
                                         odd in character for the area

Star Ratings

I've given each problem a star rating, which is some sort of subjective measure of the quality of aesthetics and movement on the route. But just like with V-grades, my opinion in these ratings shouldn't dictate your choice in climbs. I tend to like most problems, so the star ratings really just serve to highlight the ones I thought were the coolest, and to excuse the horrible ones that I probably liked anyway. Each problem is given 0-3 stars, which basically break down as follows:

0 STARS: Problems without a star are ones you'll probably pass over. They are low, chossy, dirty, low-angle, or all of the above. This doesn't mean that they're not worth doing though – a fun endurance-training "ugly circuit" could include all the zero-star problems in several areas...

★ **STAR:** Problems with one star are definitely worth doing, but just aren't the best around.

★★ **STARS:** Problems with two stars are pretty awesome. Think of them as three-star problems that didn't make the all-star team.

★★★ **STARS:** Problems with three stars are classics. Special priority was given to old-school problems, problems with an interesting story, highballs, steep problems, long problems, problems with good rock quality, and, as these things go, the scrappy few established by this egotistical guidebook author. Three star problems are the ones you simply must try. If you have to work on one of these even just a little bit, it will make your day.

INTRODUCTION

PROBLEMS WITH PROBLEMS?

PROBLEM NAMES
"Unknown" is not the preferred nomenclature, dude.

The issue of problem names presented a bit of a dilemma in the writing of this guide. The bulk of Leavenworth's boulder problems haven't carried a name down with them through the years, and all but the super-sick problems in Gold Bar are without known names. I've tried my best to track down first ascensionists and extract some sort of name from them. But many of central Washington's wonderful problems are quite old, or weren't named to begin with… In order to avoid publishing a guidebook full of unnamed problems, I've gone ahead and made up names for scores of problems. Some, like "Tree Crack," aren't very inspired, while others involved a bit more of a creative process, like "Han Solo's Lightsaber Tournament." While I conferred with other local boulderers in these areas, and I can't take credit for all the bad puns, I'll happily take all the flak for my diabolically egotistical actions in re-naming certain routes. If you feel you've established a problem incorrectly named/credited in this book, please feel free to drop me a line and let me know. A subsequent edition of this guide may include more accurate problem names. Please write to:

Kelly Sheridan
c/o Sharp End Publishing LLC, PO Box 1613, Boulder, CO 80306

PROBLEM GRADES

If the naming of all these boulder problems was something of an obstacle, cataloguing their grades presented even more of an anxiety-producing nightmare. Rename someone's choss pile, and they'll get over it. But screw up the grade, and they'll be bashing me on the internet long after this guide is even in print!

I've included a real-deal V-grade for every established boulder problem in this guide. Suffice to say, this wouldn't be a very popular guide without John Sherman's Hueco Tanks grading scale. In fact, without it, the entire world of bouldering would be quite different these days. Many climbers began climbing with V-grades, have watched their progression through V-grades, and have come to take these 'objective' measurements very seriously. Unfortunately, bouldering is not an objective experience. It is a highly subjective, pointless, and fundamentally physical activity that continues to resist quantification. How can I help other climbers transcend the base pleasure of numbers and discover "the kinesthetic soul of the art," while still providing the numbers we all love to bicker over? This is my dilemma.

More than anything else, I've strived to make the V-grades in this guide a consistent judge of difficulty within the areas covered in this guide. But more than any other area, I've used Hueco Tanks, the birthplace of the V-grade, as a rough yardstick for grading problems. I have personally climbed most of the problems in this guide, and attempted every single one. I've also consulted with other area climbers, to the limit of their patience, in an effort to make the grades in this book *accurate*.

INTRODUCTION

Many of Leavenworth's grades have been modified since the most recent publication of **Leavenworth Bouldering**, hopefully with a general increase in precision. If it was V3, it's probably now V4 and if it was V10, it's probably now V9. Many of Gold Bar's problems had not been graded, and my grades might seem off because I was having a good day or a bad day. I must beg a little understanding from each and every one of you: If a certain problem's grade doesn't seem quite right to you—please—don't sweat it. If it felt a little easy for the grade, pat yourself on the back. Great job! If it felt too tough, realize that it shouldn't detract from your experience or your self-worth as a climber. No biggie! Force yourself to imagine the area without any numbers—the goal is to have fun, right? Which climbs are the most inspiring? Which look like fun challenges? The goal is to have fun, right???

"Welcome to the smorgasboard that is bouldering. The boulderer picks a problem from the menu, **tastes the moves**, digests the sequence, then kicks back on the summit with a pleasant fullness. Shortly thereafter, out plops a V-grade, and not surprisingly, the bigger the grade, the more stink it causes. Strangely, at this buffet, most climbers act like flies, preferring to **buzz around the grade**, rather than the entrée."

- John Sherman, "To V or Not to V."

photo: Timothy Kemple

INTRODUCTION

A BIT OF HISTORY

LEAVENWORTH

Most Washington-area climbing histories start with Fred Becky, Wes Grande, and Jack Schwabland's 1948 ascent of Midway (5.5) on Tumwater Canyon's Castle Rock. This landmark climb was the first technical rock climb in the Leavenworth area, and ushered in an era of exploration and development in both Tumwater Canyon and the "Casmere Crags" of the Enchantments region. This initial buzz of development continued into the 1960s and resulted in the first white-man's ascents of most of the area's prominent towers and peaks by Beckey himself. Leavenworth's famous multi-pitch showpiece, Outer Space (5.9), was first climbed by Beckey and Ron Niccoli in 1960, and later freed in 1963 by Beckey and Steve Marts. A year later, the stale logging town of Leavenworth adopted the Bavarian 'theme.' Imagine what the town must have looked like then, a general store and a few old diners with fancy new Bavarian signs!

The Peshastin Pinnalces and the now 'lost' Chumstick Snag also received reasonable amounts of attention during this time. In 1949, Pete Schoening climbed the Trigger Finger formation at the Pinnacles, an ascent that may have been the first in Washington to employ bolts for protection. This relic was unfortunately destroyed when the tower collapsed during a winter storm in 1979 – a testimony to the rock quality in Peshastin! In 1974, Peshastin saw another landmark climb with Don Harder's free ascent of Bomb Shelter, perhaps the state's first 5.11. Fred Beckey and Erik Bjornstead's 1965 Guide to Leavenworth Rock Climbing Areas became Leavenworth's first guidebook, as well as the state of Washington's.

The 1970s and 80s saw the development of most of Leavenworth's established climbing, and is probably the only time there was anything of a climbing 'scene' in town. Leavenworth was a very different place then, as were the Tumwater and Icicle Canyons. Gustavs used to be Das Berghaus, a casual burger joint where climbers would hang out. Rumor has it that you were once able to trade climbing pictures for food – check out your server's expression if you try that one today! Icicle Creek Canyon also saw much change during the first part of the 1980s, when much of today's private land saw development. Before the extensive privatization of the lower Icicle, climbers could essentially go wherever they wanted, and climb on whichever rocks they wished. Many of the *backyard* boulders in the stretch of road following the Fridge Boulder are home to historic problems that have been off-limits since this time. This time of privatization also ushered in the era of no trespassing and no camping signs in the Icicle, and dramatically changed the nature of the canyon.

Some of the oldest established bouldering in the area can be found at Swiftwater in the Tumwater Canyon, and at the Fridge, Bolt Rock, The Pumphouse and Barney's Rubble in the Icicle. It's worth noting that two of the above areas are now off-limits, further victims of privatization. The 1990s saw the development of major bouldering areas like The Beach, Mad Meadows, and Forestland. Clamshell Cave, the JY Boulders, Egg Rock, Fuzz Wall, and similar smaller areas also saw new

INTRODUCTION

problems during the 90's, though the actual timeline is a bit hazy. The devastating Rat Creek fire of 1994 left a good deal of Icicle Canyon charred and smoldering. Many climbing areas were affected, and the entire canyon was closed until the following spring for restoration efforts and salvage logging.

The late 1990s saw the beginnings of Leavenworth's new-school bouldering era. Frequent visits by then-teenagers Cole Allen and Johnny Goicoechea resulted in the establishment of many of the area's harder lines, including The Sail (V9), Goicoechea (V9), and later, Musashi (V9) and The Peephole (V10). Other climbers actively developing boulder problems around this time included Greg Collum, Damian Potts, Ben Shrope, Chris Kirschbaum, and Ryan Paulsner. In the summer of 1999, locals Jeff Hashimoto and Damian Potts developed the bulk of the bouldering at Mountain Home Road, including such classics as Darth Maul (V5), Emperor's Lightning (V7), and Punk Ass Kid (V6).

The turn of the century also saw the self-publication of Leavenworth Bouldering, a.k.a. A Cheesy Guide to Pleasing Rock, by the late Damian Potts. Subsequent editions drafted by Leavenworth Mountain Sports' Alec Gibbons and Brian Behle have led to the guide's fifth edition of 2004. Most visitors to Little Bavaria's boulders have benefited from the happy rantings of this storied pamphlet. Leavenworth's 'old' guide sports a ton of character, and without it, Central Washinigton Bouldering would not be a reality. Check it out someday, if you can, and while you're at it, pick up Viktor Kramer's Leavenworth Rock. It's the definitive guide to Leavenworth's roped climbing, and also makes a valuable tool for the boulderer seeking to develop new areas.

The last few years have seen a surge in new development in the Leavenworth area. In Icicle Creek Canyon, new spots like The Sleeping Lady, The Pretty Boulders, and Tin Man have popped up, and established areas like the JY Boulders have been expanded dramatically. Tumwater Canyon areas such as The Labyrinth, The Range Boulders, The Beach Parking Area, The Pitless Avocado, Jenny Craig, and That Demon have all also seen development in recent years. Many of these 'newer' areas may even have seen bouldering activity in the past but have been forgotten, the slow march of time returning them to a 'natural' state. Active boulderers who've made extensive contributions in the last few years include Cole Allen, Kyle O'Meara, and Kelly Sheridan. A wide range of especially difficult problems can also be credited to Joel Campbell, a talented climber who has had as large an impact on Leavenworth bouldering as anyone else. With the publication of **Central Washing-**

INTRODUCTION

ton Bouldering, Leavenworth should see an increase in general traffic, as well as (hopefully) a bit of a shift away from over-trafficked areas like Swiftwater and Forestland. The area has such a rich, diverse array of offerings, so go climb on something you've never been to before—today!

GOLD BAR

The climbing history in Gold Bar is a bit harder to pin down. It's unclear how long people have been monkeying around below Zeke's Wall, but it's been some time — check out the abandoned mine on the way up to the western hilltop parking for a tangible sense of Gold Bar's history. While the swooped granite of Zeke's Wall saw small amounts of development in the 1980s and 90s, it doesn't see much traffic these days, perhaps due to the arduous approach and the lack of available route info. To initial developers, the bouldering in Gold Bar's Clearcut and Forest areas has been known since even before the area was clear-cut. When logging activity devastated the Clearcut area in 2000, route development began to stretch further uphill, with major developers including the likes of Joel Campbell, Cole Allen, Gabriel Cisneros, and the enigmatic Duckowitz. Aside from the main Gold Bar bouldering, the discovery of satellites like the Five Star Boulder, the Camp Serene Boulder, and the Beach Boulder can all be attributed to Bob Buckley, the former two receiving colossal cleaning effort by his hand. Much like Leavenworth, the bouldering at Gold Bar is visited by many different users with little or no connection or discussion. And even more so than in the Leavenworth section, the given names for many of Gold Bar's problems may impose on an older name. The information in this guide is merely a selection of Gold Bar's established bouldering—which is fantastic—but someday, the area will deserve a stand-alone guide of its own. Why should we dwell on the past when the future's so exciting??? Get out there!

> "A big attraction of Leavenworth bouldering is the **unexplored, adventurous side** of the sport here. If you are willing to clean a little, there is a plethora of gems to be unearthed. Just don't be surprised if some old timer interrupts your spraying about your 'new route' to show you a picture of it being **sent in EBs** 20 years ago."
>
> - Brian Behle, *Leavenworth Bouldering*

INTRODUCTION

ETHICS... A PLEA

During the course of writing this guide, I've spent a great deal of time wandering around these bouldering areas. No two spots are the same. The landscape, rock type, and atmosphere of Central Washington's bouldering areas are all exceptionally varied, one of the coolest aspects of this amazing region. Visiting and revisiting every area in this book, notebook in hand, I'd walk from boulder to boulder checking my maps and scribbling shorthand notes in the margin: "SDS sidepulls crappy" or "tall v2 actually v5." Just like the setting, the character of the climbing is different at every area in this guide, each classic guiding the climber through unique movements, each obscure choss-pile a fun, new adventure.

Wandering around the quiet north side of Swiftwater one sunny afternoon, I was reflecting on this remarkable diversity in our array of bouldering spots... our 'bouldering gardens.' I'd always liked the way that phrase sounded, and the charmed quality it seemed to lay upon the stones. Absent-mindedly bending for a scrap of tape on the ground, I looked around at the worn dirt of the trail, the chalked handholds on the boulders beyond, and the piece of trash in my hand. Seeing evidence of our climbing everywhere, I came to realize a deeper meaning in the term. Just like gardens, bouldering areas are by no means examples of unchanging, frozen Nature, but are completely affected by human presence and human intention. From conscious actions like cleaning, climbing, and coating the stone in chalk to the inevitable effects of our pads, pets, and flip-flops, we determine every aspect of the appearance of our climbing areas. Even the lush vegetation surrounding me was only a result of logging and forest fires—more human impact. I was struck by the realization that to some degree, this is the one quality shared by every bouldering area in this guide. Each area is different, yes, but they have all been markedly saturated with the presence of boulderers.

As it relates to the 'ethics' of our bouldering, this is sort of a tricky realization. We are told to "leave no trace," yet it seems like traces are the least we can leave. Furthermore, looking around, all we can see are the traces of other climbers. But to write these areas off as lost, already 'unnatural'—the "it's screwed anyway" approach—is irresponsible and stupid. Precisely because these areas are so affected by us as boulderers, it's crucial for us to minimize our impact when visiting them. As conscious, intelligent beings, making good decisions about the nature of our impact is the very least we can do. These larger-than-life rock gardens literally become extensions of ourselves—why would we treat them as anything less?

Observing the following recommendations is a good way to ensure that you're minimizing your impact as a boulderer and leaving the area the way others would want to find it. Be conscious of your actions, and demand the same of those around you. These boulders are all of 'ours,' and it is our privilege to visit them; let's treat them well.

• Stick to established trails, no matter how faint, and don't contribute to erosion by short-cutting switchbacks.

INTRODUCTION

• Please carry out ALL of your trash with you. Yes, this includes tape, cigarette butts, beer cans, chalk wrappers, anything and everything. Super-cool climbers keep an empty plastic bag in their pack and pick up trash even if it isn't theirs. It's a very cheap way to feel good about yourself.

• If you've got to use tick marks, be discreet and please have the decency to brush them off before you leave. There aren't many better ways to seem like a dumbass than being seen flailing for the edge of a six-inch rookie-stripe you've ground into the face of a beautiful boulder. Be a better climber and use your eyes and brain—or stay in the gym.

• Chipping, drilling or gluing holds to the wall will not be tolerated. These days, reinforcing holds with glue definitely falls into this category. Broken holds, no matter how unfortunate, are part of the evolution of a climb. If a climb doesn't go, just climb on one of the thousands of other boulders around. And no pof.

• The same ethic goes for cutting trees: just find another problem to climb. Playing lumberjack isn't a cardinal sin among the vast clear-cuts of Washington's National Forests, but ugly stumps reflect poorly on climbers, and the tree in front of your uber-proj may already be useful for cleaning or descending from established problems.

• Blowtorches have become a trendy way to appear gung-ho during a winter session, but the truth is they don't work very well and they absolutely do damage the stone. If you've got to resort to pyrotechnics, stick to the slopers and please be gentle. The Icicle is home to plenty of pink-hued, sandy boulders whose surface has been destroyed by the high heat of forest fires—think about it. For dry winter rock, why not just find a nice south-facing hillside like, say, all of the bouldering in Icicle Canyon or Gold Bar?

• Last but not least, don't make poopy in the boulders. Take a walk (away from water, genius) and dig a six-inch-deep hole. Fill it in when you're done. There are also free, easy-access toilets at Eight-mile and Bridge Creek Campgrounds in the Icicle, and at The Beach and Swiftwater parking areas in the Tumwater.

> "When in doubt, erect scaffolding."
> *-Warren Harding, Downward Bound*

INTRODUCTION

CLIMATE

No doubt about it, the weather in the great Northwest gets a bad rap. Non-residents enjoy citing statistics like "It rains 364 days a year in Seattle" and other such propaganda in justifying their reluctance to visit… I've even wondered if these rumors weren't started by the region's more selfish climbers, unwilling to share the Cascades' bounty with the rest of the country. All speculation aside, the truth of the matter is that the Northwest's notorious rain is really limited to the coast. East of the Cascade Mountains, one finds a desertous climate like that of Central and Eastern Washington. As a rule of thumb, the internet's enigmatic "30% chance of precipitation" forecast typically means a bit of rain for Gold Bar, but clear skies when it's given for Leavenworth.

Leavenworth is located in the 'rain shadow' at the very eastern edge of the Cascades. Such related perks as minimal summer rain, relatively mild snowfall, and more pronounced seasonal change all come as part of the package. Leavenworth is often sunny and dry when Seattle and the western slope are buffeted by Pacific rains. Spring and fall are the ideal seasons to climb in Leavenworth, with average highs in the 60s and 70s and little precipitation. The summer months can be quite warm, with highs in the 80s, 90s, and even the triple digits. June through August are still good times to visit, but be prepared to take a break and have a swim to escape the mid-day heat. Fortunately, these badass boulders never 'close,' and many enjoyable summer sessions have been had by headlamp and lantern. Winter conditions in Leavenworth can be pretty grim, but with the exception of a couple months around the turn of the year, intrepid boulderers can find dry rock during most of the snowy season. Some of my best climbing days in the Icicle have been sunny, 20 degree February afternoons. When you can find dry, south-facing rock, winter conditions are perfect in Leavenworth: the canyons are empty, the friction immaculate, and the feel of rock under your fingertips a long-lost delight. Snowshoes help to make the boulders as accessible as ever, and many layers keep you nice and toasty as you go around sending your old projects like Bruce Banner with PMS. For most climbers, however, Leavenworth is a three-season area, the climbing season overlapping quite nicely (or unfortunately?) with the town's busy festival schedule.

Gold Bar lies on the western slope of the Cascades, and experiences quite a different climate than that of Leavenworth. The spring and fall are a bit rainier than on the east side of the mountains, and it is sometimes pouring in Gold Bar whilst sunny and warm in Leavenworth; even weirder is when the opposite occurs. Still, Gold Bar remains an ideal three-season area, the summer highs rarely dipping into the 90s and the boulders remaining tolerable even on the warmest afternoons. The winters in Gold Bar are typically quite wet, though the area doesn't see too much snow accumulation. The unique side-by-side landscapes of Gold Bar's Clearcut and Forest boulders also add to the area's versatility: the open, south-facing Clearcut dries quickly after rainstorms, while the Forest area remains cool and shady during the warmer months. Gold Bar is a great place to escape Leavenworth's scorching summer temps, but make sure to check the forecast before visiting in the early spring and late fall.

Johnny Goicochea on The Coffee Cup (V10)   Photograph by Brian Sweeney

INTRODUCTION

BEST OF THE BEST

V0	The Rail, *Barney's Rubble* South Seas Arête, *South Seas* Slickfoot Sanctuary, *Sanctuary*		**V7**	The Doja, *The Forest* Premium Coffee, *Swiftwater* Obesity, *The Clearcut*
V1	Fun House Stairway, *Barney's Rubble* Beach Slab, *Beach* The Cube, *Clamshell Cave*		**V8**	WAS, *Straightaways* Pretty Hate Machine, *Prettys* Ground Zero, *Five Star*
V2	The Sleeping Lady, *Icicle* The Classic, *Sword* Royal Flush, *Swiftwater*		**V9**	Pimpsqueak, *Mad Meadows* Musashi, *Egg Rock* Lighten Up, *The Forest*
V3	Slice of Cake, *Barney's Rubble* The Sword, *Sword* El Navigante, *The Forest*		**V10**	The Peephole, *Mad Meadows* Droppin' the Kirschbaum, *Lonely Fish* The Equinox, *The Clearcut*
V4	Darth Maul, *Star Wars* Fridge Right, *The Fridge* Serenity Now, *Camp Serene*		**V11**	The Cotton Pony, *Straightaways* Ebriosity, *Five Star*
V5	Footless Traverse, *Swiftwater* Sinistricity, *The Clearcut* Road to Zion, *Sanctuary*		**V12**	The Practitioner, *Forestland* The Ram, *Mad Meadows*
V6	Answer Man, *Straightaways* Slingblade, *Pitless Avo.* Ryan's Problem, *Camp Serene*			

> "Writing about climbing is boring. I would rather go climbing."
> – *Chuck Pratt*

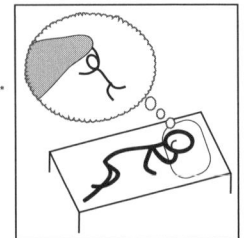

Pirate Max Hasson poised to attack **The Octopus** (V7)   Photograph by Jackie Hueftle

1 · Leavenworth

LEAVENWORTH : Introduction

LEAVENWORTH

The small tourist village of Leavenworth is nestled at the edge of the granitic Wenatchee Mountains, on the eastern edge of Wenatchee National Forest. Bizarre festival weekends, a cornucopia of kitschy gift shops, and an abundance of overpriced hotels make this faux Bavarian village in the middle of the state Washington's second-biggest tourist destination.

Visitors to the town who don't appear horribly out of shape are probably there to sample many of the outdoor recreational activities available in and around the town. Each weekend brings a handful of folks to Leavenworth to climb moderate trad climbs in the Icicle and Tumwater Canyons, and an even smaller number for the bouldering.

Leavenworth's bouldering has been well-known but underappreciated for many years, with most people seeming to equate it to much of the area's roped climbing: off-vertical, sandy, and not especially exciting. John Sherman wrote in **Stone Crusade** that "Swiftwater Picnic Area is one of the few spots with enough problems to constitute a circuit, and even then one must hunt around in the woods for some of the boulders." The venerable Verm must have donned an awfully thick pair of beer-goggles for his visit, as Leavenworth's canyons are literally lined with a diverse array of pristine bouldering areas! In addition to Little Bavaria's well-traveled classics, the area is home to many newer problems that are steep, high, or hard—or all three.

For a good sampling of the bouldering here in Leavenworth, make an attempt to check out all three major areas in this guide: **Icicle Canyon, Tumwater Canyon, and Mountain Home Road**. Each actual area within these chapters sports a unique blend of stone, a pleasant setting, and at least one problem guaranteed to make your day. So go and explore for yourself—who knows what you might find???

Getting There: Leavenworth is located roughly in the center of the state, some two-plus hours east of Seattle on US Highway 2.

From Seattle and other points west, you've got two options:
• If you're closer to I-90, head east on this interstate over Snoqualmie Pass to exit 85 near Cle Elum. Follow WA-970 N/E for 10 miles until it becomes US-97 N. Rt. 97 takes you over Blewett Pass and intersects Rt. 2 after some 35 miles. Turn left onto Rt. 2 and follow it for five minutes to the town of Leavenworth.
• If you're closer to I-405, take that north to exit 23 onto WA-522, which intersects US-2 in the town of Monroe after about 15 minutes. Leavenworth lies another 75 miles east on Rt. 2, past Gold Bar and over Steven's Pass. US-2 is also the best way to Leavenworth from points north of Seattle—take I-5 to Everett and hook up with Rt. 2 there.

From Spokane and points east, you'll be traveling west on I-90. Take exit 151 onto WA-281 north and follow it for almost 10 miles. Then turn left onto WA-28 and drive for 34 miles to US-2. Leavenworth is another 15 miles west on Rt. 2.

Vancouver, BC
U.S. / Canada Border
97
Monroe
Leavenworth
Spokane
522
2
Seattle
2
90
97
28
281
90
195
Ellensburg
12
5
N
Yakima
82
97
Portland, OR
84
60 mi

To Seattle and I-5
Leavenworth Area Overview
Wenatchee River
Tumwater Canyon
Chumstick Hwy
N
2
Leavenworth
2.5 mi
Wenatchee River
Icicle Creek
Icicle Creek Rd
E. Leavenworth Rd
Mt. Home Rd
2
Icicle Canyon
Mountain Home
Eightmile Road
97
To Cle Elim and I-90

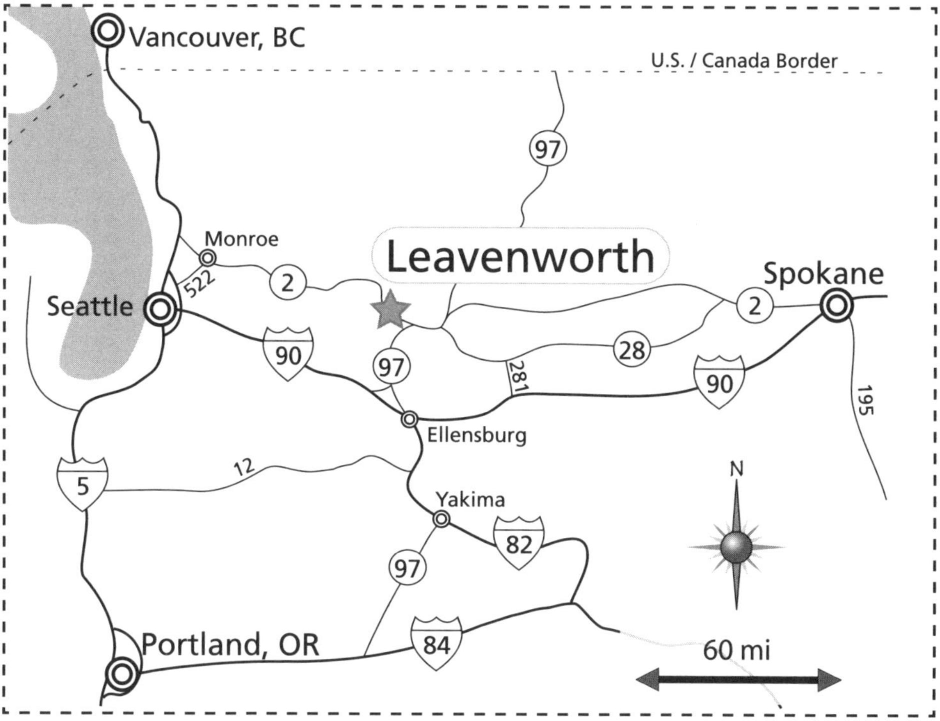

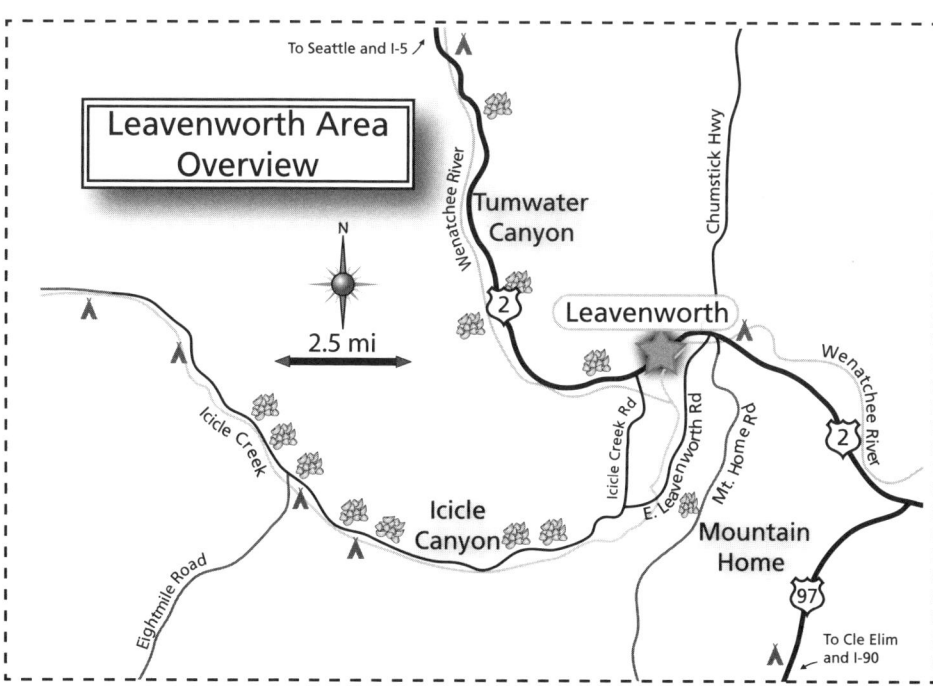

LEAVENWORTH : Introduction

LEAVENWORTH AMENITIES

As soon as you hit Leavenworth's crowded Front Street on a busy Saturday, you may be asking your friends "So… just how far away is Squamish?" Fortunately, the same things that make Leavenworth a strange and busy little tourist trap make it quite hospitable to the traveling rock climber. If you can get over the traffic, the tourons waddling on your feet, and the hokey German music blaring nonstop during festival weekends, you will easily find everything you need (and more) in town.

LODGING

Hotels: Leavenworth has more than its fair share of hotels, most of which are on Rt. 2 or Commercial St. If you can afford it, The Sleeping Lady resort is located 2.5 miles up Icicle Canyon, where you can pamper your aching muscles in an outdoor granite hot tub just minutes after sending. For the rest of us, there are a multitude of campgrounds in the Leavenworth area.

Camping: The KOA behind Safeway on the east side of town is the closest to Little Bavaria, but at $22.00 a night and up, it isn't highly recommended unless you just have to have a cable TV hookup for your Winnebago. Coming from the west and want to crash quickly? The Tumwater Campground is 10 miles west of Leavenworth on Rt. 2, with standard amenities and fancy flush toilets.

Icicle Canyon Camping: If you're looking for a little peace and quiet, as well as some first-rate scenery, camp in the Icicle. There are six National Forest campgrounds in Icicle Canyon, excluding the Black Pine Horse Camp. The two closest to town, Eightmile and Bridge Creek campgrounds, open in mid-April when the upper spots are just beginning to thaw. Both are also within walking distance of bouldering, an obvious plus. All campgrounds have vault toilets and tested water, and cost $12.00 per site ($13.00 for Eightmile). Icicle Canyon's "No Overnight Camping" signs can seem a bit unwelcoming at first, but there are still some good free sites to be found, especially after the road turns to dirt—for starters, try the pullouts on the right in the mile or two following the Rock Island Campground. **Please do not camp in the Forestland parking area or at any area in this guide.** Even badass professional climbers have been rousted for 'illegal camping!'

CAMPGROUNDS BY DISTANCE FROM LEAVENWORTH

Campground	Distance	Notes
KOA	0	(in town)
Eightmile	7.1	
Bridge Creek	8.5	
Tumwater	10	(in Tumwater Canyon)
Johnny Creek	11.5	
Ida Creek	13	
Chatter Creek	15	
Rock Island	16.5	

H2O

To stock up on water, try any of the campgrounds in Icicle Canyon, or the hose on the side of the 76 station at Icicle Junction. If you need to clean up a bit, showers can be procured at the KOA midweek for $5.00 apiece plus tax. Swimming in the river's also a great way to fake some personal hygiene when it's warm enough. Make sure you swim upstream (west) of Leavenworth in the summer, unless you want to bathe in the untreated sewage flowing your way from the kid's beach at Pioneer Park. There are some great swimming holes in the Tumwater Canyon; the parking for the Beach area is a great place to start.

LAUNDRY

Sadly, Leavenworth's sole laundromat bit the dust some time ago, and the nearest place to do laundry is in neighboring Peshastin. Drive 4.0 miles east of town on Rt. 2 and take the left turn for Peshastin. Turn left after passing under the train tracks and the Laundromat will be on your right after four blocks. For a more scenic return route, continue straight on North Road until it ends. Turn left onto the Chumstick Highway, which soon intersects Rt. 2 in Leavenworth.

GROCERIES

Located just off Rt. 2 on the east end of town, Leavenworth's Safeway chain is a pretty generic modern supermarket, with the exception of the Bavarian-themed paintings on the exterior of this pre-fab behemoth. For a bit more character and a great beer selection, check out Dan's market next to Der McDonald's on Rt. 2.

NEED GEAR?

Leavenworth is home to two gear stores: Rt. 2's Leavenworth Mountain Sports and Front Street's Der Sportsman. The latter is slightly more geared towards the tourist dollar, but you aren't going to find a really hard-core climbing shop in town. Head to Der Sportsman for shoe rentals or the best deal on block chalk, but hit up Leavenworth Mountain Sports for beta or to buy gear like shoes and pads.

INTERNET

Last but not least, access to the mighty Lethe of information: where to go for your email, weather, and slander fix. Leavenworth's public library is quite pleasant, and your only chance to use the internet without a handy laptop computer. There are four terminals with a maximum use of 30 minutes, and there is typically no wait during weekdays. The library also offers a wireless internet signal. If you're looking for free wireless internet on Rt. 2, check out the 76 station at the corner of 9th, or the Icicle Coffee Roasters by the mini-golf on the west side of town. If fast-food ambience and bourgeois spending are your thing, the Starbucks on Rt. 2 offers T-Mobil wireless internet for a price. But seriously, come on.

THE BEST OF LEAVENWORTH

Best Burger:	The Heidleburger, Rt. 2
Best Lazy Breakfast:	The Renaissance Café, 8th St.
Best Lunch Deal:	$2.50 Subs @ Dan's Market, Rt. 2
Best Quick Munchies:	The Gingerbread Factory, Front St.
Best Pint:	Uncle Uli's Pub, 9th St.
Best Last-Minute Coffee:	O'Grady's Pantry, Icicle Rd.
Best Swords:	The Australian Store, Front St.

LEAVENWORTH : Introduction

ACCESS: SPECIAL CONSIDERATIONS

Current situation: The access situation for Leavenworth's bouldering areas is good but not perfect. Perhaps Leavenworth's greatest blessing is that the neighboring Wenatchee Mountains are just within the edge of Wenatchee National Forest. But while much of Tumwater Canyon is National Forest land, Icicle Canyon includes many small pockets of private land. Most of the bouldering areas in this guide are in the clear, but several are threatened and some have already been lost.

Historic areas like the Pumphouse (a.k.a. The Government Boulders), and the wide field of boulders across from Icicle Island are now posted against trespassing. Other spots on private property, like the Footbolt Dyno and the area around Bolt Rock, have seen new development within the last year and are now considered off-limits to boulderers. A sizeable victory for Leavenworth rock climbers was won in May, 2005 with the **Trust for Public Land**'s purchase of Icicle Canyon's Sam Hill property. The effort to protect this 40-acre plot, which includes the Fridge Boulder and several popular trad crags, was led by the **TPL**, the **Washington Climber's Coalition**, and the efforts of **local climbers**.

Future: What can we do as boulderers to help preserve access to the bouldering areas in Leavenworth? Joining the **WCC** is a good idea, for one. When you're out climbing, pay attention to your presence in the area, and what kind of mark you will leave. Park your car well away from private property, driveways, etc, and always use established pullouts where you will be completely off the road. Stick to established trails. If you're exploring, take the time to avoid crossing private property

Cole Allen bouldering in 2001 at the now off-limits Bolt Rock area.
Photo: Kyle O'Meara

Introduction : **LEAVENWORTH**

even if it means going the long way. At sensitive areas bordering private property like the Millennium Boulder and the Pretty Boulders, take care to keep a low profile and minimize your impact.

Access conditions may have changed since the publication of this book. It is your obligation to be aware of current access status and to behave responsibly. In sensitive areas, less is more; it's best to respect private property and avoid creating a nuisance, letting the battles be fought by organized coalitions such as the **WCC**.

27

OTHER CONSIDERATIONS

Back Off! A coiled, defensive Rattlesnake at the Hook Creek Boulder.

Besides the dreadful threat of new "No Tresspassing" signs appearing in the Icicle, Leavenworth offers little to worry about. The town is extremely safe and generally quite friendly towards its outdoor-tourism industry.

As with most climbing destinations, vehicle break-ins can and do occur in all three of the areas in this chapter. Keep all valuables at home or well out of sight, including all those shiny metal objects used to scale rocks. Even in the Tumwater Canyon, car windows have been smashed simply for climbing gear, so why give them a reason?

Kelly Sheridan rockin' out on the Sleeping Lady (V2).
Photo: Todd Mannherz

Besides the occasional car thief, the main concern of the Leavenworth rock climber is a slightly more civilized animal, the rattlesnake. These gray-brown buggers are seen from late spring to late summer, most frequently on the south-facing hillsides of Icicle Canyon. Rattlesnakes have been spotted at most areas in Leavenworth, hiding from the sun in bushes or rocky caves. In attempt to conserve energy, many won't begin to rattle without provocation, instead sitting coiled and waiting like camouflaged land mines. Snakes will often sense the vibrations of your footsteps and start to escape well before you approach, so tread heavily, and never step where you cannot see. Those overgrown patches of the Forestland and Mad Meadows trails that block the view of your feet also make for ideal rattlesnake terrain. Snakebite kits are available at Der Sportsman for about seven bucks and come with instructions for use. In the event someone is bit, call ahead to the **Cascade Medical Center** (509 548-5815) or **Wenatchee's Central Washington Hospital** (509 662-1511) and have them begin mixing the antivenom. Less than 1% of treated rattlesnake bites are fatal.

Bears are also present around Leavenworth but aren't a real problem for hikers and campers in the area. Food is fine left in vehicles overnight, but ought to be hung if camping away from the car. Take care to make plenty of noise around dawn and dusk, especially if moving swiftly, to avoid startling Yogi. You won't like him when he's angry.

LEAVENWORTH-1
ICICLE CANYON

Johnny Goicoechea on the Teacup project in Upper Forestland, one of Leavenworth's finest Photo: Brian Sweeney

LEAVENWORTH : Icicle Canyon

ICICLE CANYON

Icicle Canyon is the heart of Leavenworth bouldering. Beginning a few miles from town and stretching almost to the 10-mile marker, The Icicle is lined with small roadside areas and larger hilltop clusters, each possessing a slightly different blend of granite.

While more concentrated areas like Mad Meadows and Forestland have become relatively popular in recent years, The Icicle is rife with smaller spots where the boulderer can find solitude. Further up-canyon, older areas like The Sword and Egg Rock are home to great medium-sized circuits as well as some difficult testpieces. Newer areas like the Straightaway Boulders, JY Boulders, and the Pretty Boulders are also home to some new-school classics just waiting to be climbed on.

For folks willing to hike to new problems, the Icicle has some of the most potential of any area in this guide. The tough-to-access south side of Icicle Creek is relatively untapped, with only several established bouldering areas and many obvious *leads*. The Icicle is a true boulderer's paradise, offering a lifetime's worth of climbing in a beautiful, accessible setting.

Icicle Canyon is also the center of Leavenworth's vibrant outdoor recreation scene, and can feel downright crowded on summer weekends. Hikers, backpackers, kayakers, mountain bikers, trad climbers, bird watchers, campers, and others all use the Icicle for their outdoor pursuits. Midweek and during the winter, however, the canyon is much quieter, even to the point of seeming empty. The Icicle is also home to yuppie vacation homes, hippy-types dwelling in yurts, and the ubiquitous drunken bubbas. I've even met one young man who had made an extended trip to Icicle Canyon to prospect for gold. The ability to absorb so many different people and present such an isolated feel is part of what makes the Icicle so special. Please be respectful of others in the canyon, keeping in mind that you represent just one of a wide range of user groups.

Approach: Icicle Road leaves Leavenworth from Icicle Junction, by the 76 gas station and the mini-golf on the west side of town. All mileages for climbing areas are given from this intersection with Rt. 2. The brown roadside mile markers in Icicle Canyon aren't 100% accurate, but can be quite helpful in getting your bearings. As you travel up most of the canyon, the road heads northwest; for the sake of simplicity in description, Icicle Creek is always south of the road, and points down-canyon are always due west. The best way to find the bouldering areas in Icicle Canyon is to read the area directions and then use the mileage to locate some sort of landmark. Unfortunately, the best landmarks for some areas are adjacent areas; between-area mileages are provided for this purpose, though they won't be precise enough for the tough-to-find areas. With time, each spot will become obvious and you'll be able to impress your friends by rattling off area after area as you zoom down the canyon.

Icicle Canyon Mileage Chart

A From Icicle Junction
B From Alpine Lakes Bulletin Board
C From Previous Area

	A	B	C
The Fridge	3.4	-1.0	NA
Starfox	3.6	-0.8	0.2
YFAW	4.3	-0.2	0.7
Sleeping Lady	5.1	0.5	0.7
Mad Meadows	5.1	0.5	0.0
Clamshell Cave	5.2	0.6	0.1
Barney's Rubble	5.5	1.0	0.3
Forestland	5.7	1.2	0.1
The Lonely Fish	5.8	1.3	0.1
Hook Creek Boulder	6.0	1.5	0.2
Straightaway Boulders	6.1	1.6	0.1
Rat Creek Boulders	6.8	2.2	0.7
JY Boulders	7.1	2.5	0.3
Carnival Boulders	7.4	2.9	0.3
Pretty Boulders	7.7	3.0	0.1
Twisted Tree	8.2	3.7	0.7
Little Bridge Creek Wall	8.5	4.0	0.2
The Machine Gun	8.7	4.1	0.2
The Sword	8.8	4.3	0.2
Egg Rock	9.0	4.5	0.2
Fuzz Wall	8.2	4.7	0.2
Tin Man	9.3	4.8	0.1

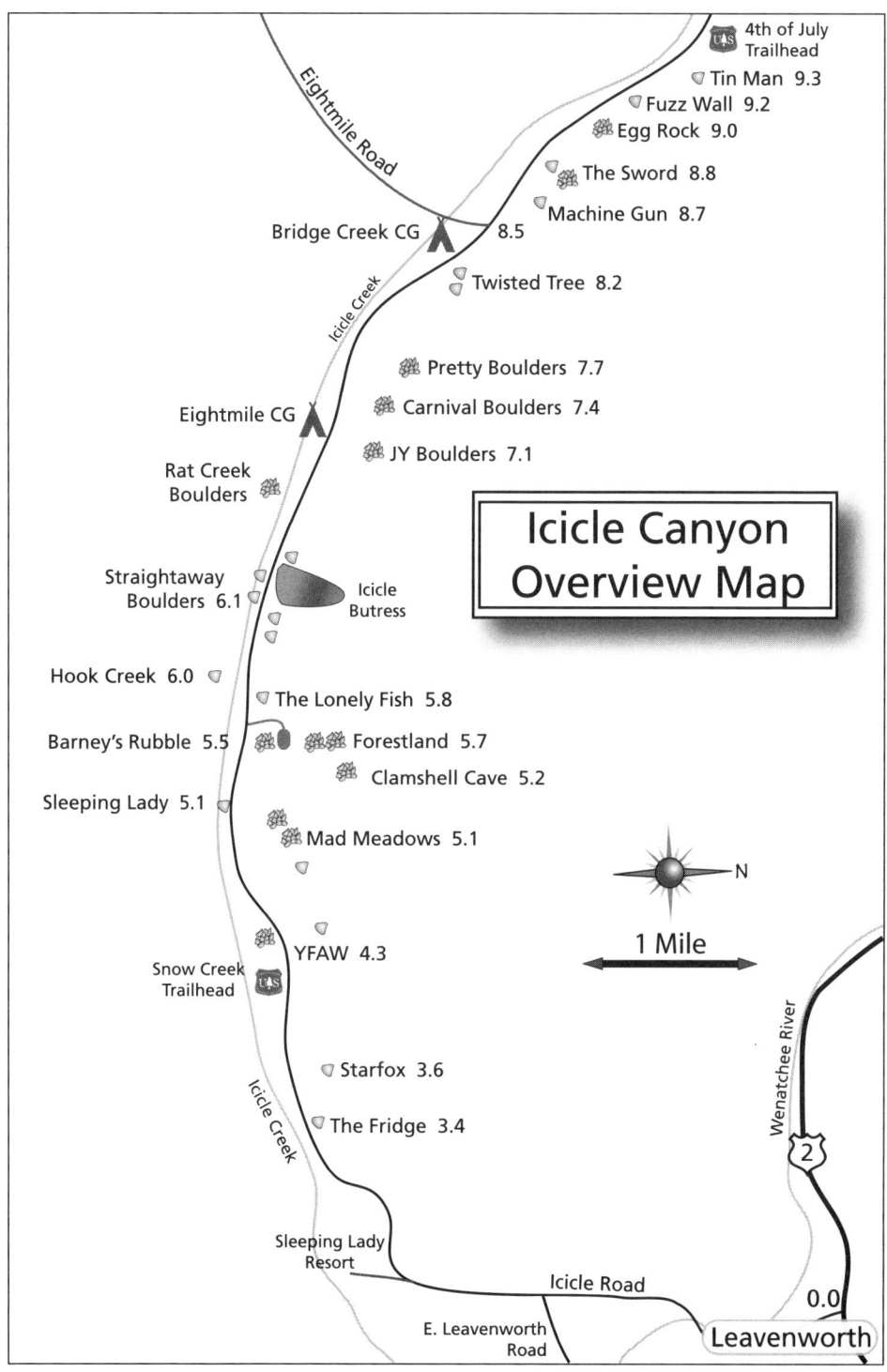

LEAVENWORTH : Icicle Canyon - Fridge

THE FRIDGE BOULDER

The Fridge boulder is the closest Icicle Canyon bouldering spot to Leavenworth, and one of the most historic. Its proximity to town as well as to the road make it a popular evening spot for those looking to crank after work or a day of route climbing. The boulder is in a south-facing corner that receives some winter sun, but the shady side is where the goods are; the **Fridge Center** (V4) and **Right** (V4) lines are aged Leavenworth classics, two proud ticks for any visiting boulderer. The Fridge vicinity has some potential for new routes, especially at the top of the steep gully and below the Trundle Dome crag. Access to the Fridge and its surrounding area was permanently secured in 2005 as part of the Sam Hill purchase by the Trust for Public Land and the Chelan-Douglas Land Trust, thanks largely to the efforts of local climbers and the Washington Climbers Coalition.

Approach: The Fridge is located 3.4 miles from Icicle Junction, and visible on the right side of the road. Park in the pullout on the left just before the boulder—it is the pullout directly after the lefthand pullout with the gated bridge marked "US Property - No Trespassing." Please cross the road carefully and help keep this popular, high-visibility spot clean.

___1. **Cool Down** V0- ★

Traverse up and left on the juggy rail, mantling whenever you feel the inclination to do so. This is also the standard downclimb for the boulder.

___2. **Cellar Door** V3 ★

Climb awkwardly over the overlap on the right side of the corner.

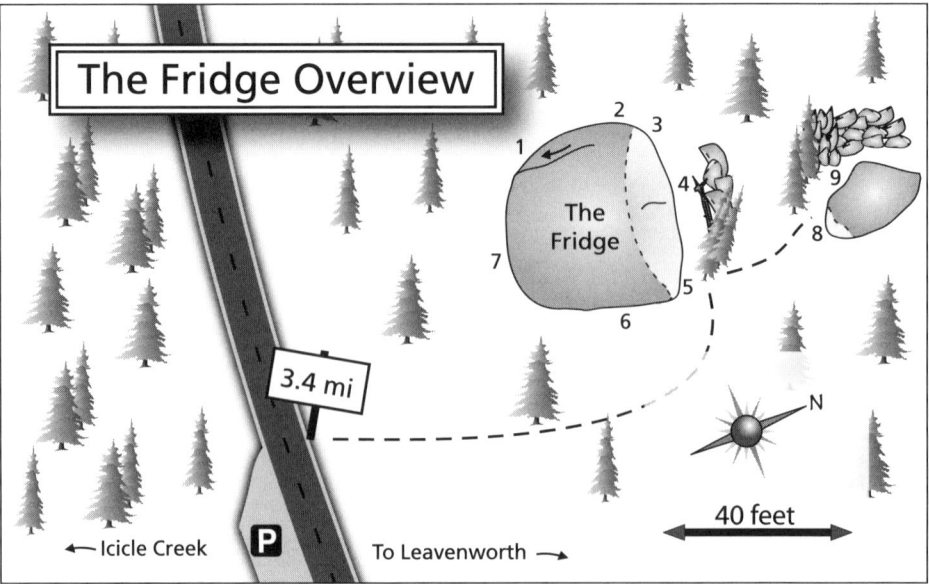

___3. **Fridge Right** V4 ★★★

Climb the slopey arête from a small crimp around the right corner. Make a tough barn-door move to a good hold on the corner, then finish up and left with some burly heel-hooking. A great sandbag.

___4. **Fridge Center** V4 ★★★

Start on crisp pinch/crimps in the center of the face. Maneuver past the tricky fingerlock and big underclings to jugs on top of the huge block and top out.
Variation (V5): Begin as for **Fridge Center** and make an iron-cross move to the good corner hold on **Fridge Right**, finishing up that problem. Definitely a bit reach-dependent.

___5. **Fridge Left** V8 ★★

Begin low on the left arête with your right-hand on a decent gaston edge. Slap to the good sloper on the right face, then climb to a super high left-hand crimp around the arête. Finish straight up on the corner; classic!

___6. **Fridge Door** V2 ★★

Start on the right side of the tall thin face, climbing straight up to grasp the left arête, finishing with an easier topout. Great balance practice. **Variation** (V1): To use the slabby footholds with a good 'railing,' begin on the left side of the face and follow the arête up and right to the top.

___7. **Fridge Slab** V0 ★★

Climb the high slab on the roadside face of the boulder. Can you do it without using your hands?

___8. **The Lizard** V5 ★

Start crouched with two low opposing edges. Paste your feet on, slap to the crimp and top out up the short corner.

___9. **Jumping Spiders** V4 ★

In the middle of the face left of **The Lizard**, grab two opposing sidepulls, paste those feet on, and lunge for the juggy lip. It's closer than it seems!

STARFOX

Starfox is another single-boulder area, sporting just one lonely problem. Established during the winter of 2005, it's pretty new to the area, though this may be owing to the unfortunate nature of the climb. Starfox is a beautiful overhung dihedral with crisp salt-and-pepper granite edges… but the crux is sneaking around the edge of an adjacent boulder without dabbing, especially frustrating for taller climbers. Save this one for a little treat when you've seen most other areas, or when it's too snowy—Starfox is well-sheltered and stays dry during most of the winter.

Approach: Drive 0.2 miles past the Fridge Boulder, and park in the Mountaineer's Dome pullout on the left, 3.6 miles from Icicle Junction. Keep an eye on the steep hillside on your right; Starfox is 60 yards uphill, a large slabby boulder with a dead log perched on top. Head straight over the right side of the small roadcut, passing a buried pipeline easement halfway up, and approach Starfox from the right. Remember to wave to the climbing classes scattered along the easy cracks uphill on summer weekends.

____1. **Starfox** V6 ★★

  Start on the chest-high crimp rail on the left side of the dihedral. Climb back and forth between small, positive crimpers in the dihedral until you latch a beefy left-hand sidepull. Keeping your rump off of the rock behind you, climb up to the jug, dyno for the lip, and top out.

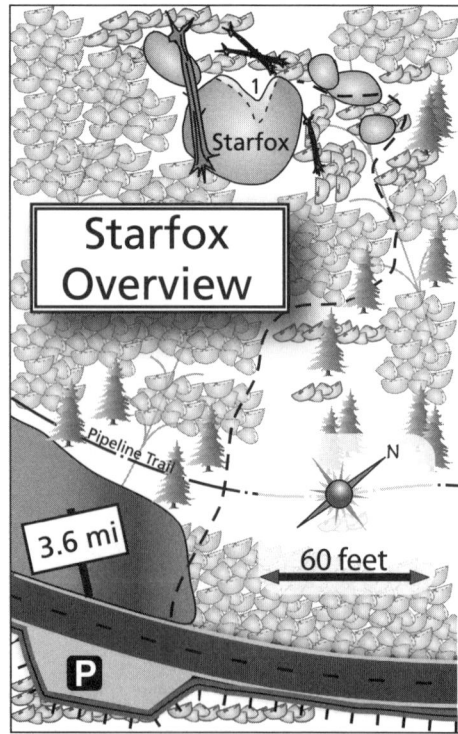

LEAVENWORTH

A rare view of a wonderful climb: Robert T. Hardage on The Sleeping Lady (V2)

LEAVENWORTH : Icicle Canyon - Your Friends Are Watching

YOUR FRIENDS ARE WATCHING

Your Friends Are Watching is found directly uphill from a small collection of riverside blocks (The Government Boulders) located just after the Snow Creek trailhead. Unfortunately, **Your Friends Are Watching** (V6) and **Nobody's Watching** (V5) are the only climbs in this section that can be visited legally. The riverside boulders are located on Icicle Irrigation Division property and are posted against trespassing. Included here for historical purposes only, the Government Boulders are home to the **Pumphouse** (V2), one of Leavenworth's classic old-school challenges. While there may be a way to access the Government boulders without passing "No Trespassing" signs, the area is definitely off limits. Vehicles parked at the pullout do attract attention, and sheriffs have been spotted peering down the hill.

Approach: The parking pullout for **Your Friends Are Watching** (and the Government Boulders) is located on the left side of the road 4.3 miles from Icicle Junction. It is the first pullout after the Snow Creek trailhead, and also makes for a good spot to shirk the cumbersome Forest Service parking fee. To find **Your Friends Are Watching**, walk roughly 20 yards further up-canyon, cross the road, and follow the rough trail up a steep talus slide. YFAW is the stout boulder located in an alcove just behind a huge tree. There is also a good deal of potential on the plateau above this tiny area to reward the hardcore hiker.

The Government Boulders are downhill and slightly upcanyon from the pullout, on the other side of signs that clearly say "**No Trespassing, Icicle Irrigation Div.**" Try pleading ignorance on that one...

____1. **The Pumphouse** V2 ★★★
A.K.A. **The Sandbox**. This old-school classic starts on the left arête of the tallish face adjacent to the gravel access road. Climb the arête and face using large flat holds to a committing finish. A fun variation eliminating the arête bumps the difficulty up a notch.

YOUR FRIENDS ARE WATCHING

____2. **Your Friends Are Watching** V6 ★★
Start sitting on the left side of the flat platform with a good edge. Climb the short overhanging face on nice crimps to a jug at the lip. F.A. Kyle O'Meara.

____3. **Nobody's Watching** V5 ★
Climb the narrow overhanging face from a chest-high jug. May need a little cleaning... grade unconfirmed.

LEAVENWORTH : Icicle Canyon - Sleeping Lady

THE SLEEPING LADY

Welcome to Washington Bouldering... **The Sleeping Lady** is perhaps the best climb in the Universe, undoubtedly Leavenworth's finest easier climb. This gorgeous line of river-polished jugs overhangs the turbulent rapids of Icicle Creek. Like the serene retreat a few miles closer to town, the Sleeping Lady gets its name from a certain resemblance in the ridgeline of Wedge Mountain at the southern mouth of Icicle Canyon. Most recently 'discovered' in 2004 by Kyle O'Meara, this roadside gem is the perfect scenic warm-up or cool down for the confident boulderer. When you're not climbing, be sure to savor the view of Wedge Mountain, the beautifully-sculpted granite across the stream, and the energy of the rushing water echoing through this small amphitheater. The Sleeping Lady is annually inaccessible during the better part of the spring; during the flood season of 2006, it was at one point half-submerged and not totally dry until mid-July! This fantastic hang is a great first stop in Little Bavaria…

Approach: The Sleeping Lady is nestled beside the parking pullout for the Mad Meadows area, 5.1 miles from Icicle Junction. Park on the left side of the road roughly thirty yards before the brown wooden sign containing Forest Service fire information for Icicle Canyon (This sign contains various messages during the summer months, but is regularly blank during the winter). A few short trails lead down to the Sleeping Lady from the east end of the pullout.

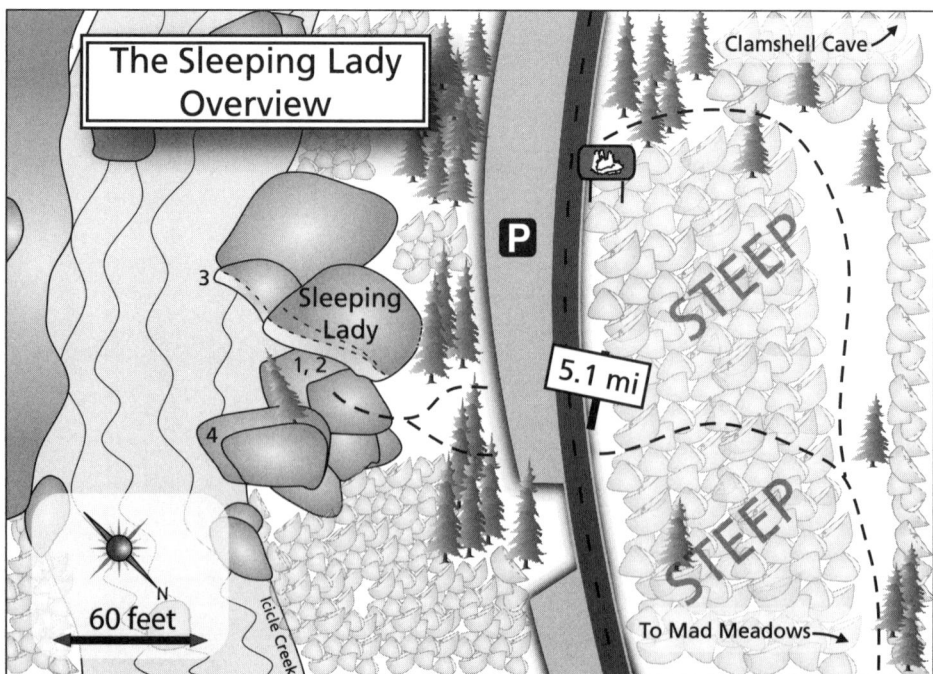

Icicle Canyon - Sleeping Lady : **LEAVENWORTH**

___1. **The Sleeping Lady** V2 ★★★
Start on the little platform at the edge of the stream, grab the lowest polished shelf, and make increasingly larger moves up the overhanging blocks. After a committing lunge to a huge hold, climb right to rock up on jugs and top out slightly left. The start is annually inaccessible during a portion of the spring thaw. A fall from anywhere on this climb is highly inadvisable!

___2. **Sound Asleep** V1+ ★
Start as for **The Sleeping Lady**, but at the second flat shelf traverse right on jugs instead of lunging straight up. Move right to the thin left-facing flake in the scrunched corner and finish with a nice mantel on the juggy lip above.

___3. **Sleeping Lady Extension** V2 ★★
Scramble down the upstream side of **The Sleeping Lady** to access the start of this problem. Begin on the sharp corner overhanging the stream in a good left-hand sidepull and climb rightwards around the lip to the start of the previous two problems. Finish as for **The Sleeping Lady**, or for the full pump value, continue right to **Sound Asleep**. A late summer problem, and another good one not to fall from.

___4. **The Pee Problem** V1 ★
To reach the riverside start of this prolem, traverse carefully left from the middle of the short descent to **Sleeping Lady**. From a small platform, climb straight up the sloping shelves to a slightly insecure topout. What's that smell???

LEAVENWORTH : Icicle Canyon - Mad Meadows

MAD MEADOWS

This is one of Leavenworth's premier bouldering areas, home to classic moderates and some of the area's sickest hard problems. Located on a flat plateau above Icicle Road, Mad Meadows is a nebulous group of boulders stretching from the dense first cluster to the distant Pimpsqueak area some 10 minutes down-canyon. Mad Meadows proper is home to **The Sail** (V9) and **The Peephole** (V10), perhaps the proudest duo in Leavenworth's pantheon of super-problems. Heading further uphill, don't miss creatively-named classics such as **The Pocket** (V4), **The Rail** (V3), **The Hole** (V5), and **The Undercling** (V5). The former-classic-turned-testpiece **Pimpsqueak** (V9) may be Leavenworth's best boulder problem, with the nearby **Amphitheater** (V4) well worth the hike as well. Mad Meadows offers something for everyone; potential for more easy problems can be found uphill of the approach or in the jumble just past **Pimpsqueak**. Expect all-day sun in the summer, and snakes are commonly observed on the approach and in the upper boulders below the Playground Point crag.

Approach: Park on the left 5.1 miles from Icicle Junction, just before the second Forest Service fire information sign. The Sleeping Lady is just downhill, while Mad Meadows is on the hillside above. Start up the steep hill across from the parking, following dusty switchbacks to the level ground above. Follow the well-worn trail to the right (towards Leavenworth) through an open 'meadow,' crossing a swampy area before emerging onto an open, a gentle open hillside. The first cluster of boulders are straight ahead, stretching up the shallow gully to Hanta Man. **Pimpsqueak** lies some 10 minutes beyond.

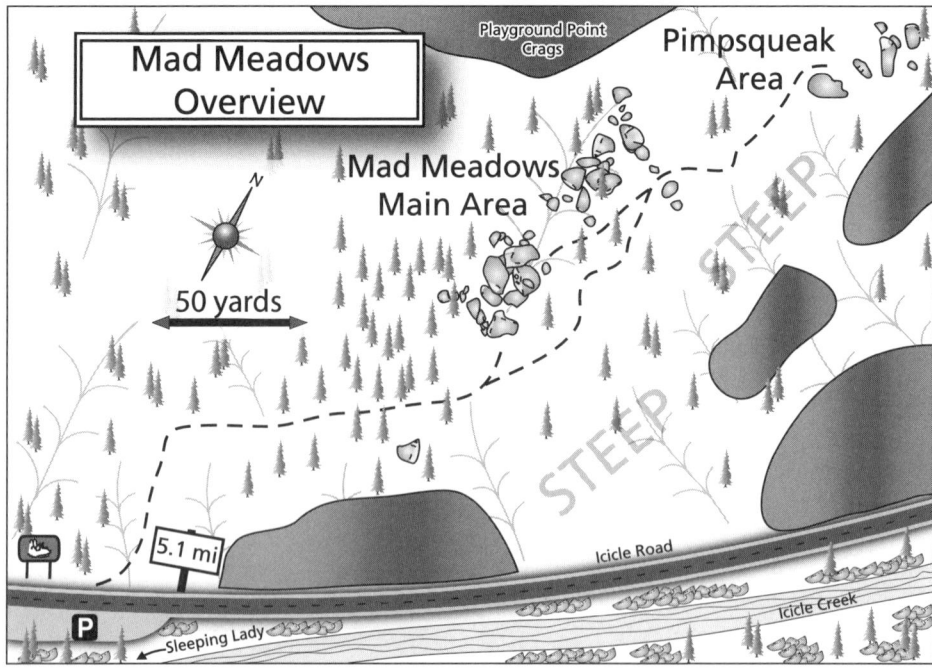

Icicle Canyon - Mad Meadows : LEAVENWORTH

___1. **Pocket Rocket** V3 ★★
 Climb the short overhang from a sit start on the slab with a low crimper. Cool holds!

___2. **Hairy Spotter** V5
With the torched tree at your back, climb up and right on sloping edges in the faint seam.

___3. **Squarepusher** V3 ★
 Climb the short, blocky arête on the downhill side of the boulder, finishing straight over the grainy lip after a cruxy lunge.

___4. **Flounder** V2 ★
 Start sitting on the right side of the blunt overhang, climbing straight up on slopers to a thrutchy finish onto the slab above.

___5. **Swordfish** V4 ★★
  Start sitting on slopers as for **#4**, climbing up and left on fun grips to a lefthand crimp around the corner. Stick the lip and finish on the left side of the arête.

___6. **The Lamb** V3 ★
Start sitting, matched on the low flat hold in this little overhang, climbing a few stout moves up both arêtes to finish straight up. Can you do it in sneakers?

___7. **Drugstore Cowboy** V3 ★★★
  Start sitting with two shallow pockets just right of the wild bulge of **The Peephole**. Climb up and right with a big foot ledge to rough jugs in the crack, finishing up the pumpy steep jugs between the boulders. The stand start is a great problem on its own, and can be made more difficult by eliminating the boulder on the right.

___8. **The Peephole** V10 ★★★
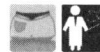 The famous bulge. Start matched on the 'peephole' jug under the teardrop feature, heading up and out on pinches to match the big undercling in the steepest part of the roof. Steep, technical climbing leads up and right through tricky crimps to a final slap for the lip. One of the best; the emblem of hard Leavenworth bouldering. F.A. Cole Allen.

___9. **Occum's Razor** V5 ★★
Start matched on the quartzy sloping crimps in the shallow corner left of **Peephole**, climbing a few tenuous moves to an easier finish straight up. Slippery, and harder than it looks.

___10. **Alpine Feel** V0 ★
Climb the nice, featured slab from the top of the low platform. Easy but somewhat high, so beware of that 'alpine' rock quality.

___11. **The Hueco Route** V1 ★★★
Start sitting on the left end of the steep swiss-cheese wall in the sheltered room. Climb up and right on juggy huecos to the final two pockets halfway up. Drop off from here, or kick your feet onto the boulder behind you, finishing 'Fred Nicole style' on the other rock. Finishing straight up the striking right arête is still a project.

___12. **Barnacles** V1 ★★
In the second 'room,' climb incut ripples up the vertical wall behind **The Sail**. Stemming off of the other boulder is poor style, but many will welcome its help during the tricky mantel.

___13. **The Sail** V9 ★★★
This super-steep, super-cool line climbs directly out the steep bulge of this suspended boulder. Pull on with a decent lefthand pinch and a poor right sloper, slapping twice to a square-cut edge on the right side of the bulge. Then grab the incut slot in the face, climbing straight up to jugs on the arête. F.A. Johnny Goicoechea.

LEAVENWORTH : Icicle Canyon - Mad Meadows

___14. **The Ram** V11/12 ★★★

 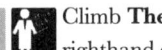 Climb **The Sail** to the square-cut righthand edge. Slap to a decent crimp on the blank left face of the boulder. Squeeze and slap to bring your right hand onto the left face and finish up the sloping edges above to mantel and walk off. Or, skip all that work and simply campus straight to the left crimp from the start like Johnny G! F.A. Cole Allen.

___15. **The Jib** V8 ★

Start with a sharp right-facing crimp on the left side of the steep face, pull on, and stab to the hidden jug up and left. Finish up and right as for **#14**. F.A. Johnny Goicoechea.

___16. **The Rudder** V1 ★

Climb the face and left arête on the uphill side of the Sail boulder. Might need some cleaning, and definitely a pad or two.

___17. **Flex The Matrix** V6

This neat flake of granite sits on top of the **Hueco Route** boulder. Start sitting with two tiny crimps and chuck to the flat shelf above. Take care not to fall off the landing…

___18. **Wooly Mammoth** V0

On the first boulder reached walking up from the lower cluster, climb the left arête of the short face, making use of the seam as you go.

___19. **The Dish** V1 ★

Climb the center of the short face on neat sloping huecos. A little harder than it looks…

___20. **Dr. Doom** V2

Around the left side of the tall pocketed face, climb the crack from a grove of bushes to a high, easy finish.

___21. **The Pocket** V4 ★★★

Climb the center of the tall face on strange huecos and pockets to a high finish at the boulder's apex.

___22. **Madvillian** V2 ★

Climb the right arête, using holds on the face when necessary. Finish just right of the nose on jugs.

___23. **Heir Apparent** V0

Traverse up and right with big ledges on the trailside lip.

___24. **Bushmen** V4 ★

Around the corner from **#23**, find this short face overgrown by bushes. On the left side of the overhang, grab a small crimp, step on, and dyno for the lip. Dab.

___25. **Pruning Shears** V1

Climb the right arête of the overgrown face from a good incut at head height.

___26. **The Break** V2 ★★

From the blocky ledge in the little alcove, climb up and slightly left to the incut crack. Finish straight up with a strenuous mantel to the right of the tiny corner. Great fun.

___27. **The Crimp** V5 ★★

Starting on the blocky ledge as for **#26**, grab the crimp on the face and make a big move right to the arête. Finish straight up with big moves on the juggy corner. A bit reachy, but that's no excuse!

___28. **The Rail** V3 ★★★

Begin on the corner with two low opposing sidepulls and a good heel hook. Cross back to 'the rail,' a good pinch on the arête, and finish straight up the corner. Awesome!

Icicle Canyon - Mad Meadows : **LEAVENWORTH**

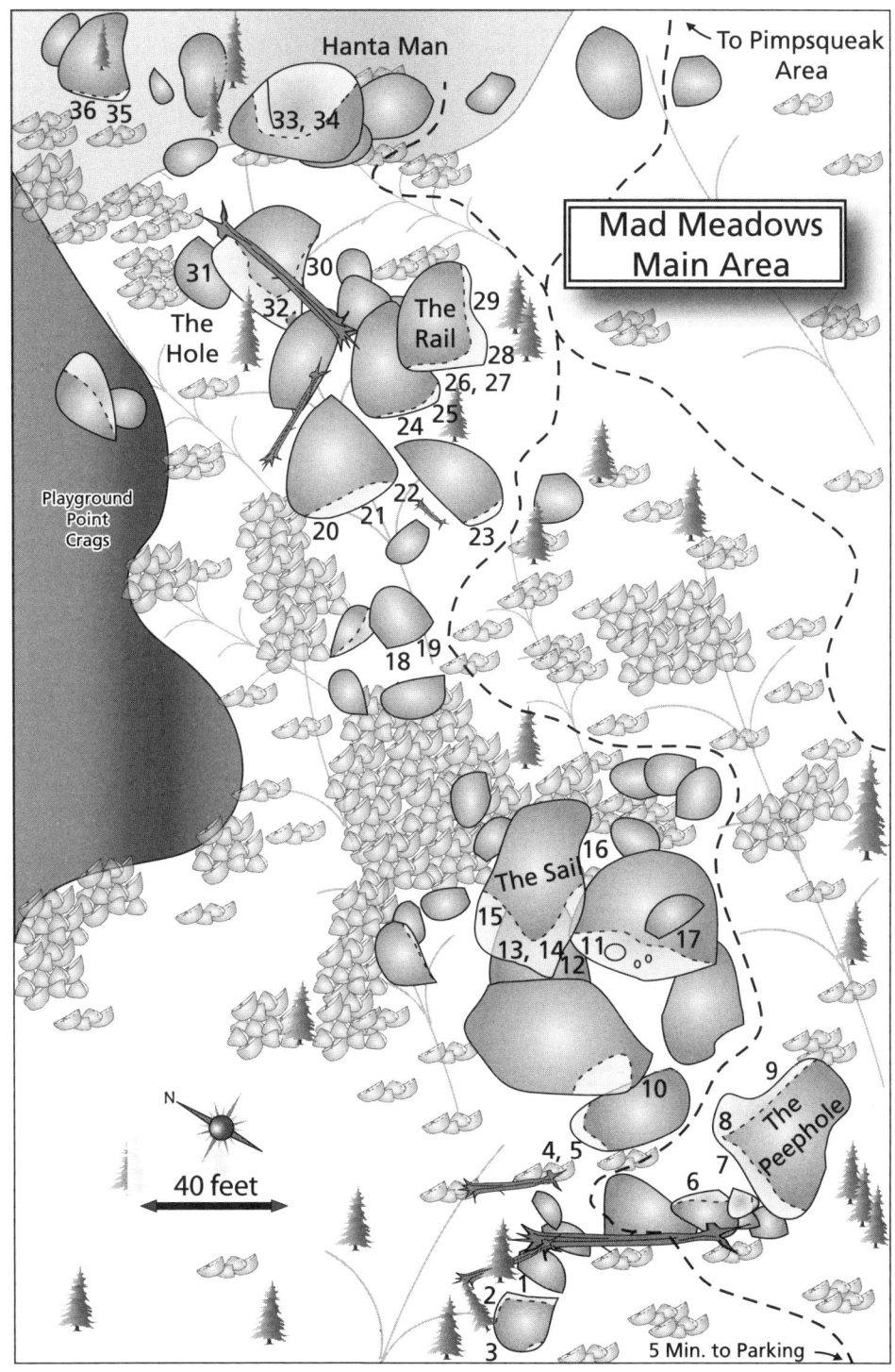

LEAVENWORTH : Icicle Canyon - Mad Meadows

___29. **The Scoop** V2 ★★
Start sitting in the left side of the obvious polished scoop right of **#28**. Climb up and right in the cool seam to a crimp and good holds over the lip. **Variation** (V3): Start as for **The Scoop**, but climb straight over the lip on little crimpers.

___30. **The Undercling** V5 ★★★
Starting with a big, smooth hueco in the narrow alcove, climbing past a tricky undercling to the top of the slightly overhanging face. Finish up the left side of the slab over the sketchy landing. Awesome!

___31. **The Flake** V4 ★
From a sit start on the other boulder in the left side of the overhang, follow the big flat rail up and right to a jug on the lip. Finish up the low-angle slab.

___32. **The Hole** V6 ★★★
Start sitting in the hole under the overhanging face, matched in a huge undercling in the hueco. Climb straight out of the steep overhang with some foot trickery, finishing up the easy slab above. This climb can be super-technical or super-burly—you pick.

___33. **No Pain No Grain** V5 ★
Find this steep, featured cave on the back side of the huge boulder visible uphill of **#30**. This near-horizontal crack climb starts with two hand jams in the deepest part of the roof, climbing straight out to the lip on painful locks in the low fissure. F.A. Jens Holsten.

___34. **Hanta Man** V9 ★★
Starting in the deepest part of the cave, climb through an undercling in the steep roof to a good crimp near the lip of the cave, finishing via the two cracks. Fun and technical, this would be a much better climb if not for the small boulder in the cave.

___35. **Spongebob Squarepad** V3 ★★★
Climb the square arête from a stand start, slapping and hugging your way to an easier finish. Super fun. Can be made more difficult by eliminating holds on the left face.

___36. **The Tentacles** V3 ★★
Starting in the sweet hueco pockets on the face left of **#35**, climb straight up to the juggy crack and top out.

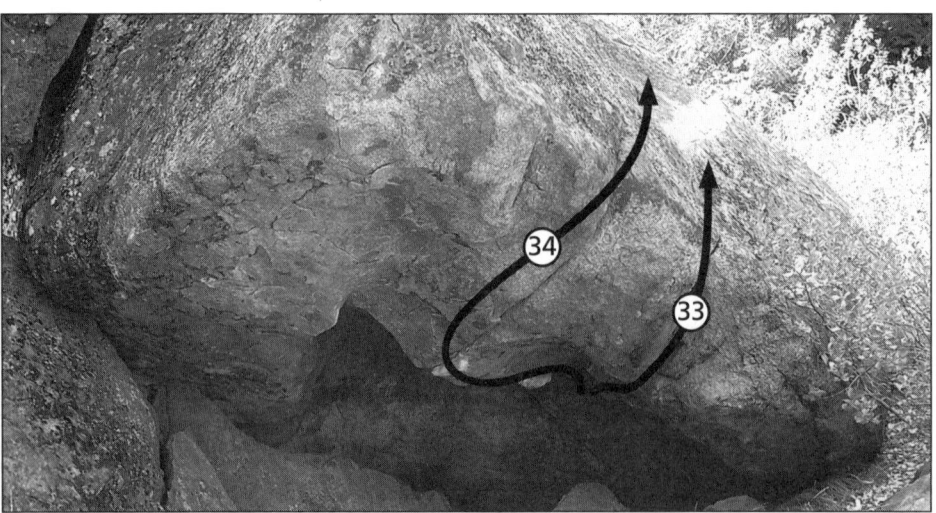

Kyle O'Meara flexing on The Peephole (V10)

LEAVENWORTH : Icicle Canyon - Mad Meadows

PIMPSQUEAK AREA

To find Pimpsqueak, continue traversing straight across the hillside from problems #26–#29, following the main trail past a small balanced boulder and slightly downhill as you head down-canyon. After a minute or two, the mini-crag on the backside of the Amphitheater will appear on the right. Follow the trail up and left over the small ridge, then dip into the shallow drainage above. Pimpsqueak can also be accessed from Hanta Man by following the trail down-canyon and eventually downhill. The upper Mad Meadows area is a bit confusing, but believe me, you'll know Pimpsqueak when you see it.

____1. **The Ampitheater** V4 ★★★

Start on the two chest-high pods on the right side of this neat, secluded wall. Climb to a small crimp, then hit the flat ledge above and mantel. Dynoing directly from the pockets adds several grades; using the crack to the right makes for a fun V0.

____2. **Crank** V1 ★

Climb the crack on the left side of the scooped face to a juggy top-out.

____3. **Winterbottom Arête** V3

Climb the short arête left of **Crank** from a sit-start, slapping up slopers and face edges to a mellow finish.

____4. **The Kiddie Pool** V1 ★★

Just down from the **Ampitheater**, you'll find another scooped face sporting this fun traverse. Start on the right end of the sloping ledge, traversing left to good holds next to the tree. Drop from here or mantel out of the 'pool' onto the dirty, low-angle face above.

____5. **Thirty Seconds** V3

That's about as long as this one will entertain most people... Start sitting in the middle of the low face, your right hand on a sidepull crimp in the incipient crack. Pull on over low smears and fire for the ledge, finishing up the dirty slab above.

____6. **Tweedle Dee** V0- ★

On the small 'corridor' boulder between the **Amphitheater** and **Pimpsqueak**, climb to the lip from a head-high jug and top out.

____7. **Tweedle Dum** V0

The rightmost crack on the boulder. Start on scooped sidepulls down and left in the discontinuous crack, moving right to layback up the short flake.

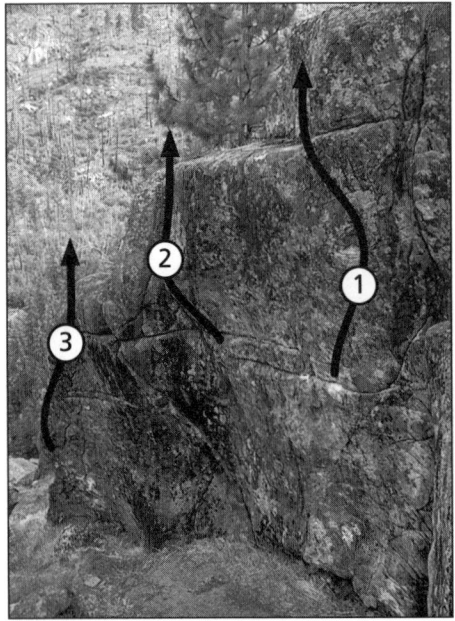

46

Icicle Canyon - Mad Meadows : **LEAVENWORTH**

Jessica Campbell demonstrating the beta on Pimpsqeak (V9)

LEAVENWORTH : Icicle Canyon - Mad Meadows

___8. **Pimpsqueak** V9 ★★★

One of the coolest features around. Start up the clean right arête to a jug at the edge of the cave, then head straight out the horizontal prow, squeezing between the slopey lip and better holds under the roof. This problem has become much more difficult since the departure of the thank-God jug on Greg Collum's **Pipsqueak**, though it's still one of the best lines in the area.

___9. **Crimpsqueak** V7 ★★

Start in the deepest part of the cave with sloping hueco features in the roof. Using strange heel hooks and slopers, climb to the lip opposite **Pimpqueak** and a good crimp on the face. Chuck to a good left-facing sidepull and top out.

___10. **Dog Log** V2 ★

Climb the scooped face on friable edges from a high right-leaning crimp rail. A one-move exercise in pain tolerance; at least it's a cool move.

___11. **Size Wise** V5

Start crouched on the right side of the short, steep arête spread wide between the toothy left arête and a low right undercling. Slap to a jug on the corner and finish straight up. Either I'm missing something or this one is incredibly reach-dependent.

___12. **V13s Don't Have Kneebars** V1 ★

Start standing with a low lefthand undercling and right on the edge of the sharp right-facing corner. Work around the small bomb-bay corner with weird kneebars to mantel straight over the bulge. Can also be started sitting on the right arête for a decent V2.

___13. **The Firefly** V1 ★

Climb the short arête on the back of the smallish boulder.

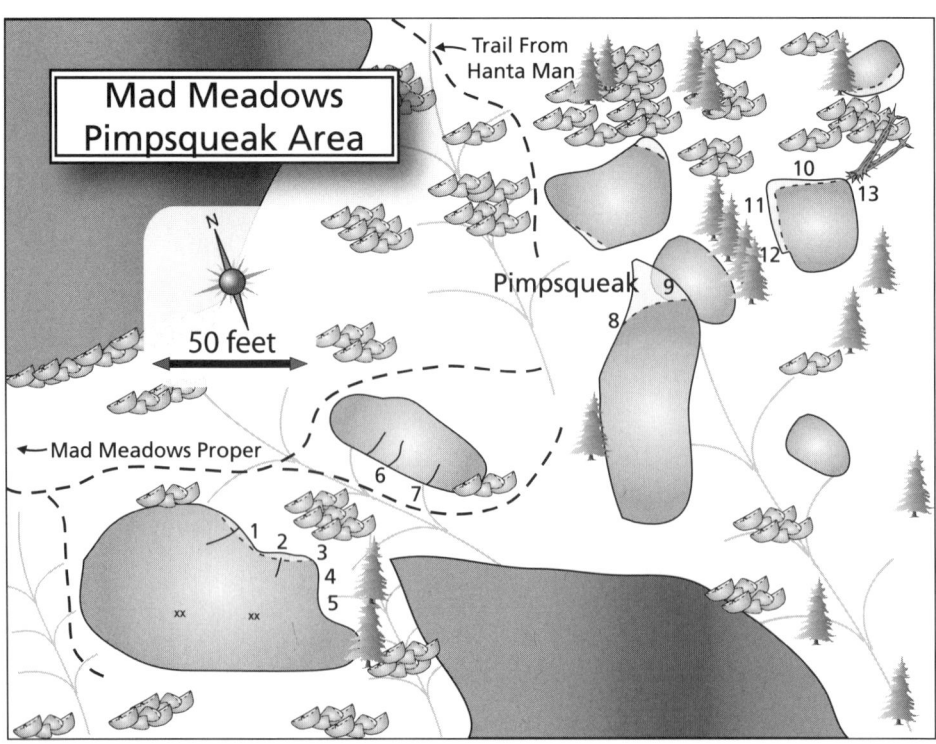

LEAVENWORTH : Icicle Canyon - Clamshell

CLAMSHELL CAVE

Clamshell Cave is a popular crag on the hillside well above Icicle Creek, also home to a good variety of boulder problems. With one of the most arduous hikes of the Icicle Canyon bouldering areas, the bouldering at Clamshell Cave is a well-earned treat. Older highball classics on the Cube, a large square-cut boulder at the base of the cliffs, are supplemented by several cool 'new-school' problems such as **Crimp, Crimp, Slap, Throw** (V3), and **The Octopus** (V7).

Clamshell Cave itself is a sheltered room created by a giant hueco in the undercut bottom of the cliff. Sadly, the rock quality in this neat hangout isn't quite what it could be. Marking the beginning of Clamshell's uphill trudge is The Hand and the neighboring Rob's Corral, home to a couple of interesting problems of their own. Check out Cole Allen's **More Cushin For Your Tushin'** (V10) on the east side of The Hand if you're feeling up to a bicep-slaughtering one-mover. The boulders at Clamshell Cave get a good amount of sun but can be comfortable even in summer heat with a nice breeze... Don't expect too much solitude in return for your legwork, however, as Clamshell Cave is relatively popular with novice craggers.

Approach: The hike begins just down the road from the brown fire information sign that marks the approach to Mad Meadows, 5.25 miles from Icicle Junction. The Hand, a large fist-shaped boulder that nearly overhangs the road, lies across from the far end of the long pullout and marks the beginning of the trail. Follow the well-worn trail up a short hill and left through a flat meadow, then across a small stream and up a series of steep switchbacks. The cliffs and boulders will become apparent after 10 or 15 minutes of hiking.

Alternatively, Clamshell Cave can be reached from Upper Forestland. From the trail above the Ruminator, bushwhack due east and slightly uphill for roughly 100 yards, with only a slight gain in elevation. Crimp, Crimp, Slap, Throw will be one of the first boulders encountered, just below Clamshell Cave itself.

The Hand from Icicle Rd

___1. **The Octopus** V7 ★★
This ascends the right arête of the first boulder the trail reaches. Pull on using a crimp on the arête and a small lefthand sidepull on the face. Slap to the sloper and finish up the corner. The jump start clocks in around V3.

___2. **Pentaphobia** V5 ★
Climb the scooped vertical face on tiny edges. May feel a bit tough 'til you warm up to it...

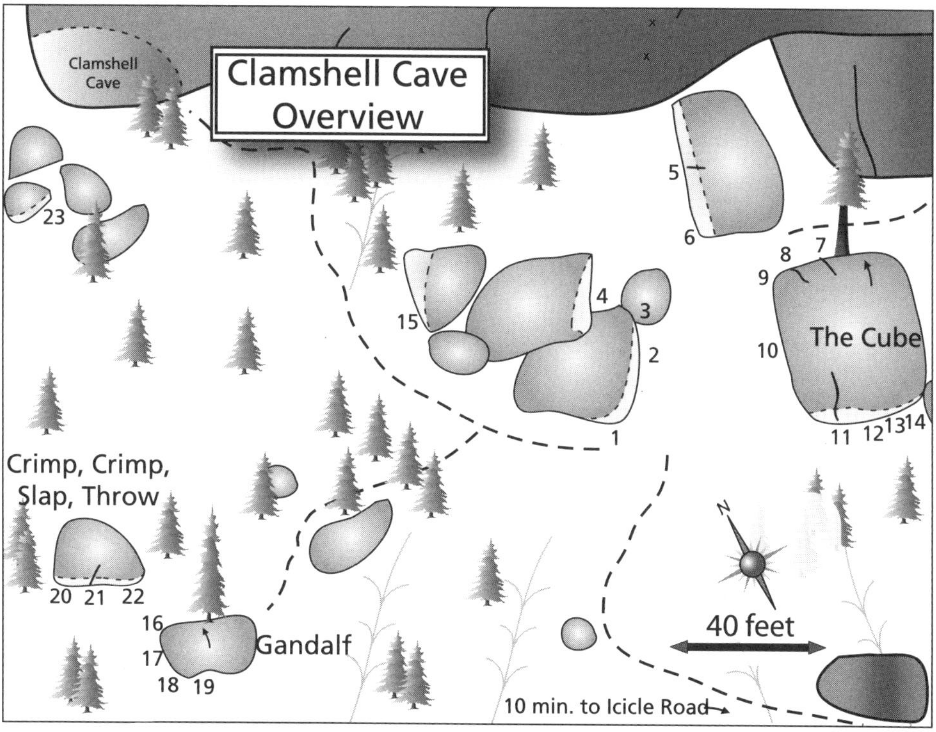
Clamshell Cave Overview
Clamshell Cave
5
6
7
8
9
4
3
2
1
15
23
The Cube
10
11 12 13 14
Crimp, Crimp, Slap, Throw
20 21 22
16
17
18 19
Gandalf
N
40 feet
10 min. to Icicle Road

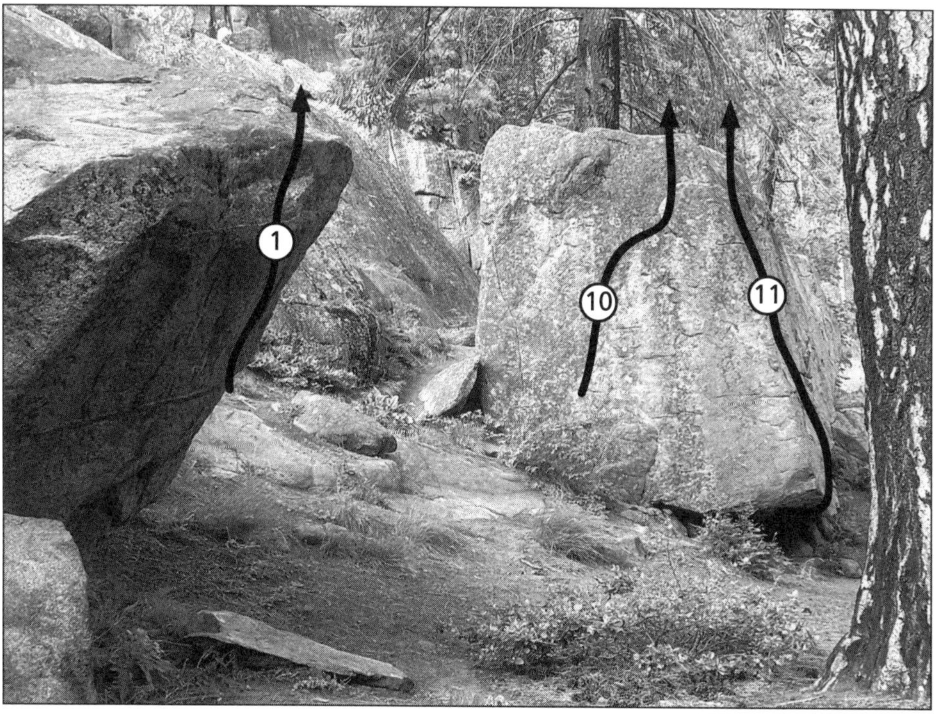
1
10
11

LEAVENWORTH : Icicle Canyon - Clamshell

____3. **Cornucopia** V2 ★
Start on a jug at head-height in the cramped corner and climb the blunt arête on somewhat dirty slopers.

____4. **Slice of Tea** V3 ★★
Start in the hole between the boulders behind **Cornucopia**. Up the left-leaning flake to a cruxy move for the lip. Best not to fall!

____5. **Playback** V1 ★★
A strenuous layback up the obvious right-facing flake in the middle of the overhanging face. Finish straight up with a bit of a mantel onto the slab. Sweet!

____6. **Terminal Traverse** V2 ★
Start on the downhill side of the overhanging face, traversing left on slopers on the lip to mantel just past the crack.

____7. **The Segment** V0 ★★
Climb the short hand crack just right of the tree. A great beginner's climb.

____8. **Tron** V0
Climb the broken hand crack five feet right of **The Segment**. May be a bit dirty.

____9. **Rubick's Arête** V0 ★
Climb the north arête of the Cube on big holds. Quite easy and short with a bit of exposure.

____10. **The Cube** V1+ ★★★
Climb delicate face moves up the left-facing flake in the middle of the tall face. Finish up and right on crimpers and better holds. Classic!

____11. **Cube Crack** V2 ★★★
 Be a boulderer... start sitting in the small roof under the high face and make a hard reach around the lip off a fist jam. Finish up the tall 5.7 crack, a very enjoyable climb in its own right.

____12. **Shallow** V1 ★★★
Climb the tall face right of the crack on big holds. The sit-start with a sidepull jug on the lip bumps the grade a notch.

____13. **Cube Traverse** V0 ★

Traverse to the left above the low lip of the boulder from underclings in the scoop of whitish rock. Finish up the crack.

____14. **Under the Bleachers** V5 ★

Climb the right arête of the tall face from an undercling at waist height. The small boulder to the right is a bit awkward, but the moves are great. Top out straight up the arête.

____15. **Scram** V2 ★★

Traverse up and left on the grainy lip, finishing with a fun mantel on the left side of the point.

____16. **The Hobbit** V2 ★

Climb the short corner. Look around for the good holds! Descend next to the tree.

____17. **Elfen Magic** V1 ★

Start in the middle of the slab with a good edge foothold, climbing straight up to finish on sloping holds.

____18. **Greed** V2

SDS on the foothold of **#17**, climb up and right on edges to finish up the right arête.

____19. **Gandalf** V2 ★★

The left arête of the tall scooped slab. Exit left to better holds at the notch in the arête, or head up the dirty slab if you're "feeling saucy."

____20. **Crimp, Crimp, Slap, Throw** V3 ★★★

Can I get some beta here??? Climb the left arête of the modest boulder from a stand start with two small crimps, gaining jugs on the lip with a fun toss. Awesome!

____21. **Cleaver Crack** V0 ★★

Climb the obvious hand crack in the middle of the face, jamming, laybacking, or pinching the side like a true boulderer…

____22. **The Goods** V4 ★

From high edges on the right end of the lip, traverse left on slopers, eventually mantling on good slopers near the left arête.

____23. **Boll Weevil** V2 ★

Start with two head-high gastons in the tiny overhang. Slap to the lip and mantel… actually way more fun than it looks.

Erin Bingham working on her heel hook technique on Scram (V2)   Photo: Jackie Hueftle

LEAVENWORTH : Icicle Canyon - Barney's Rubble

BARNEY'S RUBBLE

Barney's Rubble and the nearby Bruce's Boulder comprise one of the most popular toprope destination in Icicle Canyon. Despite the ever-present helmet brigades around the corner, the mellow bouldering at Barney's Rubble makes for one of Leavenworth's better warm-up spots. Many of the problems here provide a gentle wake-up call for both the psychical and mental sides of your climbing day. Sheltered by trees and relatively well-trafficked, The Rubb' remains dry throughout most of the winter and shaded during summer heat. Prepare to feel a bit sandbagged on the classics **Fun House Stairway** (V1+) and **Slice of Cake** (V3). Some of the neighboring toprope climbs can also make for fun scrambles, like the low-angle corner on the river side of Bruce's Boulder (5.2). To see a different side of Barney's Rubble, look for the river-polished squeeze arête of **The Fin** (V7)… but expect to find yourself on the sandy landing quite a few times first. If you're feeling warmed up and want to test your mettle, the trail to Forestland begins just up the hill…

Approach: Barney's Rubble is located across from Bruce's Boulder, a roadside granite dome on the left 5.5 miles from Icicle Junction. Park in the pullout on the left, cross the road, and follow the well-worn trail to the visible boulders. The approach takes about one minute. Alternatively, turn right onto the small dirt road 5.7 miles from Icicle Junction and follow it to the Forestland parking area, just uphill from Barney's Rubble. Please remember to carry out your trash and tape, and brush your chalk from the rock to help keep this popular spot pristine.

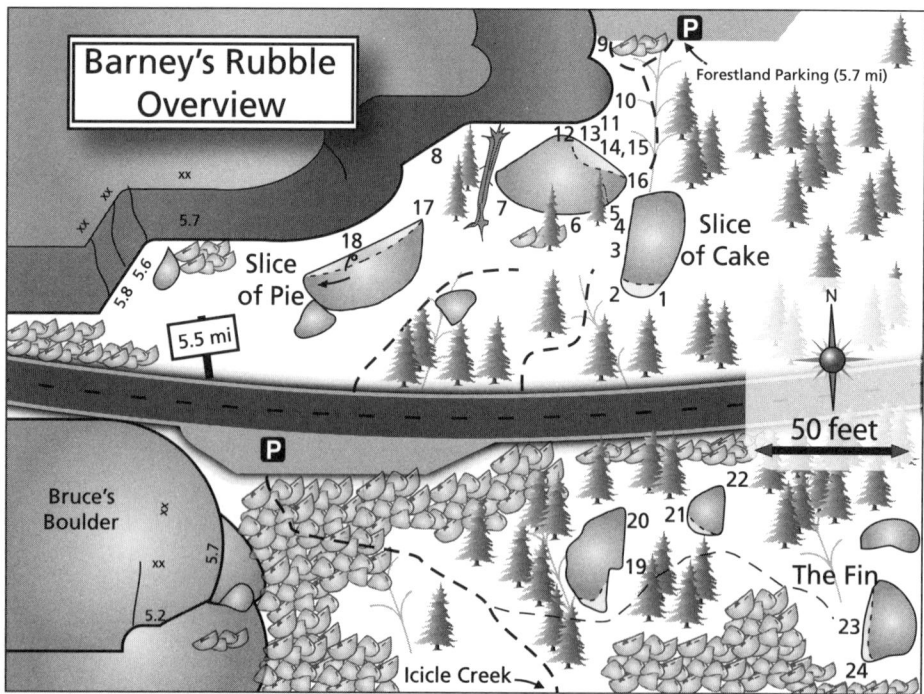

Icicle Canyon - Barney's Rubble : LEAVENWORTH

___1. **The Rail** V0 ★★★

Climb the right side of the prow from low triangular slopers to a juggy rail. Finish on either side of the corner.

___2. **Fun House Stairway** V1+ ★★★

Start sitting with low crimps, and use deceivingly sloping edges to climb straight up the left side of the prow. Harder than it looks and well worth the effort, an area classic.

___3. **The Rubb' Dyno** V8 ★★

Begin with a waist-high righthand sidepull on the right side of the wide flake. Stand up, cross over and establish on tiny crimpers then hurl yourself up and right to the arête. **Variation** (V9): For the more statically inclined, a variation begins as for **Rubb Dyno** but continues straight through a poor gaston to join the arête higher up.

___4. **Slice of Cake** V3 ★★★

Formerly a toprope, this classic line climbs the tallest part of the boulder's high vertical face. Start with exfoliating holds on the left-facing flake, then climb up the thin seam and rock to the fragile flake. Awesome! **Variation** (V3): For full badass value, follow the seam up and right to the top.

___5. **Tree Crack** V1 ★★

Begin on the head-high jug and climb the incipient crack behind the small tree. Superclassic.

___6. **The Hesitatator** V2 ★★★

Climb the center of the tall slab. Mantel into the large divot two-thirds of the way up, then stand and make one committing move to the top… it usually takes a minute or two to muster the willpower.

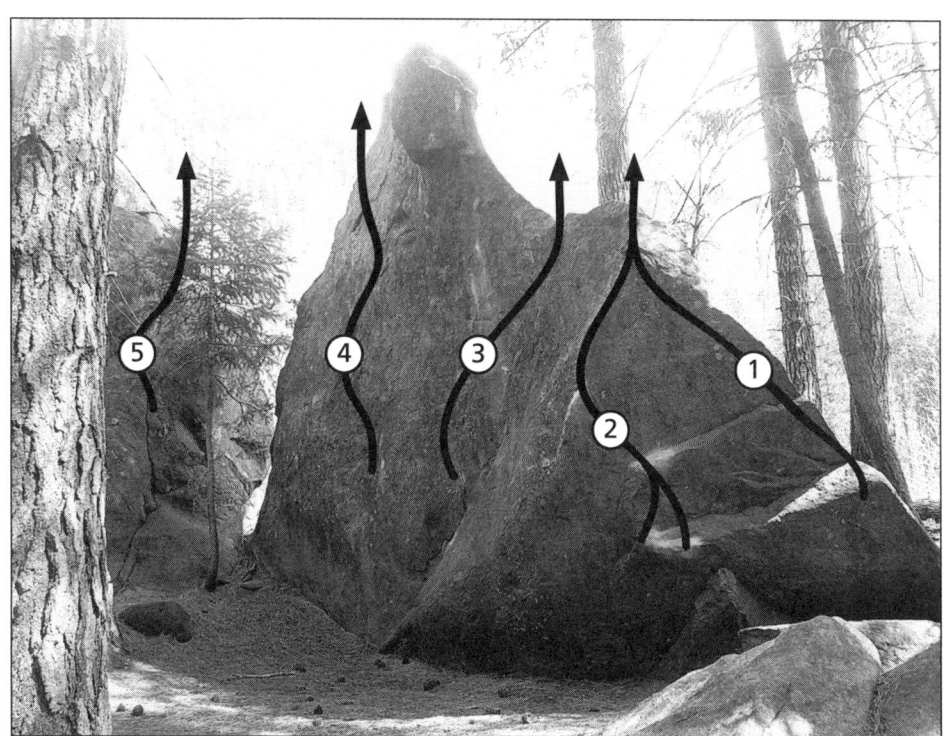

LEAVENWORTH : Icicle Canyon - Barney's Rubble

___7. **The Phatness** V2 ★

Climb the not-too-tall left side of the big slab, starting from the jug foothold and moving up and left to the arete. A good climb for working on your slab technique without the fear.

___8. **Chunky** V4 ★

A sustained traverse across the well-featured face that can be done in either direction, usually starting from a good undercling pinch at right-center and finishing in the high juggy crack on the left side.

___9. **Firebelly** V7 ★★

On the right side of the beige wall directly adjacent to the Forestland parking lot, climb this blank bulge from a stand start with a high right edge and your left hand in the lower dish feature. Work up on small edges and mantel… the sit-start on juggy huecos is still a project.

___10. **Fat Lip** V2 ★

Traverse the grainy black slopers across the lip to a dirty topout just right of the notch.

___11. **Ouchies** V6

From a sit-down start, climb the sequential path of sharp sidepulls and crimpers to the same topout as **Fat Lip**. Stemmers will suffer a subtraction of several style points.

___12. **Why?** V2 ★

Begin in the mouth of the narrow little opening with two hand jams. Thrutch out the dirty crack, and top out however you wish.

___13. **Alcove Right** V3 ★

Begin crouched in the corner with a good left-hand sidepull and a marginal right-hand crimper in the cave. Cross up and left to the jug, then top out straight up.

____14. **Alcove Center** V4 ★★

Start on the large horizontal shelf and climb up and right to the jug. The top is a bit harder than it looks. **Variation** (V5): Dyno straight from the shelf to the jug and top out.

____15. **Alcove Left** V3 ★★

Start as for **#12** and climb up and left through several left-hand sidepulls.

____16. **Rudy** V4 ★

Start squeezing the leftmost corner of the Alcove boulder and climb the arête into the top of **#13**. A decent intro to compression climbing.

____17. **Rainbow** V1 ★★★

Climb the left arête of the huge flake. A few powerful moves on awesome pinches leads to an eye-opening traverse on the juggy lip. Top out wherever you wish, and descend by shuffling along the back side of the fin towards the top-ropes. A direct start on flexing face edges adds several hard moves to join the arête, at least while the holds are there. The entire flake can also be traversed from the other side at a similar difficulty as **Rainbow**.

____18. **Slice of Pie** V2 ★★★

An old 5.11 toprope problem that sees mostly unroped ascents these days. Climb from the large sandy hueco into the incipient crack up and right. Make a long reach to the notch in the lip, and don't fall. A beautiful line whose unthinkable landing is its only detractor.

____19. **Alfalfa or Spanky?** V5 ★★

The first boulder reached on the hike down from Bruce's Boulder. Climb the tall dihedral on the downstream side of the big boulder. A hidden hold transforms something frustrating into something fun…

____20. **Musk** V9 ★★

Start on high micro-crimps at the bottom of the slight scoop on the right end of the face. Delicate footwork unravels the strange sequence of sidepulls and slopers above. Yet another tough one from Mr. Joel Campbell, grade unconfirmed.

____21. **Lowpers** V3 ★

Start crouched under the small bulge with two flat opposing rails. Slap straight out the bulge and finish up and left on the arête. Low but good.

____22. **Therête** V0

Climb the arête on the roadside corner of the short boulder. Could use a bit of traffic…

____23. **Sandy Man** V8 ★

Make a desperate jump to a high sloper on the lip and top out in the dirty right-facing corner above. Like Swiftwater's **Chicken Man**, the difficulty of this one may fluctuate annually with the level of the sand… most of us will have to wait for a really good year to get this one…

____24. **The Fin** V7 ★★★

Start sitting, hugging the polished fin of rock with hands and feet. Stab to a left-hand crimper and continue up the blunt arête with some involved heel-hooking. A classic problem on very unique granite. The landing also fluctuates seasonally.

"Boulders are small windows **to enlightenment.**"

- *Kyle O'Meara*

LEAVENWORTH : Icicle Canyon - Forestland

FORESTLAND

Forestland has been Icicle Canyon's premiere bouldering area in recent years, with one of the highest concentrations of problems found in the Leavenworth area. Forestland's collection of problems is divided into two tiers, Upper and Lower Forestland. Lower Forestland is a good spot to warm up, with a wide range of enjoyable problems on gritty granite. Upper Forestland is a bit more spread out, with a slightly finer texture and some truly classic lines. Moderates such as **Feel the Pinch** (V4) and **The Physical** (V4) ought not to be missed, nor should the difficult old-school mantel of **Backdoor Ass Attack** (V7). Located in the upper reaches of Forestland's established bouldering, the side-by-side classics **The Coffee Cup** (V10) and **The Practitioner** (V12) are some of the hardest in the area. Lower Forestland can be quite sunny and warm during the summer, while Upper Forestland offers a bit more opportunity to hide in the shade. This is one of Leavenworth's most popular bouldering areas, and several parties can typically be found here on spring and fall weekends. If 'crowds' aren't your thing, the area surrounding Upper Forestland is home to some good climbs and a bit more potential, offering solitude and fresh rock for those willing to bushwhack and scramble. Rattlesnakes are frequently observed in Forestland throughout the summer; pay special attention on the trail from the parking lot, as well as in the talus of Upper Forestland.

Approach: Forestland bouldering is easily reached from the parking lot above Barney's Rubble. Turn right onto the easy-to-miss dirt road 5.8 miles from Icicle Junction, following it a couple hundred yards back towards Leavenworth to a large parking area, formerly a staging area for firefighting efforts during the 1994 forest fires. A well-worn trail leaves the northeast end of the parking lot by a few small boulders. After crossing a log bridge and passing a small boulder, the trail reaches the boulders of Lower Forestland. To find Upper Forestland, follow the trail through Lower Forestland and turn left up a short hill on switchbacks.

____1. **Squeezer** V2
This scrappy little hopeful is virtually impossible from a low start. A stand start can be done from a high flat edge. A bit silly, but it's there…

____2. **Lock and Pop** V2 ★
Start sitting matched on the trailside jug, climbing the arête and right side of the short face. Finish straight up in the groove.

____3. **Runner** V0 ★
Climb the slab near the left side of the short face on small edges. Alternatively, discard all technique and hop to the finish from a running start.

____4. **Marathon Man** V0 ★★
Climb the right side of the slab using smears and small edges.

____5. **Abstraction** V0
The short slab around the corner from **#4**.

____6. **Lock and Load** V4 ★
Start on the far left side of the rounded bulge with a high knob in the seam. Climb straight up on slopers to a devilish mantel.
Variation (V7): Start on small head-high edges down and left of the knob, climbing right along the lip into **Lock and Load**. Finish as above.

Icicle Canyon - Forestland : **LEAVENWORTH**

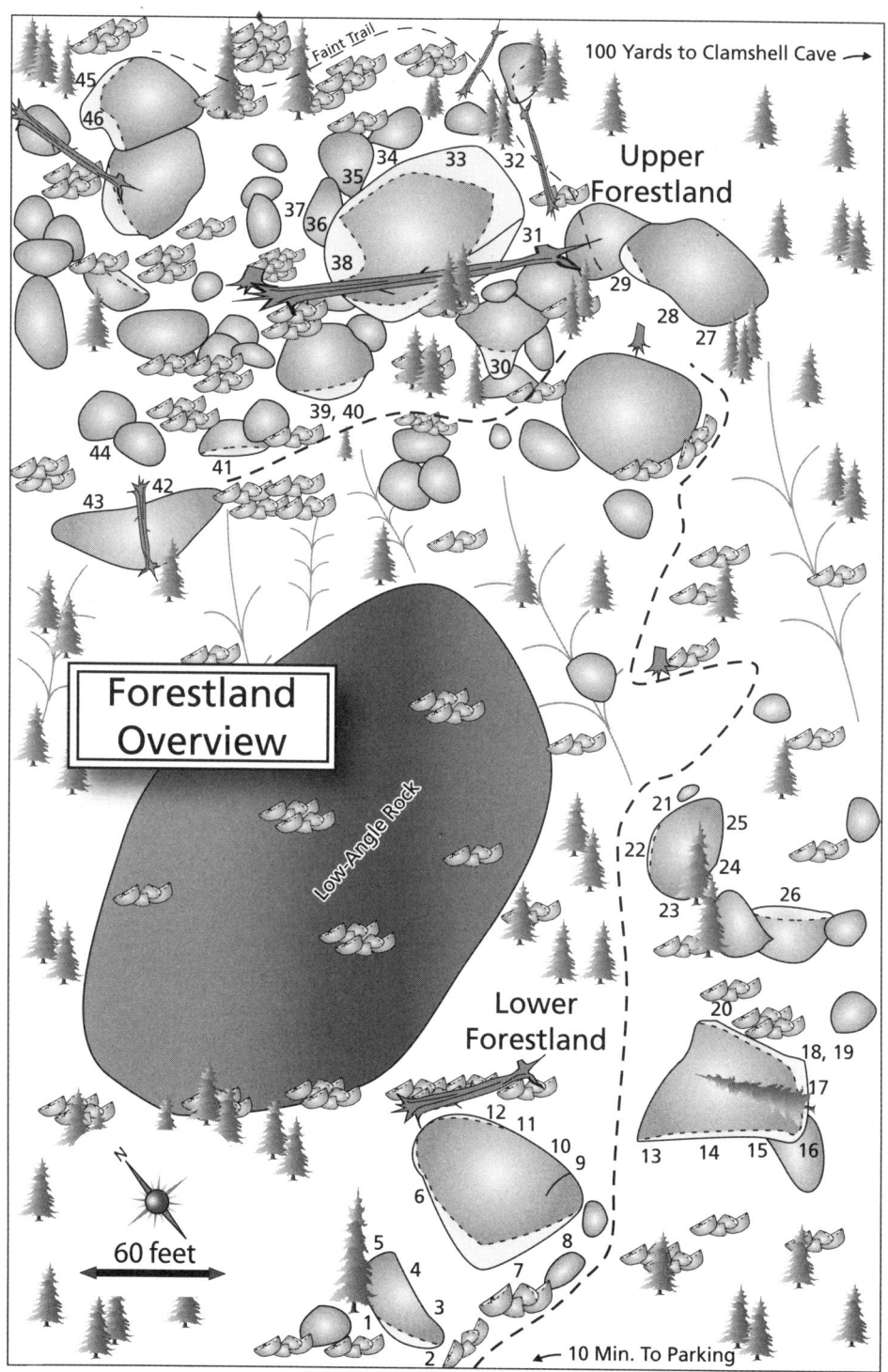

LEAVENWORTH : Icicle Canyon - Forestland

___7. **Backdoor Ass Attack** V7 ★★★

Start hanging from a nice head-high jug next to the trail. Throw your heel up, and rock up on poor slopers to an insecure mantel finish. **Variation** (V8): Start sitting with a sloping righthand sidepull and a small left undercling, make a powerful chuck to the jug and finish as above.

___8. **Project**

A tough future line follows poor slopers up the wide seam from a sit start on a right-facing sidepull.

___9. **Breadline** V0+ ★★★

Climb the fatty right-facing flake to finish straight up with some delicate footwork.

___10. **One Summer** V5 ★★★

Start standing with small crimps, step high and lunge to the obvious flat ledge. The crouch start down and left with an incut crimp trades a star for an extra grade.

___11. **The Real Thing** V4 ★★★

Climb the vertical face using small edges and a prominent left-facing sidepull. Great technical face climbing.

___12. **Concavity** V0 ★

Climb the juggy crack up and right. Tackling the scooped face straight up from low jugs in the crack is a slightly loose V1.

___13. **Arrested Development** V3 ★★★

Hop to a good square-cut hold on the left arête, climbing up and right on the face to a committing finish high on the corner. **Variation** (V5): From the righthand starting holds, climb up and right to a right-leaning gaston on the face and finish straight up.

___14. **The Shield** V7 ★★★

Grab two wide sidepulls in the center of the face, paste your feet, and dyno to an incut righthand sidepull at the 10-foot level. Move left to another sidepull and finish direct, aiming for a small notch on the lip. Classic movement!

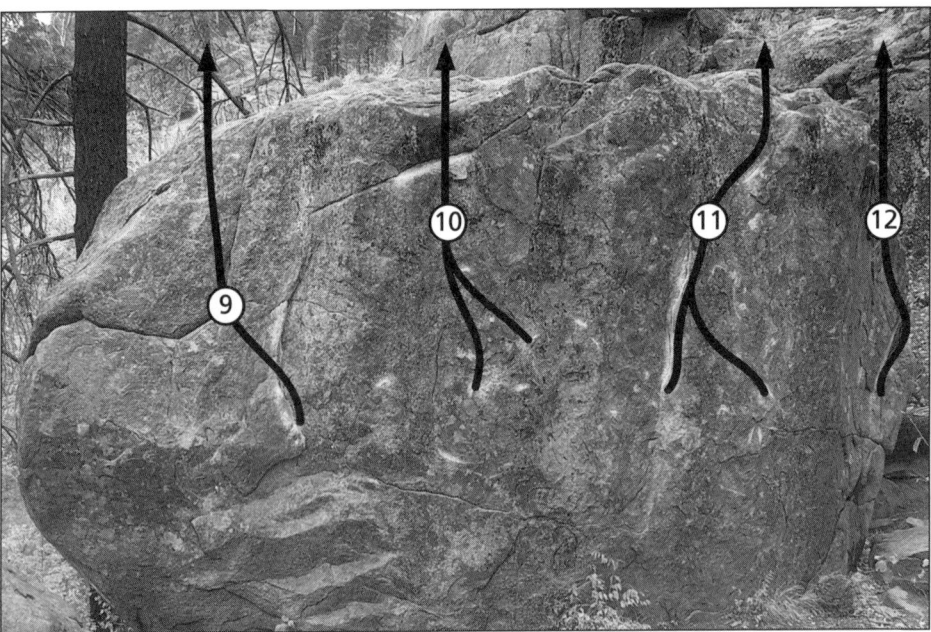

60

Icicle Canyon - Forestland　　**LEAVENWORTH**

Angela Payne on the all-out dyno of The Shield (V7)

___15. **Bedroom Bully** V8 ★★

Start with two head-high crimps on the right side of the face and stab to the incut fingerlock up and right. Hit the lip and mantel straight over. You might want to tape a finger for this one… Starting with the fingerlock and mantling clocks in around V2.

___16. **The Drill Sargeant** V8 ★

Climb the short corner just right of **#15** from two low sidepulls. The stand start to this one also clocks in around V2. F.A. Joel Campbell.

LEAVENWORTH : Icicle Canyon - Forestland

___17. **Feel the Pinch** V4 ★★★
Start crouched on a sloping rail on the right side of the face. Climb up and left through another sloper to a neat-o pinch and gaston crimp, topping out a few feet right of the tree. A definite must-do.

___18. **Fiend it Like Crack** V3+ ★★
Start sitting on the corner on flexing holds. Climb up and left to the start of **#17**, then right on decent holds in the crack. Finish straight over the corner with a somewhat heady mantel.

___19. **Busted** V8 ★★
Start on a flexing jug as for **#18**, climbing straight up the arête on incut sidepulls. Gain the rail via a hard move from a tiny right-hand sidepull. This one would be three stars if the start weren't going to break…

___20. **Cruise Control** V6 ★★
Start with a sloping knob and incut gaston in the overhang, moving right to better holds on the corner to finish straight up. This one's all about the feet…

___21. **Silly with an S** V0
Start sitting on the left side of the trailside slab. Pull up, mantel, and top out.

___22. **Hearthstone** V0 ★
Start with high jugs on the right side of the lip, mantel, and climb to the top. Fun!

___23. **Dredge** V1 ★
Climb the slab left of the tree on small edges to a flat jug near the top.

___24. **The Scarecrow** V1 ★★
Climb the thin face just right of the tree to the good right-facing ledges below the lip.

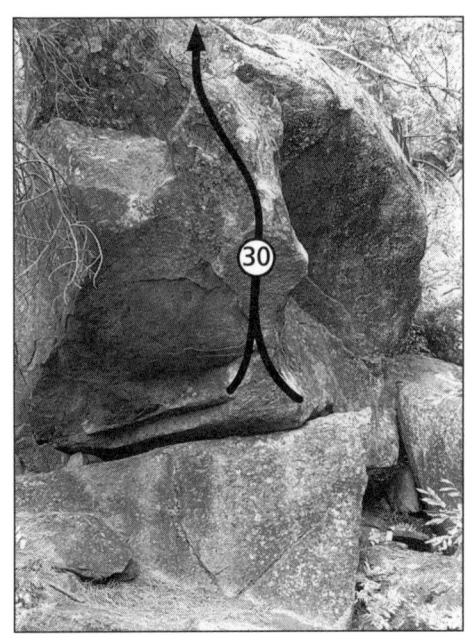

___25. **Cowardly Lion** V0 ★
Climb the slight scoop in the right side of the face to mantel onto the arête and top out.

___26. **Toto** V4 ★
This problem can be found in the small alcove to the left of **#24** and **#25**. Start matched on the flexing flake in the small overhang and bust to the lip.

___27. **Fedge** V2 ★★
Start on the corner with a small triangular crimp, climbing up to an incut sidepull and through neat features on the slab. Starting down and right on small gastons is fun and possibly almost easier.

___28. **Slickfoot Holiday** V1 ★★
Start on the big rounded edge 10 feet left of the arête, climbing up and right on small edges to the high slab finish of **#27**. A sneaker testpiece!

____29. **Lovage** V3 ★★★
Start sitting matched on the big ledge on the left end of the face. Climb straight up to the hidden jug on the corner and top out.

____30. **The Physical** V4 ★★★
Start this strong problem on the slab below the flying arête. Punch up and left using opposing holds on either side of the bulge. Great movement and a high commitment factor make this another must-do.

____31. **The Ruminator** V6 ★★★
You may have to think about this one for a minute… Climb the steep left-leaning crack on the biggest face of this giant boulder. Long moves between big holds in the 45-degree crack lead to an insecure mantel at the lip. One of the area's proudest, though not especially hard for the grade.

____32. **Cole's Jump** V6 ★
On the right side of **The Ruminator** overhang, two terrible crimps are perennially chalked in the hopes they can provide V-sick passage to the slopers above. While the stand remains an impossi-proj, the jumpstart to the lip goes. Grade unconfirmed.

____33. **Dangle** V7 ★★
Start sitting with a flat low edge on the left side of the steep overhang. Make a hard move to the obvious incut flake three feet above, then hit the slippery lip and mantel (crux).

____34. **Kobe Tai** V8 ★★★
Roughly 20 feet right of **#33**, climb the overhanging face over the gap between the boulders. Start from a rounded righthand crimp and a low lefthand undercling. Harder and harder moves on beautiful crisp edges lead to a heady lip encounter over the abyss.

Jens Holsten on Cruise Control (V6) Photo: Max Hasson

LEAVENWORTH : Icicle Canyon - Forestland

___35. **Curtis Suave** V5 ★
Climb the blunt arête from the top of the boulder a few feet right of **Kobe Tai**, starting with a huge move to the lip from a righthand sidepull. Powerful, but much less dangerous than it looks. We promise.

___36. **Clod-Hopper** V2
Start sitting with slopers on the very low corner, moving up and left to a jug and mantel. Finishing way up and left would be quite scary…

___37. **The Cro-Magnon** V6 ★
Start with a decent right-facing sidepull on the smallish undercut face and dyno to the lip. Moving to the right arête and up is a less contrived V1. F.A. Joel Campbell.

___38. **Bananas** V8 ★★
Start standing at the edge of the rocky cave, matched on a sloping rail at head height. Pull on, chuck to a small, sloping crimp below the lip, and hold it together for the topout. F.A. Kyle O'Meara.

___39. **Sunny and Steep** V2 ★★★
Climb the left side of the beautiful featured face on rounded jugs. Feel free to add a grade in the summer!

___40. **Funny and Cheap** V4 ★
Start as for **#39**, climbing directly right to a low sidepull and a big undercling. Bust for round slopers on the shelf up and right, then head to the lip via flat ledges. **Variation** (V3): Skip the low move; Climb straight up and then right to the slopers, finishing as above.

___41. **Tahitian Moon** V0 ★
Start on a big jug on the left side of the small boulder and traverse the crisp lip right to mantel just before the corner.

___42. **Bad Moon Rising** V2 ★★★
The clean black water streak just left of the fallen tree. Beautiful friction climbing.

___43. **Moondog** V0 ★
Follow the mossy ledges up the slab. The most convenient downclimb for **#42**.

___44. **Death to Rednecks** V2 ★
The tricky slab by the base of the fallen tree.

___45. **The Coffee Cup** V10 ★★★
Start on a high sloping rail on the left side of the undercut bulge. Pull on, stick the crimp above, and move to the lip. A super proud old-school line that will unfortunately lose a key hold someday…

___46. **The Practitioner** V12 ★★★
Start under the square roof with a good undercling, slap right to the shelf on the lower lip, then crimp and slap straight up the blunt corner. This uber-classic bulge was a longstanding project until several ascents were made in the last year or two. Leavenworth's hardest—so far. F.A. Herman Feissner

Icicle Canyon - Forestland **LEAVENWORTH**

Cole Allen feelin' the buzz on The Coffee Cup (V10) Photo: Brian Sweeney

LEAVENWORTH : Icicle Canyon - Lonely Fish

THE LONELY FISH

The Lonely Fish, a.k.a. Another Roadside Attraction, is the large roadside boulder just 0.1 miles past the turn for the Forestland parking area. Along with the Millennium Boulder across the road, the Lonely Fish is home to some of Leavenworth's most unique problems. If you enjoy traverses but don't feel like scraping along in the dirt, you will be in sideways heaven here. The desperate campus traverse on Joel Campbell's **Lonely Fish** (V9) requires some serious crimping before the hanging dihedral exit, while Cole Allen's **Millennium Traverse** (V8) will have you stretching out on some slopers. The Millennium boulder also makes for a decent place to warm up, with several moderate problems on beautiful white granite. Check this area out in the spring and fall when the temps will make the sun refreshing.

Approach: The Lonely Fish is visible on the right side of the road 5.8 miles from Icicle Junction, 0.1 miles after the turn to Forestland parking. Park off the pavement on the right side of the road. The small crag up and right from the Lonely Fish is the Roto Wall, a popular spot for beginners and climbing classes. The Millennium boulder is visible directly across the road from the Lonely Fish, though a bit more distant. The Millennium boulder is in relatively close proximity to a private residence, but access has not been problematic and the land is not posted. Please stick to the trails, be on your best behavior at the Millennium, and respectful of any folks you may encounter.

___1. **Dirty Dude** V10 ★★
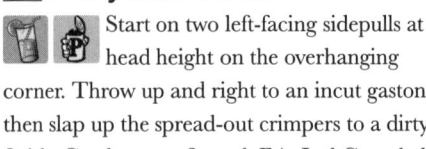
Start on two left-facing sidepulls at head height on the overhanging corner. Throw up and right to an incut gaston, then slap up the spread-out crimpers to a dirty finish. Grade unconfirmed. F.A. Joel Campbell.

___2. **The Lonely Fish** V9 ★★★
Using the smaller boulders and the sloping hueco, establish on the obvious crimpers at the nine foot level. Climb right to a good sidepull in the high face, ninja-kick your foot over, and haul yourself into the dihedral above. A classic testpiece that became slightly harder in fall 2005 with the departure of a portion of one of the starting holds. F.A. Joel Campbell. **Variation** (V8): Jump to the footholds down and right of the dihedral, finishing as for **Lonely Fish**.

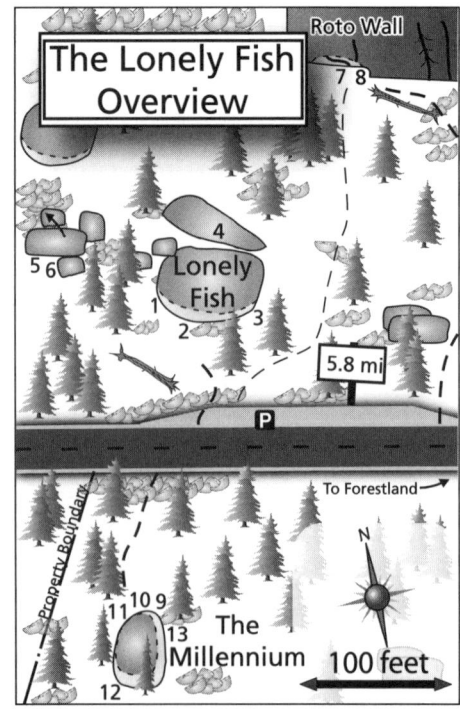

Icicle Canyon - Lonely Fish : **LEAVENWORTH**

___3. **Caught Red-Handed** V4 ★
 Climb the left side of the tall face from a good sidepull jug just overhead. Work to the obvious incut seam, then up you go!

___4. **Unknown** 5.11
This line is an old toprope climb. Perhaps it has seen ropeless ascents?

___5. **Easy One** V0 ★★
Climb the tallish face on good holds. Usually done in sneakers.

___6. **Easy Two** V0 ★★
Grab the good jug at head height and use the juggy corner to mantel and top out.

___7. **Droppin' the Kirschbaum** V10 ★★★
This former longstanding project is located on the left end of Roto Wall, approximately 50 yards uphill from the Lonely Fish. Start in the middle of the wall on low right-facing holds. Punch left out the overhanging rail on sloping crimps then traverse back right across the entire lip on perfect granite to reach the wide crack top-out. A mammoth endeavor, although there are no stopper moves. F.A. Kyle O'Meara

LEAVENWORTH : Icicle Canyon - Lonely Fish

___8. **Bombs Away** V7 ★

Jump start to the slanting crimps at the nine-foot level on the right end of the alcove. Climb up to the lip and move right to the crack to top out.

___9. **The Corner** V2 ★

Start on the left corner of the round boulder with your left hand on a good crimp and your right on a low sloper. Climb awkwardly up and right on edges, eventually mantling onto the corner.

___10. **Millennium Mantel** V1 ★★

Begin on the sloping shelf overhead with large footholds. Mantel. Eliminate the crimpers up and left or remove your climbing shoes for more of a challenge.

___11. **1999** V2 ★★

Climb the low arête beginning with your left hand on a good sloper and your right on a teensy crimp on the face. Slap up to a crimp and top out up and left. Great fun.

___12. **2001** V4 ★★★

Start with a sharp lefthand sidepull and sloping right crimp on the blunt arête. Paste your feet high, hit the crimpers above, and rock up to an edge high on the face. Burly and balancey.

___13. **The Millennium Traverse** V8 ★★

Start next to the ankle-biting boulder on the right end of the steep face with a sloping pinch on the lip. Make a reachy move out left to the dark divot, and continue across the lip to a good edge. A final difficult move from the small left-facing corner leads to an enjoyable topout. F.A. Cole Allen.

Kyle O'Meara eyeing the crimps on Droppin' the Kirschbaum (V10)

Icicle Canyon - Lonely Fish : **LEAVENWORTH**

Kyle O'Meara enjoying early spring friction on Tall Boy (V5)

LEAVENWORTH : Icicle Canyon - Hook Creek

THE HOOK CREEK BOULDER

The Hook Creek boulder, a.k.a. the Rat Creek boulder, is one of the few developed bouldering spots on the south side of Icicle Creek. Several classic toprope climbs can be found on this large, square-cut bloc, as well as a few nice boulder problems. Home to the lowball testpiece **Atomic Energy** (V9), the Hook Creek boulder is a pleasant sunny hangout as well as a great place to test your finger strength. The shaded alcove on the east side stays dry all winter, and cool in the summer when the tall faces are baking in the sun. The Hook Creek boulder has been climbed on for ages with seemingly problem-free access, but the land has recently changed owners and future development may affect the access situation. As always, observe all posted restrictions and make an effort to educate yourself about the area's current status.

Approach: Park for the Hook Creek boulder in the Alphabet Wall pullout, on the left 6.0 miles from Icicle Junction. Walk down the hill and slightly down canyon towards the obvious white bridge. Cross the bridge, turn left, and take the middle of three driveways. The large, free-standing Hook Creek boulder will be visible on the right after a couple minutes. The bridge services two private residences, so it is crucial as climbers that we keep a low profile in this area and obey posted signage. The area surrounding the Hook Creek boulder has a bit of potential, though much discretion should be used in exploring on private property.

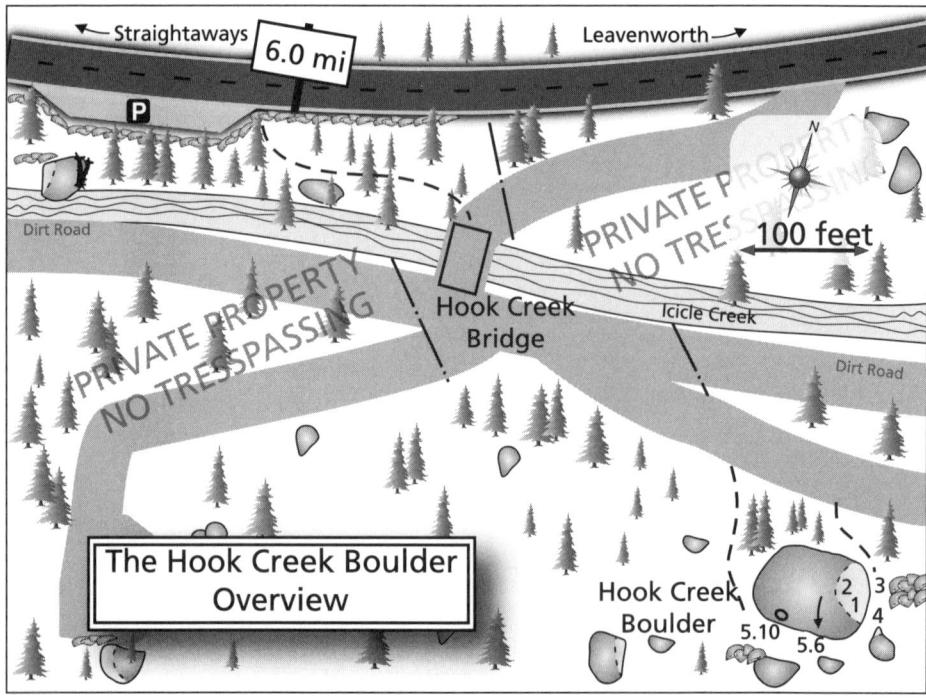

Icicle Canyon - Hook Creek : **LEAVENWORTH**

___1. **Atomic Hole** V4 ★★

Start with a chalked sloper under the left side of the overhang, climb left to a neat hueco on the corner, and traverse the lip rightwards. Finish up the tall face. **Variation** (V6): Start as for **Atomic Energy** and make a shouldery move left to finish up **Atomic Hole**: the **Atomic Link**.

___2. **Atomic Energy** V9 ★★★

Start on the innermost crimp in the right wall of the overhang, following the beautiful low seam right to jugs. Climb up and left on good holds to finish as for **#1**. FA Cole Allen.

___3. **Dalai Lama** V8 ★

Grab two poor crimps at the eight-foot level in the center of the lip of the overhang. Burl down and huck to the jug above however you can.

___4. **Sweenis** V3 ★

Start sitting, hugging the small boulder next to the **Atomic Energy** alcove. Slap up on opposing holds, finishing out left along the juggy lip. Low but fun.

Several toprope climbs on the Hook Creek boulder also make for fun boulder problems. The descent on the right side of the south face is 5.6 or so, and the obvious layback flake on the left side is 5.10. The **Thermal Energy** project is accessed from the same bridge, roughly a ten-minute walk from the Hook Creek boulder (see map).

LEAVENWORTH : Icicle Canyon - Straightaway

THE STRAIGHTAWAY BOULDERS

The Straightaway Boulders are a spread-out cluster scattered on both sides of the road, stretching from the large Hook Creek pullout to the slabby base of Icicle Buttress. The Straightaway Boulders give credence to exaggerated boasts that one could park their vehicle every 50 yards in Icicle Canyon and find a gorgeous roadside boulder… That said, they are not a place for high problem concentration, nor are they much of a warm-up destination. The Straightaway Boulders contain some of the best hard problems around Leavenworth, including the iconic **WAS** (V8) and the impeccable mantel of **Batman** (V8). For a serious challenge, check out the 45-degree dyno of the **Cotton Pony** (V10) or the fly-on-the-wall crimping of the **Ladder Project**. The latter will someday be Leavenworth's proudest testpiece, an independent line of widely-spaced edges and shelves up a 20-foot overhang. For warm winter sun, check out the south-facing classics The **Icehouse** (V4) and Leavenworth's granitic answer to Hueco's Babyface, Answer Man (V6). The Straightaways offer a few hours' worth of solitude for a few minutes' hike. Many of the Straightaway Boulders are in the sun during most of the day; check out the Icehouse and the Cotton Pony for some shadier climbs.

Approach: The Straightaway Boulders begin just after the large lefthand pullout 6.0 miles from Icicle Junction, and end at 6.3 miles, where Batman has crumbled from the base of Icicle Buttress. The approaches here tend to be short but steep, and all the boulders mentioned here are within 50 yards of the road. *The easiest way to locate all the Straightaways the first time through is on foot:* Park in the Alphabet Wall pullout directly across from the six-mile marker and head up the road. While you're walking (well to the side of the road) be sure to check out both the directions and the map. Each area has a small landmark, though none are too obvious, especially if you're whipping by in your car. Batman is pretty easy to find even from a vehicle; just park next to the last cluster of rocks on the right and wander up.

THE ICEHOUSE

The Icehouse is the first large boulder on the right after the Alphabet Wall parking area. Fifty yards after the six-mile marker, there is an orange pole on the right marking a buried telephone cable. Leave the road here and follow the trail uphill and slightly left from the mini pullout. The Icehouse is clearly visible at the top of the steep incline, 20 yards from the pavement.

____1. **The Icehouse** V4 ★★★
Start on low crimpers on the right side of the scooped face. Climb past the unique tufa-like pinch to a jug, and finish straight up the technical face.

Icicle Canyon - Straightaway : **LEAVENWORTH**

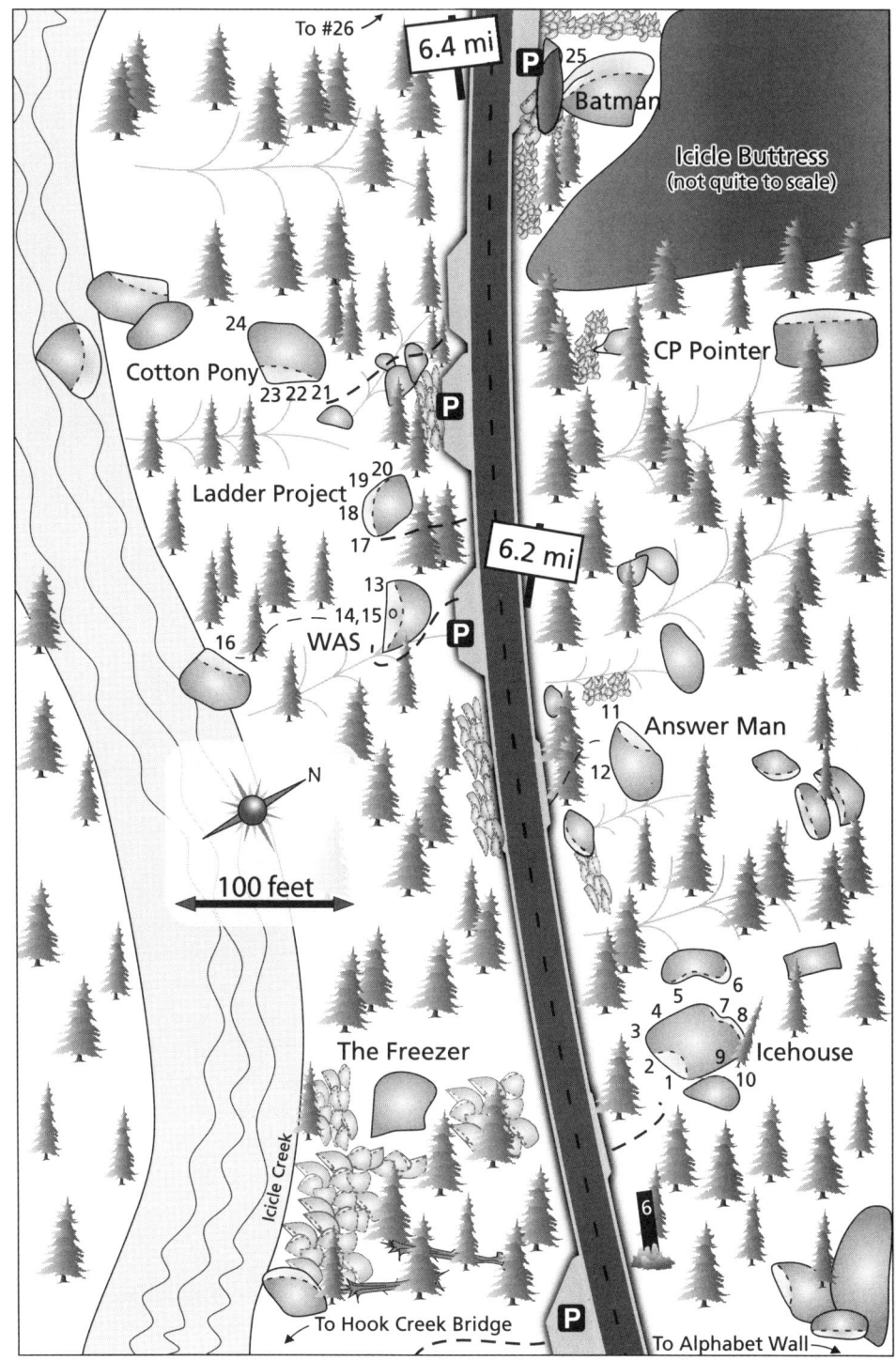

LEAVENWORTH : Icicle Canyon - Straightaway

___2. **Tall Boy** V5 ★★

Begin with a righthand sidepull on the right arête of the tall slab. Climb left, then up past a sloping rail and through two tiny crimps. The reach-challenged should expect to do twice as many moves as others.

___3. **Ice Age** V5 ★

Begin on a low right-hand undercling and climb the off-vertical arête to a gripping finish. Technical and hard for the grade.

___4. **Ice Grip** V4 ★★

Climb from a high righthand sidepull to sloping shelves in the shallow dihedral. A nice mix of power and technique.

___5. **Fat Lip** V3 ★

Begin with sloping edges on the left end of the low boulder adjacent to the Icehouse. Traverse right along the lip to the cool fin and finish around the corner. Silly but fun.

___6. **The Icicle** V3 ★★

Climb the small bulging arête from low opposing sidepulls. Great climbing on a tiny rock.

___7. **Little Bear** V5 ★★

Start crouched with low holds on the corner and make a big move up and left to the basketball sloper. Slap straight up the small prow to finish.

___8. **Bear Hug** V4 ★★

Begin with your arms spread between the left arete and the opposing rail underneath the bulge. One burly move for flat edges above leads to a thrutchy finish.

___9. **Claustrophobia** V3 ★

Climb the vertical face between the tree and the other boulder. A bit sandy, and harder than it looks.

___10. **Bearly** V0

Climb the dirty little face.

ANSWER MAN

Answer Man can be found roughly 6.1 miles from Icicle Junction, on the north side of the road roughly 100 yards past the Icehouse. A small, blank roof nearly overhanging the right side of the road marks the beginning of Answer Man's faint approach. The boulder's eponym is a tall overhanging arête that can vaguely be seen from the road, definitely one of Leavenworth's better moderates. Bring some determination and a friend to spot.

___11. **Answer Man** V6 ★★★

 Sit-start on the small boulder below with two flat edges and climb the tall arête on opposing sidepulls to an insecure finish.

___12. **Taller** V5 ★

The high face, with questionable rock… does not see many ascents.

WAS

WAS is on the left side of Icicle Road, roughly 100 yards past Answer Man. Look for a low blob of rock on the left as you drive up; this is the top of the WAS boulder. WAS may be the most difficult boulder to find in the Straightaways, but is well worth the mission. The large overhang 20 yards up the road and a bit more downhill than WAS is the **Ladder Project**, itself a landmark that's home to several fun climbs and Leavenworth's proudest future problem. The faint trail to the Ladder Project descends from the mini pullout just west of the boulder's steep corner.

___13. **Maybe** V4 ★

 Climb the left arête of the tall scooped face from a small incut sidepull. Work up the arête to good edges on the left face, then mantel to the dirty lip and top out.

74

Andrew Philbin cranks to the lip on WAS (V8)

LEAVENWORTH : Icicle Canyon - Straightaway

___14. **WAS** V8 ★★★

Jump to the basketball hoop hueco in the middle of the face, and climb to the top using the left arête. An incredibly pure line that is one of Leavenworth's finest. F.A. Johnny Goicoechea.

___15. **IS** V7 ★★

Begin in the hueco as for **#14**, but climb up and right on sloping crimps to a wide reach for good edges near the arête. Make an awkward mantel onto the slab around the corner to finish. F.A. Kyle O'Meara.

___16. **Hemp** V3 ★★

Follow the faint trail to the water's edge from **WAS** to this scenic riverside problem. From a good edge under the overhang, climb left to the lip. Pop right to the good rail, and mantel; descend via the ramp.

___17. **Rex Flex** V3 ★★

From high jugs on the corner, climb up and left on sketchy jugs to the flat lip and press it out. Scary!

___18. **The Ladder Project** (Project)

Climb the tall, clean overhanging face from two high crimps in the shallow groove. Sadly, the stopper first move is not the crux.

___19. **Dog Named Rehab** V4 ★★

Start on the right side of the featured scoop left of the tree with an incut lefthand and a right sidepull at the bottom of the ramp. Slap up the mini-bulge, then make a long move to the lip and press out the mantel. Not bad at all.

___20. **I Know, Dyno!** V9 ★

Start on the head-high crimp around the corner from the ladder project and dyno to the notch up and right. Grade unconfirmed.

The Cortton Pony Pointer

THE COTTON PONY

The Cotton Pony is located on the left side of the road another 80 yards past **WAS**. Named for a certain canine's predilection to retrieve roadside litter for her owner—whether appreciated or not. Park in the second medium-sized pullout on the left, directly across from the Cotton Pony Pointer, a small spike of rock on the opposite hillside. Follow the trail downhill and slightly left from a cluster of small trees to find this super-steep overhang.

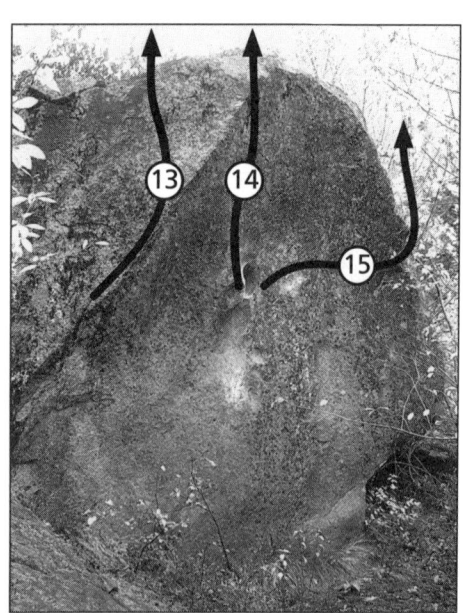

Icicle Canyon - Straightaway | **LEAVENWORTH**

___21. **The Pony Ride** V4 ★★

  Begin low on the right side of the steep face. Follow the shrinking crack up and left until you're forced to make a big move left to the edge of the notch. The finish is more puzzling than difficult.

___22. **The Cotton Pony** V11 ★★★

Start on the horizontal 'minus bar' rail in the middle of the roof. Move up to the Star Trek pinch and small right-hand crimp, then paste your feet on and dyno to the V-shaped groove at the lip (V10). Bring your guns! F.A. Joel Campbell.

___23. **The Cotton Pony Low** V12 ★★★

Begin sitting with a low undercling on the left arête of the sheer face. Traverse right along small crimps to the minus bar, continuing into the dyno of the **Cotton Pony**. Steep and hard, this heinous line is actually still a project at time of writing…

___24. **Tampax Arête** V4 ★★

Climb the tall arête around the corner downhill of **The Cotton Pony**. Super-cool jugs at the start lead to scarier climbing above the sloping landing. Finish to the left on top of the bulge and walk off the slab to descend.

BATMAN

Batman is the last of the Straightaway Boulders included in the map, located just after the road winds around the base of Icicle Buttress, a large low-angle cliff on the right. Batman is 6.4 miles from Icicle junction, hidden in a roadside cluster of rocks next to a medium-sized pullout. Park well off the road and clamber up talus to find the wide west-facing scoop that houses this classic problem, which is visible for a brief second when driving towards Leavenworth.

___25. **Batman** V8 ★★★

  Begin on the right end of the overhang with your left hand locked in the incipient crack and your right hand on the low sloping shelf. Cross up to poor holds on the lip, and traverse leftwards until you can slap to the faint depression in the slab above. Mantel and walk off the slab to the left. This super-classic problem gets a bit of runoff from the slab above, and will probably need a good brushing from time to time. F.A. Kyle O'Meara.

___26. **Throwin' The Houlihan** V4 ★★

This sole problem lies another 100 yards past Batman, and roughly 50 yards downhill. Park as for Batman and walk along the road to the small brown "Leaving Private Land" sign. The steep trail to **The Houlihan** descends from a small pullout roughly 40 yards past the sign. Start sitting, squeezing the angular block on the boulder's uphill side. Work through sloping edges to finish atop the short slab above. Tricky and unique.

LEAVENWORTH : Icicle Canyon - Rat Creek

THE RAT CREEK BOULDERS

Just upcanyon of Icicle Buttress lies a nice collection of medium-sized boulders in a flat, open setting on the tricky-to-access south side of Icicle Creek. Home to a handful of tough gear climbs, the Rat Creek Boulder proper is a huge block located just east of Rat Creek at the edge of the steep hillside below Rat Creek Buttress. The developed bouldering in the area, however, is scattered over the wide meadow to the west of Rat Creek. Several quaint classics like **The Optimator** (V3) and **Bubble Boy** (V4) can be found here, though there are more unclimbed boulders than established problems. I have not included a map for the Rat Creek boulders; access is difficult, and exploration is the name of the game here. Bring good hiking shoes and a light load, as you'll be doing plenty of walking.

Approach: The main concern in accessing the Rat Creek boulders is avoiding private property. The boulders are scattered roughly 6.7 miles from Icicle Junction, with the large white boulder visible on the south side of Icicle Creek at 6.8 miles marking the western boundary of the array.

The Rat Creek boulders should be visited in late summer and fall, when the river can be crossed in several spots. Perhaps the easiest crossing is beside the Straightaway Boulders' **Throwin' The Houlihan**, though this requires a slightly longer approach. To find your own crossing, park in the lefthand pullout at 6.8 miles and head down the steep hill. Bring a tall walking stick for balance, and don't cross alone; the current here is still pretty strong at its lowest. **Bubble Boy** can be found on top of the small ridge a short ways downstream of the big white boulder, while the rest of the bouldering is spread over the open area beyond.

During the remainder of the year, Icicle Creek is too powerful to cross and the Rat Creek boulders can only be accessed from downstream via the Hook Creek Bridge at 6.0 miles. Furthermore, after crossing the bridge, one is forced to bushwhack well onto the steep hillside to avoid the private property stretching west from the bridge to Rat Creek. Approaching the Rat Creek boulders this way takes so much time and energy that you'll be disappointed when you get there, and is not recommended; nor is an interaction with the landowner.

The Western Edge of the Rat Creek Boulders

Icicle Canyon - JY Boulders : **LEAVENWORTH**

Kelly Sheridan hangs tough on Mad Max (V7), JY Boulders   Photograph by Brian Sweeney

JY BOULDERS

The boulders below JY crag host quality problems in a beautiful meadow setting. Don't miss the powerful **Nosebleed** (V7) or the striking **Yosemite Highball** (V4). The JY boulders don't see a ton of traffic and are a good place to get off the beaten path. The area has seen a bit more attention recently, with classic climbs like **Mad Max** (V7), **King Kong** (V6), and **Right Angles** (V8) all appearing in 2006. There are still projects to be done in the JY proper, or if you're feeling more adventurous, check out the potential on the hillside up-canyon from the JY boulders, in the talus field below Small World Buttress. With all-day sun, the JY boulders can feel warm even in winter. Shaded boulders such as the Gamecube and the Mad Max cave also remain cool during summer heat, making this a pretty nice spot all year.

Approach: The JY boulders are located on the hillside directly across from the entrance to 8-Mile campground. Park on the right 7.1 miles from Icicle Junction, roughly 20 yards past the brown Forest Service sign across from the campground entrance. Follow the climber's trail up and right past the diminutive XY Crag, then left to the flat meadow and the Yosemite boulder. Nosebleed is the large boulder at the west side of the meadow; Mad Max can be found in the cluster of large boulders below the crag. Alternatively, to visit the Gamecube, park just east of the campground entrance and head straight uphill. The Gamecube lies one drainage to the right of the Green Lung boulder. This route also makes for the most pleasant winter approach.

____1. **German Acres** V0 ★
Ten yards downhill from **Nosebleed**, climb this short arête from the loose sidepull. Commonly climbed in sneakers.

____2. **Sassy Chipmunk** V2 ★
Start on the low jug 10 feet right of the nose, make a big move up and right to another jug, and finish with an easy mantel.

____3. **Nosebleed** V7 ★★
Start on low opposing sidepulls, slap to the nose, and make an awkward press with the left arête in hand. The one-move-wonder that isn't… F.A. John Wiley.

____4. **Gradisfaction** V2 ★
Climb up and left on the dirty face from the obvious chest-high undercling. Doesn't see much traffic, but definitely worth your while.

____5. **One-Mover** V2
This one really is. Start on two high, wide crimps on the small boulder, chuck to the lip, and top out.

____6. **The White Traverse** V7 ★
Vaguely like the Peak District's famed **Green Traverse**, but on sharp white granite… with painful granite crimps. Start on the left end of the short face and climb right on the strange incuts, avoiding the lip. Topout on the right arête.
Variation (V2/3): Slap to the lip from the start and traverse right. Top out via **#7** or **#8**.

____7. **Max Attacks** V3 ★
Start on the chest-high rail a few feet left of the arête. Climb straight up on sharp holds to an engaging mantel. A quality line that could use some more traffic.

Icicle Canyon - JY Boulders : **LEAVENWORTH**

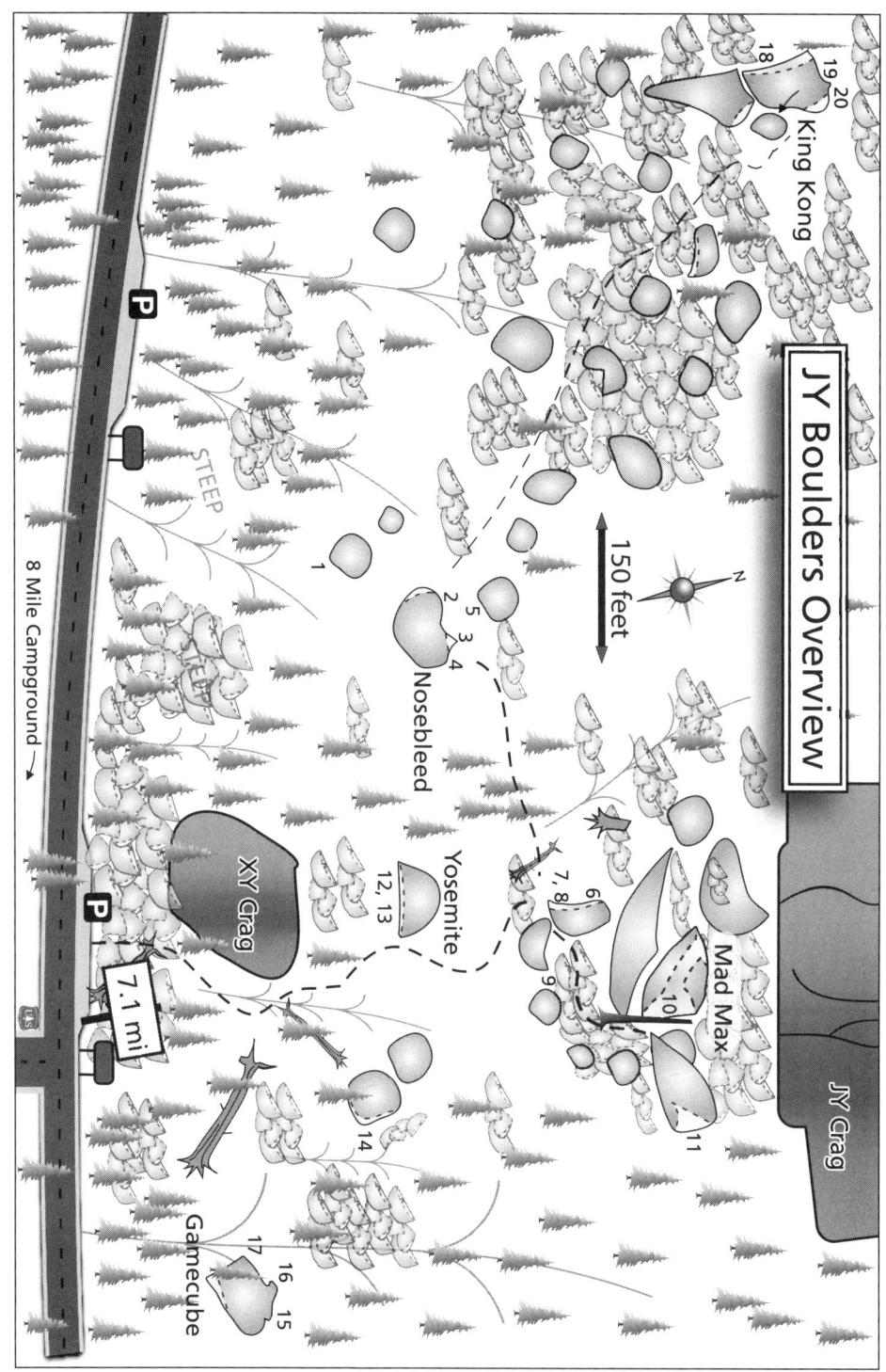

LEAVENWORTH : Icicle Canyon - JY Boulders

___8. **The White Arête** V5 ★★

Start as for **#7** but follows crimps right the arête. Stab for a chunky crimp on the corner and power to the lip. Finish with an awkward mantel on the corner. Great fun.

___9. **Private Pile** V2

Climb the short arête in the sheltered corridor from two chest-high edges.

___10. **Mad Max** V7 ★★★

Begin low in the cave underneath the tall slab. Start with your left hand on the lowest sloper and your left heel in the jug nearby. Punch up through slopers and pinches, gaining edges on the lip after a wide-open compression move. Finish up the tallish slab. Wildly steep for featured granite, this climb stays dry nearly all year. F.A. Kelly Sheridan.
Variation (project): The right exit to **Mad Max**, which follows the obvious left-facing rail to a series of sloping crimps up the steep wall, remains undone.

___11. **Guano Slap** V2 ★★

Just uphill from **Mad Max**, start this reachy problem on head-high slopers at the edge of the cave. Climb to the calcium-coated jug and stand tall to reach the lip. Super-sweet. The cramped sit-start is still a project.

___12. **Right Angles** V8 ★★★

Start sitting by the square corner on the left side of the tall face. Slap up and right to the cool sloper and follow the vertical, left-facing rail straight up to a jug.

___13. **The Yosemite Highball** V3 ★★★

Start sitting on the left end of the tall face as for **#12**. Make a big move to the sloper, then continue right along the shelf to an incut flake. Head straight up, then left to better holds, finishing with an interesting mantel. Beautiful.

82

Icicle Canyon - JY Boulders : **LEAVENWORTH**

____**14. Green Lung** (project)
Start standing on the blunt corner and climb through a few desperately thin pockets to a large sidepull and the top. I'd love to see this one climbed.

____**15. Sega** V3 ★
Hug the short off-vertical face with your right hand on a sloper in the cleft and your left on the arête. Slap up to slopers and mantel. Great texture.

____**16. Wario** V0
Climb the dirty face from the flat top of the right-facing 'ear' feature. If the sit-down interests you, go for it.

____**17. Bowser** V3 ★★
Climb the right-leaning rail to a heady finish up the arête near the tree.

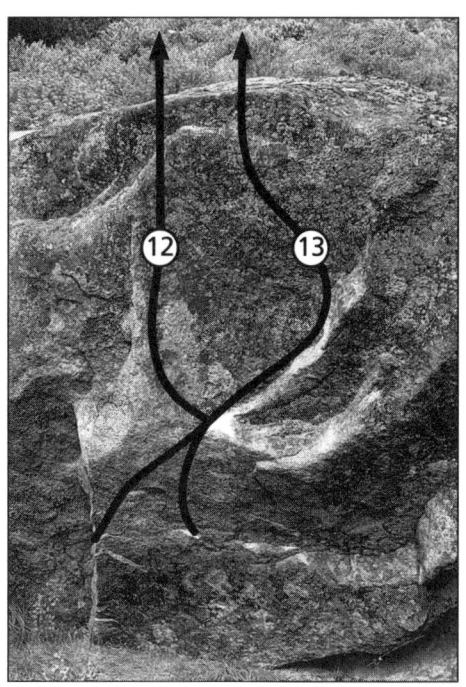

____**18. King Kong** V6 ★★★
Climb the tall left-leaning arête on right-facing holds. Finish directly up the corner on the left arête. Starting from the small boulder eases the challenge, but won't make the top any less scary. Thumbs up!

____**19. Ex-Pat Scotsman** V0 ★
Start on the right of the vertical rib on the uphill side of the boulder. Climb the left side of the tall face on good but crumbly crimpers.

____**20. Donkey Kong** V4 ★★
Start standing on the left side of the vertical rib with a righthand crimp/pinch and a good foothold. High step and stretch for a small edge in the notch, finishing straight up the juggy arête.

83

LEAVENWORTH : Icicle Canyon - Carnival Boulders

THE CARNIVAL BOULDERS

This dense cluster of talus is located just down the road from Icicle's Eightmile Campground, on the hillside overlooking the private Eightmile Island. An eponym of **Carnival Crack** (the locally notorious 5.11 offwidth uphill) these boulders see little traffic despite their close proximity to the road. The Carnivals see so little traffic, in fact, that several people have *discovered* them for themselves in recent years. Before you begin the web-spray about your new secret spot, take a look at classic highballs like **The Rib** (V4) and the flexfest of **The Brawl** (V1) to see what's been established here. Most of the Carnival Boulders' problems have pretty mellow landings. This is a great spot to escape weekend crowds for some solitude and that fresh (read: sharp) texture. More potential can also be found in the talus just above these established problems. This is a good spot for prolonging a fall day, as The Carnivals stay sunny much longer than most Icicle spots through the Mountaineer Creek Valley across the canyon.

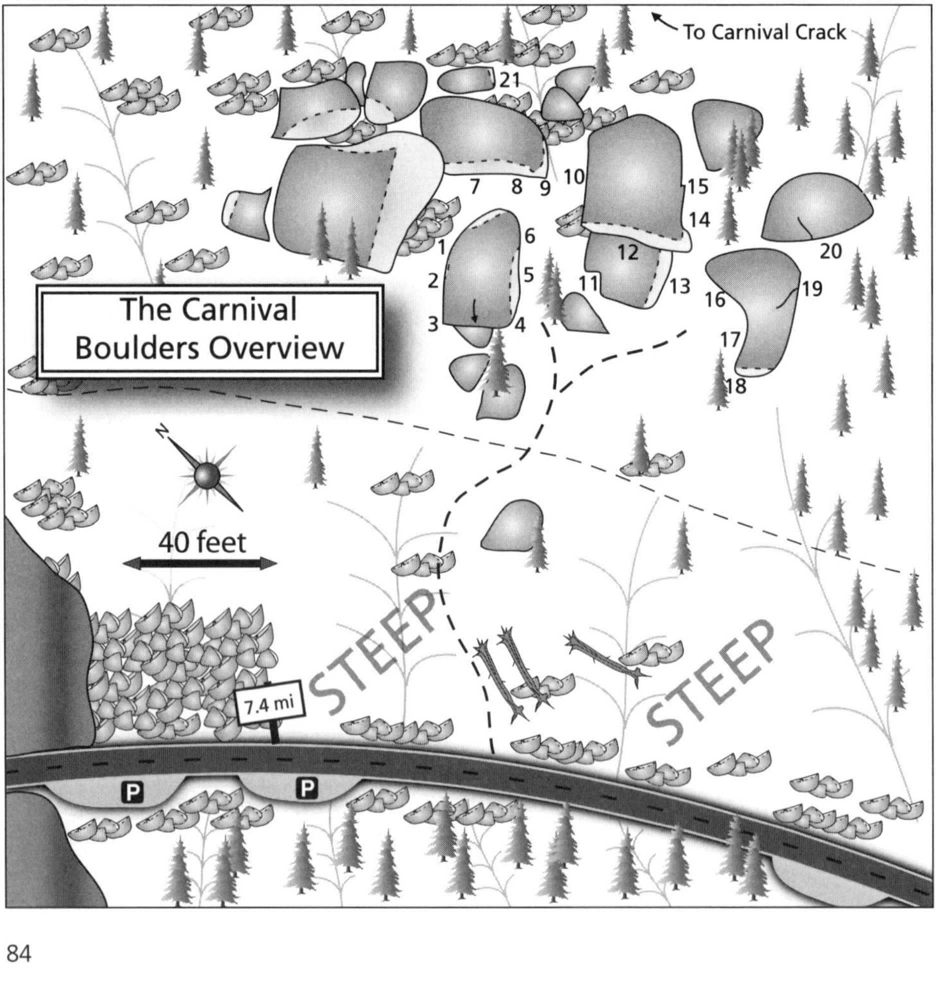

Icicle Canyon - Carnival Boulders : LEAVENWORTH

Approach: The Carnival Boulders lie 7.4 miles from Icicle junction on the hillside above Icicle Road. Park in the lefthand pullout just before the large roadcut, the crumbling cap of Eightmile Buttress. Walk back along the road for roughly 40 yards, then follow the faint trail up the short, steep incline. The Carnival boulders are visible uphill from the road, the most notable landmark being the huge roof on the western edge of the cluster.

___1. **Extreme Duck** V7 ★
Start just right of the adjacent rock with a poor head-high undercling. Work your feet super-high and lunge for the edge up and right.

___2. **Against The Wall** V1+ ★★
Climb the flake up the center of the face from a tricky start with left-facing edges and a good foothold.

___3. **The Campus Problem** V0+ ★★
Starting from a high jug on the downhill arête, climb the arête on large holds using Sly Stallone campusing or tricky heel hooks.

___4. **Heeler** V2 ★
Traverse right along the lip of the overhang from an overhead jug on the left end. Finish in the notch with a strenuous mantel.

___5. **Mine** V2/3
Start with a weird pinch in the center of the overhang, following painful holds up the seam to the lip and an awkward mantel. Super-painful and really just no fun.

___6. **Butt Surfing** V1
Start sitting with a low jug flake on the right end of the overhang, climbing straight up on grainy holds to the low lip.

Joel Zerr on The Yosemite Highball (V3) JY Boulders
Photo: Brian Sweeney

LEAVENWORTH : Icicle Canyon - Carnival Boulders

____7. **The Ferret** V3 ★★
From a chest-high edge in the tiny alcove on the left side of the face, move up and right to a strangely-solid bar hold—the Ferret. Finish up the dirty right-facing rail to the left, or dyno up and right for the block on the lip.

____8. **Fen Fin** V0+ ★★
Climb the featured intrusion just left of the arête, enjoying big holds as you head to a cruxy mantel up and left.

____9. **Grain Brain** V3 ★★

Starting matched on a grainy chest-high shelf with a low left foot, climb the slightly overhung arête to a committing move for the lip then press out the crux mantel. Perhaps a bit intimidating, but spot-on for the grade.

____10. **Giant Man** V4 ★★
Climb the center of the tall face, moving delicately up and left through sidepulls and edges.

____11. **The Stem** V0 ★★
Climb the stem corner on the small boulder right of **#9**, pinching both arêtes as you go. Great fun. Can you do it in sneakers? Facing outwards? No hands??

____12. **Mr. Joel's Wild Ride** V8/9 ★
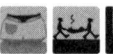
Starts on top of the slab above **#10**. Start sitting with a low lefthand incut, move up to crimps in the seam and then the lip. You may want to get creative with the padding and spotting on this one to avoid rolling backwards down the slab. F.A. Joel Campbell

____13. **Feelin' Sappy** V2
Start with a low left-facing jug in the tiny overhang. Move to the sappy lip, traversing to the left to make the crux mantel. Kind of fun, but also kind of embarrassing…

____14. **Project**
The tall overhanging arête has not been climbed from any start. There are holds, they're just really far apart…

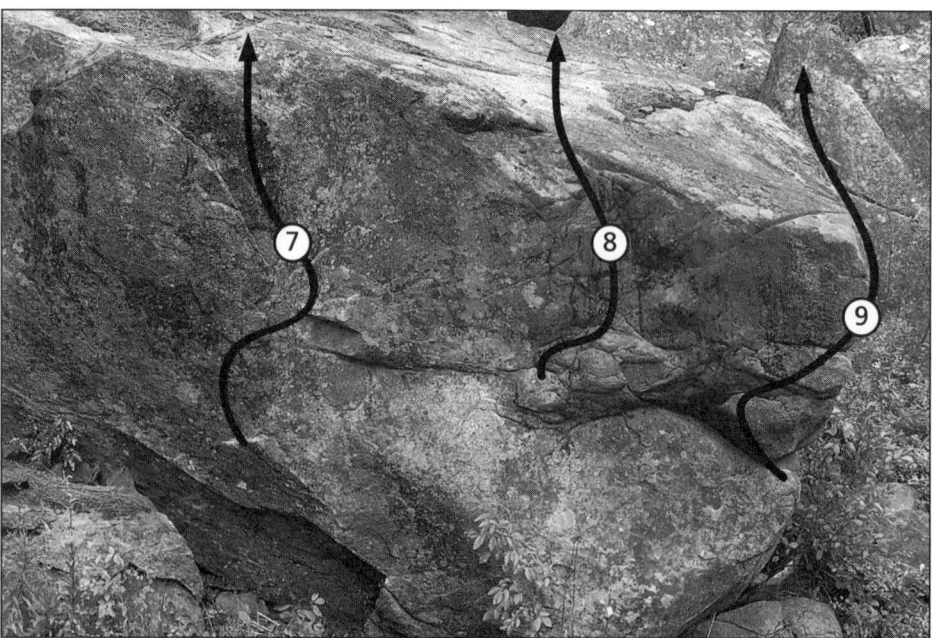

Icicle Canyon - Carnival Boulders : **LEAVENWORTH**

20. Over Myself V1 ★★

Climb the semi-clean slab at the edge of the cluster. The easiest line seems to start on the right side, mantling on edges before making a smeary traverse left to the layback seam. An adventure in modesty...

21. The Pickle V3 ★★

Start sitting on the small boulder with a low left crimp on the arete. Slap up both sides of the 'pickle' feature to a committing move for the lip. Good fun.

15. The Rib V4 ★★★

In the hidden little room, climb the tall rail feature from a stand start with a good flake foothold. At the top of the rib, make a committing move left to the shelf and finish with an easy mantel. Classic.

16. Dan Akroyd V0- ★

Climb the shallow scoop on the left side of the face on questionable jugs.

17. Rick Moranis V0-

Climb the off-vertical scoop on the right side of the face.

18. The Brawl V1 ★★

On the downhill side of the tall boulder, climb the dirty double arêtes from a head-high jug. Pretty easy, but pretty high, and very chossy... watch the burnt tree at your back!

19. Dutty Rock V1

Climb the left-leaning crack to a dirty finish in the corner. Walk up and left on the vegetated ramp to top out.

Kelly Sheridan on The Pickle (V3)
Photo: Kyle O'Meara

87

THE PRETTY BOULDERS

The Pretty Boulders are one of the newest additions to the Icicle Canyon's cache of bouldering areas. 'Discovered' in early 2006, the Prettys may very well have been climbed on previously, but, like many 'new' areas around Leavenworth, forest fires, weathering, and general neglect may have returned these boulders to something of a natural state, allowing new generations to re-pioneer this frontier. Historical speculation aside, the Pretty Boulders are home to some very fine climbs on well-textured granite, with an ambience that's hard to beat. The stunning fin of **Pretty Girl** (V3) is one of the best moderates in the entire canyon, while the timeless arête of **Pretty Hate Machine** (V8) requires some serious power. Hit the Pretty Boulders on a chilly afternoon or summer evening; between the middle-of-nowhere atmosphere and the views of Mount Stewart up the Mountaineer Creek valley, the Pretty Boulders also make for a great hangout.

Aproach: Park on the left 7.6 miles from Icicle Junction, just after the large roadcut. Roughly 50 yards down the road, an orange telephone cable marker on the right indicates the roadside Pretty Boy. To find Pac-Man and Pretty Girl, follow the climber's trail up the eroded slope directly across from the parking pullout. Head straight uphill through the open area, eventually cutting left and dropping into the gully. Pac-Man is the large boulder lying in the high flat spot across the seasonal streambed. For Pretty Girl, stay just to the right of the gully, following a series of switchbacks up the open slope. Pretty Girl is in the small cluster at the top of the hill; at the crest of the gully, continue up and left over a short rise to the large boulders. The land downhill and up-canyon from Pretty Girl is private property; please respect the landowner's privacy by keeping noise and exploration to a minimum.

Things that go bump in the night... Pretty Boy (V7) after dark

Icicle Canyon - Pretty Boulders — LEAVENWORTH

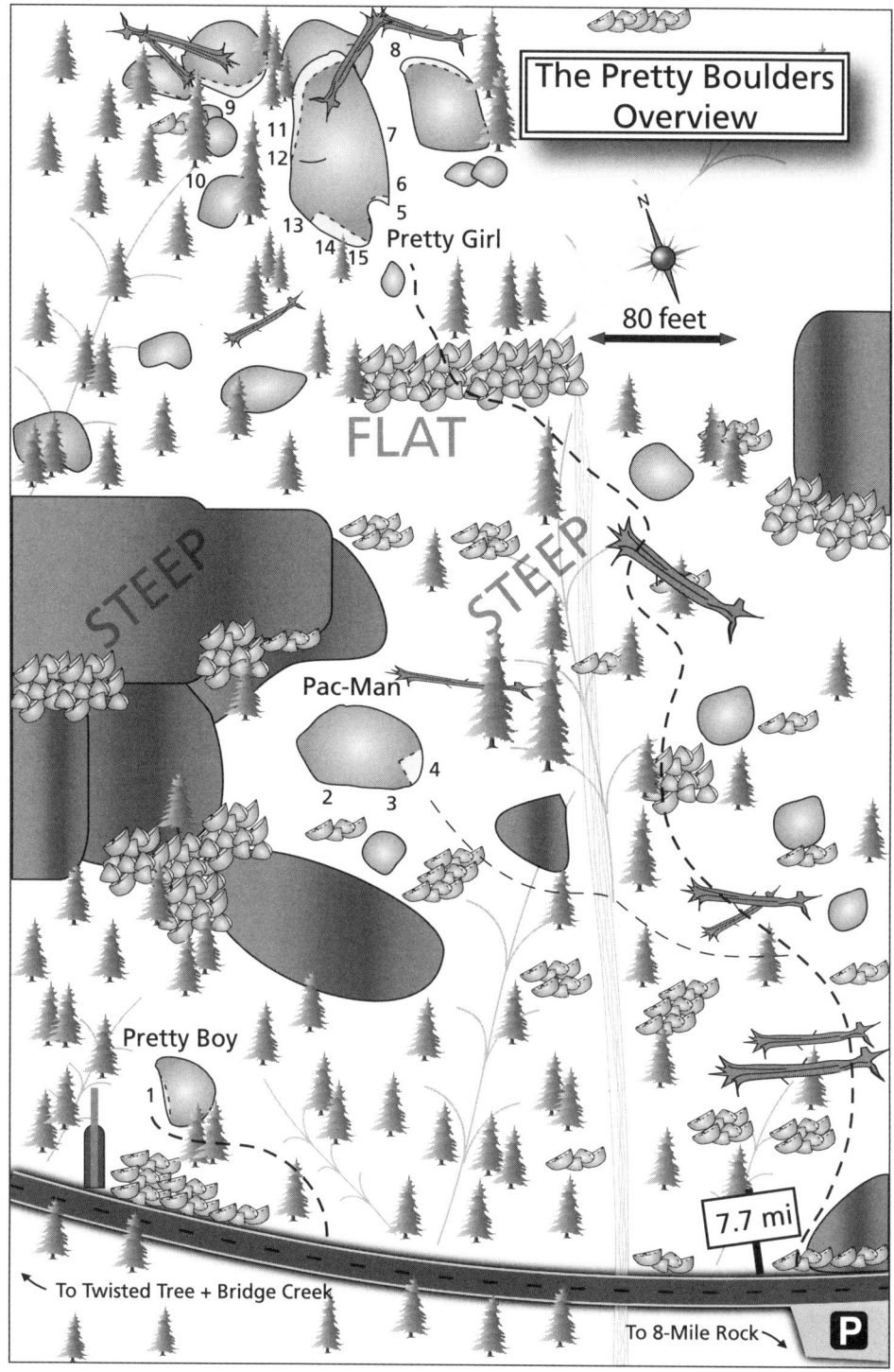

LEAVENWORTH : Icicle Canyon - Pretty Boulders

___1. **Pretty Boy** V7 ★★
A little harder than it looks… start with your left hand in the sloping hueco and the large flake for your foot. Pop to a small crimp just below the lip and finish straight up.

___2. **Pizzaface** V1+
Climb the left side of the downhill face from a high start with the calcium-coated jug. A bit loose but still fun.

___3. **Ms. Pac-Man** V3 ★
Press awkwardly onto the tallish face just right of the slight rib feature. Follow sloping crimps to a dirty mantel finish on the slab.

___4. **Pac-Man** V3 ★★
Start sitting on the east corner of the large boulder. Slap up to a pinch on the corner, then mantel on the mini-bulge and stand up using grainy slopers.

___5. **Pretty Girl** V3 ★★★
Start with a good righthand sidepull on the outside of the curved fin. Move left to good sidepulls, then slap and stem up the perfect corner. Classic!

___6. **Pretty Woman** V5 ★★
Start as for **Pretty Girl**, but climb straight up sloping edges right of the fin to a jug on the lip. Grainy and good.

___7. **Pretty Easy** V0- ★
Climb the sandy left-leaning rail in the middle of the face to an easy-as-pie mantel.

___8. **Pretty Hard (Project)**
Climb the blunt corner from two fat crimpers. It will go, but it's pretty sharp…

9. **Pretty Hate Machine** V8 ★★★

Pretty Hate Machine can be found in a small alcove behind the rear side of the Pretty Girl boulder. Start from an undercling under the chest-high bulge and climb up and right to the corner. Reach high to a poor pinch on the arête with your right hand, set up, and dyno to the juggy lip. A beautiful testpiece on impeccable rock. F.A. Kyle O'Meara.

10. **Alexis C. Jolly** V1+ ★★

Climb the hidden slab on the west side of the smallish boulder, squeezing between the arête and good rails on the face as you go. Scary in sneakers.

11. **Pretty Burly** V4 ★★

Start in small underclings in the overlap on the rear of the Pretty Girl boulder. Slap up to the sloping edge on the lip, match, and lunge to a fat pinch at the apex. Awesome.

12. **Cracked Out** V1 ★★

Start on juggy underclings in the seam at waist height. Move to a sloper, then finish up the juggy right-facing crack above.

13. **Miller** V1

Climb the undercut face from a left-facing edge at head height.

14. **John He-Man** V2 ★

Start sitting with the flat edge in front of the tree. Climb up and right on flat edges to a fun finish right of the overlap.

15. **Noland** V1

Climb the arête on the downhill corner of the Pretty Girl boulder. Fun from either side.

LEAVENWORTH : Icicle Canyon - Twisted Tree

TWISTED TREE

Twisted Tree boulder vies with Clamshell Cave's Fist Boulder for the "most obvious boulder in the Icicle" award. A stone's throw from the road, the Twisted Tree (a.k.a. the Bridge Creek Boulder) is easily identifiable by the ancient ponderosa pine wrapped around its left arête. A handful of classic problems adorn this granite nugget; the grainy slopers of **Twister** (V7) beckon for your skin as you drive by, while the standard **Twisted Tree** (V4) lurks just behind the tree. A few other fine problems can be found in the area surrounding the Twisted Tree, including **Scrambled Eggs** (V8) and **The Dildo** (V3). Visit the Twisted Tree any time of the year, though some may want to save Twister for a crisp winter afternoon!

Approach: The Twisted Tree is easy to find. Park adjacent to this roadside boulder, 8.2 miles from Icicle Junction. Please park completely off the road and avoid the usual tailgate parties; with five more campgrounds up canyon, this wide curve can be busier than you think.

For the Scrambled Eggs boulder, it's easiest to walk back along the road for 50 yards or so, re-entering the thin forest just down canyon of the stream. Scrambled Eggs is roughly twice as far from the road as the Twisted Tree.

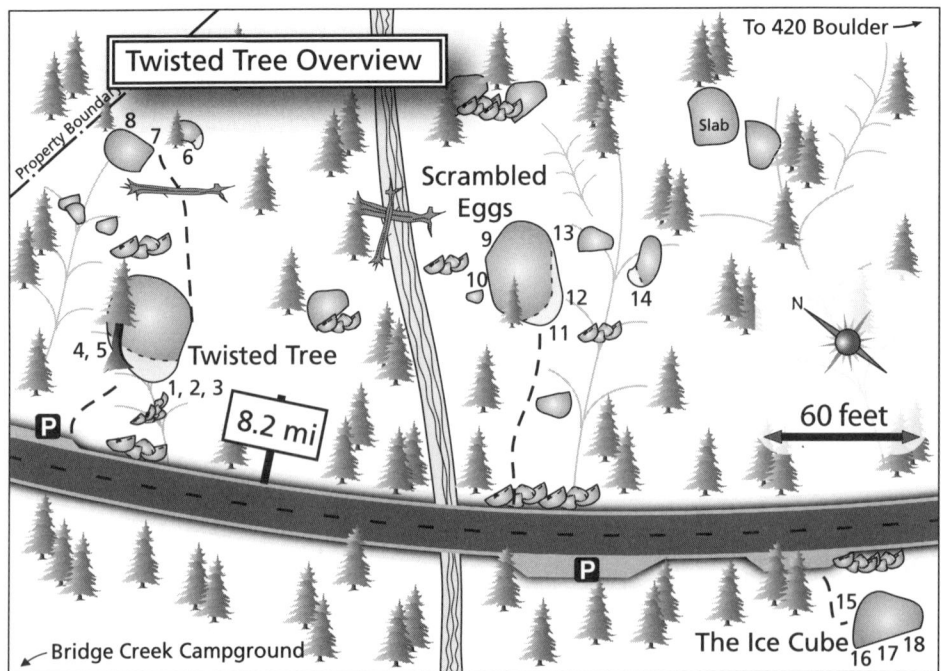

The Ice Cube and 420 Boulder are a little closer to town and take a little more cunning to find. The Ice Cube is located just below the road roughly 40 yards east of the trail to Scrambled Eggs. A modest boulder alone on the south side of the road, the Ice Cube is near the edge of the Bridge Creek Campground group site; please be respectful of others in the surrounding area while visiting this spot.

Finally, the 420 Boulder can be found on top of the hillside across from the Ice Cube. Walk up the wide drainage past a large slabby boulder, and curve right at the top of the hill into an open area. The 420 Boulder sits alone at the northern end of the pleasant meadow. Explorers ought to limit themselves to the boulders mentioned in this section, avoiding the property boundary just uphill from problems **#6–#8**.

____1. **Straight Shot** V0+ ★

Start on the chest-high flat jug in the small corner. Climb straight up to better holds, finishing up and right on dirty buckets.

____2. **With A Twist** V1 ★★

Start as for **#1** but finish up and left on a large, rounded gaston in the crack.

____3. **Twister** V7 ★★★

 Start as for the previous two prolems. Climb left to the nice round slopers at head height and continue past crimps to better holds and a scary finish. "Quit reading and do it."

____4. **Twisted Tree** V4 ★★

Start low on the big jug just left of the tree. Climb the steep corner to a tough mantel and top out straight up the slab. Short and stout, an area classic.

____5. **Mr. Leftist** V6 ★

Start as for **#4** but climb left past a sloper on the lip to a sidepull flake and mantel.

____6. **Little One** V2 ★

 Climb the mini overhanging prow from a crouch start. Sharp but pretty fun. **Variation** (V2): Start on the good edge three feet left of the prow and finish as above.

____7. **Nuthin'** V3

Climb the short arête from a crouch start. The sit is inviting but awkward…

____8. **Sumthin'** V0

Start with the big sidepull on the uphill face of the boulder. Climb to the lip and mantel. Something to climb…

____9. **Over Easy** V0 ★

Climb the textured slab from the small boulder in front of it. Head straight up using the left-facing sidepull, or step right to good edges near the arête.

____10. **Deviled** V2 ★

Start from the rocking boulder with the good waist-high sidepull in the small dihedral, climbing straight up the arête with a pinch and cool slopers to a slightly insecure finish. Good fun!

____11. **Scrambled Eggs** V8 ★★

 Start on two small crimps on the road-facing corner of the large boulder. Climb straight up the blunt arête to a good high crimp and top out. A typical Joel Campbell problem; finger and core strength a must. The stand start clocks in around V2/3.

LEAVENWORTH : Icicle Canyon - Twisted Tree

___12. **Angelina Jolie** (Project)
Climb the slanting rail up and right. Much tougher than it looks, this gorgeous line shares a really, really vague resemblance with a certain famous Peak District problem. "It's hard but it's not that hard…" – Ben Moon

___13. **Twisted Stone** V3 ★★
Start on the right corner of the tall face with a flexing jug and muscle up the arête. A bit dodgy, but great fun.

___14. **The Dildo** V3 ★★
Climb the short arête on gritty holds from the big low rail. Quite the workout.

___15. **Raptorman** V3 ★
The uphill arête. Grab a high crimp on both sides of the arête, pull on, and shoot for the lip. Once a sit-start, the departure of several holds has made this more of an exercise in pain tolerance than anything else.

___16. **Gatorade Bowling Balls** V4 ★★
Start on low opposing sidepulls, stab to an incut sidepull pinch on the arête, and top-out straight up on the right of the dirty corner.

___17. **Etna Mantel** V3 ★★
Begin with both hands on the good head-high incut in the middle of the face. Climb to sloping holds on the lip and thrutch over to small crimps. Classy!

___18. **Ben Carney's Bowling Balls** V5 ★
Start sitting with one hand in the obvious low slot. Pull on and stand to the sloping lip, finishing with a short mantel into the scoop on the slab. Very odd indeed.

___19. **420 Slab** V0 ★★★
An insecure start leads to easier climbing on this tall slab. A beautiful, isolated problem slightly marred by the unfortunate installation of a bolt anchor by some gutless wanker. Sadly, suffice to say that this poor boulder has endured worse at the hands of misguided climbers…

Right hand sloper, left hand to crimp... Herman Feissner playing Twister (V7). Photo: Jackie Hueftle

LEAVENWORTH : Icicle Canyon - Little Bridge Creek

LITTLE BRIDGE CREEK WALL

Just across from Bridge Creek Campground, the hidden Little Bridge Creek Wall crag is home to several bolted climbs, as well as Dick Cilley's burly toprope **Gutbuster** (5.12+). This short cliff really doesn't offer too much unroped entertainment, with the exception of the striking hit-the-jug-and-drop problem **The Lefty** (V7). Check this one out when you're looking for yet another hidden challenge, or if you've got to climb in a light rain. The overhanging wall shields this section of the cliff, even for several hours in a light drizzle.

Park 8.5 miles from Icicle Junction for Little Bridge Creek Wall, in the small pullout on the left at the beginning of Eightmile Road. Walk a few feet up the driveway across the street, then turn left onto the worn trail, following it northwest and slightly uphill to the base of this 50-foot crag. Find **The Lefty** on the right end of the crag, easily spotted by the prominent quartz vein running across the face. There are a couple other boulders in the area, though the cluster of talus above the driveway is most likely on private property.

___1. **The Lefty** V7 ★★★

Start hanging from the sloping shelf at chest height, working up the clean face via three sidepulls in and around the quartz dyke. Slap to the juggy horizontal crack, hang out, and drop. Beautiful.

THE MACHINE GUN

Upper Icicle's solitary Machine Gun makes a great quick stop or beginner destination. This modestly-sized granite boxcar is home to some quality easy climbs including the enjoyable **Machine Gun Funk** (V2). It's a great spot to catch a quick warm-up, and well worth the one-minute walk for the fun, inviting climbs.

Approach: The Machine Gun is 8.7 miles from Icicle Junction, 0.2 miles past the junction with Bridge Creek Campground and Eightmile Road. A great way to find the Machine Gun is to drive to the Sword area pullout (next pages), turn around, and park in the small south-side pullout 0.1 miles closer to Leavenworth. The Machine Gun boulder is visible on the north side of the road, roughly 50 yards away; Follow the faint trail through the older trees on the left.

____1. **Band of Gypsies** V0+ ★

A few feet left of the tree, start standing or sitting and climb flat edges to the lip and an engaging mantel. Good, but may be a bit dirty.

____2. **Dirty Harry** V1+ ★★

Start just right of the tree with hands matched in two rounded scoops just overhead. Get your feet on, set up, and lunge to the friable flat jug on the lip. Thrutch straight over the stepped lip to finish. **Variation** (V2): Start sitting on the flat shelf down and right of the scoops, climbing through crimps to finish as above. A little footwork goes a long way.

____3. **Machine Gun Funk** aka Susan's Arete V2 ★★★

Start sitting on the corner with two good opposing sidepulls. Climb to the rounded jug on the arête, finishing up the left side of the little prow via the good crimp below the lip. Fun movement!

____4. **Buddy Miles** V3 ★

Start sitting a few feet right of the corner with a low lefthand undercling and a right crimp. Hit the gaston above and paw up the sloping shelves to top out. An extreme drop-knee earns extra style points.

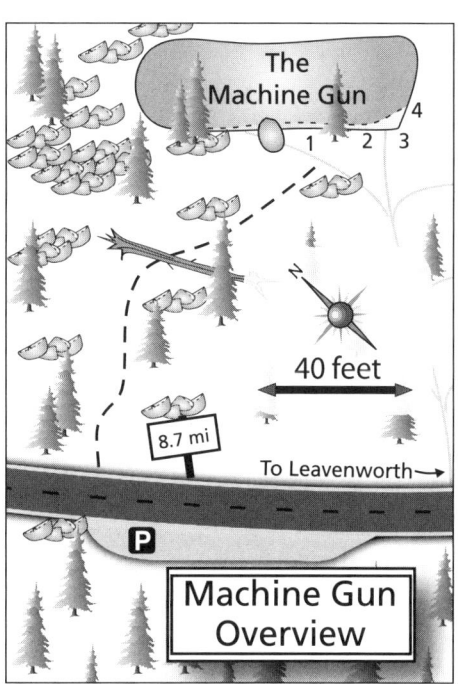

Machine Gun Overview

LEAVENWORTH : Icicle Canyon - Machine Gun

Machine Gun Boulder

Kyle O'Meara en garde on Zorro (V8)

Jens Holsten looking solid at the halfway point of The Sword (V3)

LEAVENWORTH   :   Icicle Canyon - The Sword

THE SWORD BOULDERS

The Sword Boulders comprise one of the best areas in Icicle Canyon, and enjoy a very remote feel despite their proximity to the road. For a relatively small group of boulders, **The Sword** sports a wide, varied array of classic problems including **The Classic** (V2), **The Sword** (V3), and **Resurrection** (V8). Underwear Rock, the roadside landmark for this area, makes for a great place to warm up or a nice introduction for beginning boulderers.

The Sword is an especially nice summer area, as many problems stay shaded, nestled within the open forest. The Sword Boulder itself has a finer grain than found elsewhere in Icicle Canyon, with plenty of off-the-deck challenges for the confident boulderer. If you enjoyed the rock quality at the Swiftwater north boulders, you will be pleasantly surprised by the tall, clean, and nicely textured lines at The Sword.

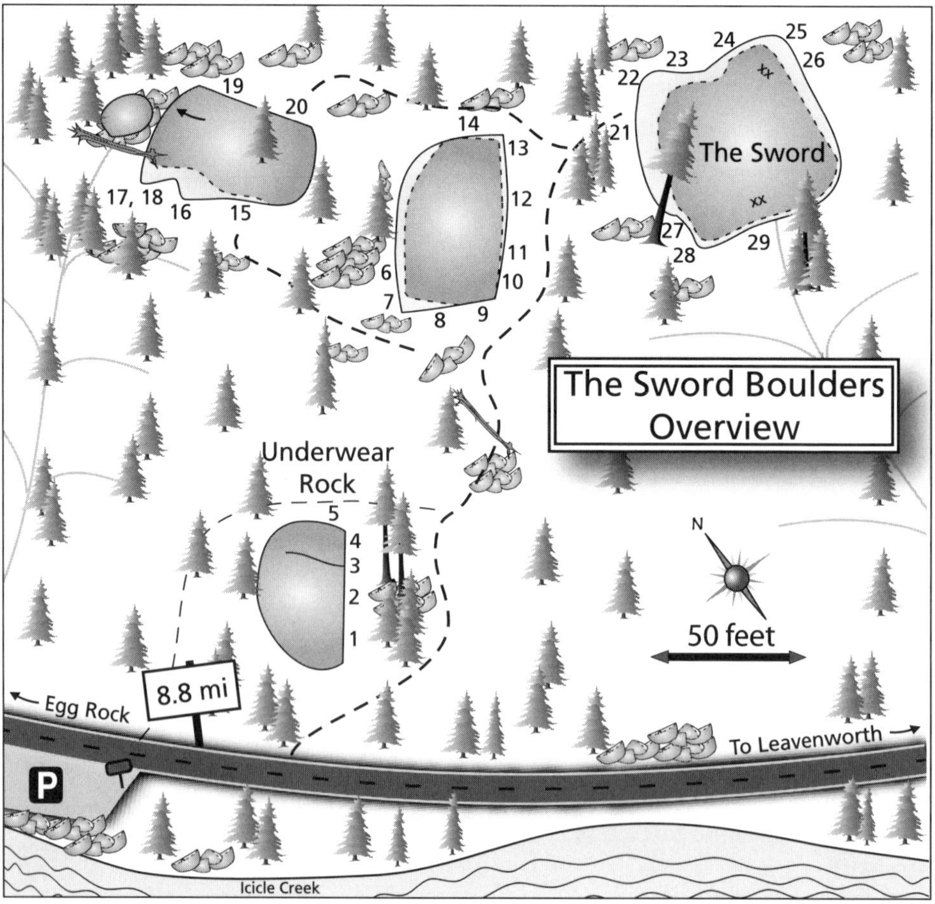

100

Icicle Canyon - The Sword — **LEAVENWORTH**

Approach: Park in a lefthand pullout 8.8 miles from Icicle Junction, easily identified by the small wooden sign stating "Knapweed Control, Check Your Vehicle," a precaution against noxious weeds that seem to have overrun the area. Walk roughly 40 yards back downcanyon and follow the well-worn trail to Underwear Rock, visible from the road. To reach the Sword proper, follow the trail up a slight hill and right into a small clearing at the edge of the cluster.

___1. **Boxers** V0 ★★
Start on a chunky edge, climb right to better holds, and finish straight up crimps on the bulge.

___2. **Briefs** V3 ★
Begin on small edges in the middle of the face, making crimpy slab moves up and left to a tall-seeming finish.

___3. **The Crack** V0- ★★★
Climb the well-featured crack to a nice topout ledge.

___4. **The Taint** V0-
Climb the featured face right of **The Crack**, finishing up and left via the dirty foot ledge.

___5. **Dingleberry Junction** V0
Climb the dirty face right of the corner.

___6. **Bowled Over** V3 ★
Start in the corner with the small boulder at your back and climb straight up on interesting holds. A bit cramped, but climbs well.

101

LEAVENWORTH : Icicle Canyon - The Sword

___7. **The Prism** V9 ★★★
Climb the steep arête from a stand start. I'm not giving any hints for this one—it's too classic and too cryptic!

___8. **The Hourglass** V7 ★★
Walk up the slabby bottom half of the tall face to high crimps in the overhang. When you're about to teeter off, leap to the good knob just over the lip and top out on flat ledges.

___9. **White Sands** V2
Climb the right side of the tall face on sloping shelves. A bit dirty, could use some traffic.

___10. **X1** V0 ★★
On the left end of the large slab, follow blocky ledges to a thinner finish up and right.

___11. **X2** V2 ★
Climb the line of small quartz edges just right of **X1**, finishing the same.

___12. **Cubicle Gangster** V0 ★★★
Follow the quartz vein up the center of the tall slab to a thank-you jug one move below the lip. The log is definitely on for the start of this one...

___13. **Played Like A Poop Butt** V0+ ★★★
Climb the rightmost quartz vein up the undercut slab from an awkward high-step start. Start matched on the low lip for extra entertainment.

___14. **Cole's Corner** V8/9 ★★
Climb the stout little arête. Start on a small lefthand sidepull and a low righthand crimp. Follow the quartz tick marks up and right to a jug on the lip.

___15. **Off The Couch** V7 ★★
Start matched on the low sloping rail in the middle of the face. Climb slightly left, then straight up on small crimps, finishing up and right. F.A. Ryan Paulsness

___16. **Sofa King** V0 ★
Climb shelves up the corner to a dirty finish.

___17. **I ♥ Jugs** V2 ★★★
Start on blocky low jugs, making cool moves up the corner to a delicate topout. Great problem.

___18. **The Wizard** V2/3 ★
Start on the square jugs of **#17** but move left around the corner to a small sidepull. Pinch the tiny pebble and slap left to the lip.

___19. **The Classic** V2 ★★★
Climb the tall right-facing rail to a jug at the 15-foot level and a heady high-step top-out. Super-classic.

___20. **The Stairway** V0+ ★
Start on the large shelves on the left side of the tall face, climbing straight up to the lip with the use of a miniscule gaston. Top out straight up and walk up and around the back to descend.

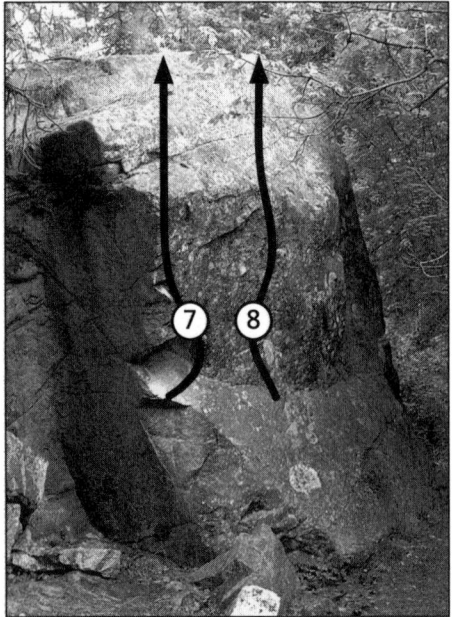

___21. **Go Baby!** V6 ★

The trail leading to the Sword boulder arrives at a chest-high bulge several feet right of the prow of **Resurrection**. Starting with a decent righthand pistol grip and a small lefthand crimp, paste your foot by your navel and chuck for the sloping edge above. Drop after mantling on the lip, or continue to the top through loose holds in the dihedral for full value.

___22. **Resurrection** V8 ★★★

This semi-old-school classic climbs the undercut prow seen when first arriving at the Sword boulder. Start standing on the corner, iron-crossed between a good lefthand sidepull and a bad righthand sloper. Paste your left foot on a high knob, slap to the lip, and grapple around the right side of the corner to top out in the dihedral high above. Descend via the tree to the right of **#27**.

___23. **Zorro** V8 ★★★

Start crouched on the left side of the prow with a low righthand undercling and a small lefthand crimp at the lip. Climb up and left to a long move for a crimp in the dihedral. Then slap up sloping holds on the corner to finish up the ramp and top out around the corner as for **#22**. Wild!

___24. **Seam of Pain** V5 ★★

Start standing in front of the tree with crimps in and around the nebulous seam, climbing straight up on edges to better, if slightly inobvious, holds below the ramp. Top out either up and right with a delicate traverse along the high dirty ramp, or move left and around the corner to finish as for **#25** and **#26**.

___25. **The Dagger** V3 ★★

Start just left of the corner with two crimps around head height. Climb directly up through two sloping ledges, finishing left on the better holds of **The Sword**, or up the scary slab to the top for full value.

___26. **The Sword** V3 ★★★

An old-school 5.11 toprope climb that is now a highball classic. Start on a head-high jug and climb strong face moves to a heady finish, eventually topping out by rocking onto the slab right of the corner. A SDS variation adds a bit of pump but barely ups the grade. Awesome!

Herman Feissner on Cole's Corner (V8/9)
Photo: Jackie Hueftle

LEAVENWORTH : Icicle Canyon - The Sword

___27. **The Tree Problem** V8 ★★
Climb the bulge in front of the descent tree, starting matched on two small right-facing sidepulls in the corner. Move left to the sloper, pinch the sideways credit card, and slap for better holds up and right. Once you've mantled onto the jug in the corner, step right to a big ledge on the arête and top out; feel free to grab the tree and descend from the no-hands stance if you want to be a wimp (like me).
Variation (V6): Skip the business and the bulge by moving straight left to the micro-gaston and rocking up to the jug around the corner to the right. Finish as above.

___28. **The Sheath** V4 ★★

Climb straight up the tall corner right of **#27** from holds at head-height, making delicate reaches between sloping holds to a good crimp halfway up. For those of us less inclined to air it out over the uneven landing, a toprope can be rigged from the **Sword** anchors with a long sling on the anchors of **#29** as a directional guide.

___29. **The Sword Toprope** 5.13
The tall downhill face of the Sword boulder sports an extremely thin toprope route. A ropeless ascent of this climb would definitely be considered a solo, and not a boulder problem—the crux move is a highly insecure reach just three feet below the lip!

"In this modern age, very **little remains** that is real. Night has been banished, so have the cold, the wind, and the stars. They have all been neutralized; the **rhythm of life** itself is obscured. Everything goes so fast and makes so much noise, and we hurry by without heeding the grass by the roadside, its color, its smell and the way it shimmers when the wind caresses it. What a strange encounter it is then between us and the high places of our planet! Up there, we are surrounded by the **silence of forgetfulness**."

- Gaston Rebuffat, Starlight and Storm

Icicle Canyon - The Sword : **LEAVENWORTH**

Drew Schick sloper-gropin' on Musashi (V9), Egg Rock Photo: Todd Mannherz

LEAVENWORTH : Icicle Canyon - Egg Rock

EGG ROCK

A.K.A. The Jerry Garcia Boulders. Egg Rock is another great place to get off the beaten path and onto some superb rock. The granite here is quite different from the neighboring Sword area, whiter and with a slightly larger grain. Though Egg Rock is a smaller area, classic moderates such as **Dark Hollow** (V5) and **Weather Report** (V3) should definitely not be missed, and there really isn't a bad problem here. For those seeking a cool challenge, the techno-burl sloper-squeezing of **Musashi** (V9) is a perfect complement to the fingery face of the unclimbed Jerry Garcia project. Egg Rock sees a good deal of shade, and is pleasant most times of the year—though in winter it's a half-mile trudge from the nearest dry pavement. Most of the landings at Egg Rock are pretty mellow, although it would be wise to keep an eye out for poison ivy lining the edges of the trail and some landings.

Approach: Egg Rock is 9.0 miles from Icicle Junction. Park in the narrow pullout on the lefthand side of the road directly across from the nine-mile marker. The "I ♥ Jerry Garcia" graffiti on the first large boulder is vaguely visible from the road, as is the small, round egg rock itself.

Icicle Canyon - Egg Rock : **LEAVENWORTH**

___1. **Sunshine Daydream** V4 ★★
Climb the vertical arête on crimpers, starting from a low right-hand sidepull with a large flake foothold.

___2. **I ♥ Jerry Garcia** (project)
Climb the tall painted face on sharp crimps and micro sidepulls. Technical and hard, but probably 'only' around V10.

___3. **Ace** V4 ★
Climb the right arête of the Jerry Garcia face, finishing straight up to the left of the notch. May be a bit dirty.

___4. **Funiculi Funicula** V0- ★★
Start on a big sidepull, climb to the obvious shelf, mantel, and top out. Very pleasant indeed.

___5. **Carlisle** V2+ ★
Begin sitting with a decent undercling on the left side of the face. Move to a good flat hold, and again to the large jug. Fun, strange stone.

___6. **Unnamed** (project)
Climb the dirty face on little crimpers to two strange little pinches and up. Just needs some cleaning.

___7. **Weather Report** V3 ★★★
Start crouched with your left hand on the fin and your right on a good sidepull. Smear your feet and lunge to the rounded jug, finishing up and right. Save some juice for the top! **Variation** (V7): Start matched on the fin and climb straight up.

___8. **Dark Hollow** V5 ★★★
Climb the shallow finger crack on the left side of the corridor, trending slightly left to edges at the top. F.A. Joel Campbell.

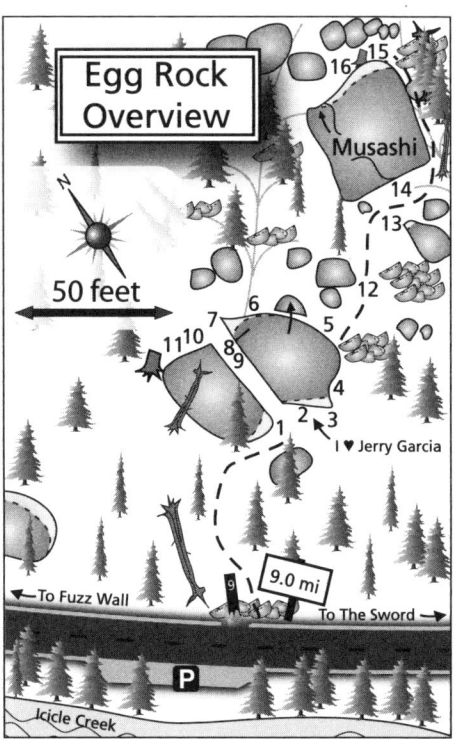

Kyle O'Meara on Dark Hollow (V6)

LEAVENWORTH : Icicle Canyon - Egg Rock

___9. **Terrapin Station** V0+ ★

 Climb the chimney between the boulders.

___10. **China Cat** V2 ★★

Climb the slab to the right of the corridor. A little footwork will go a long way…

___11. **Rider** V0 ★

Climb the small bulge just left of the tree trunk with sidepulls in the crack.

___12. **Deal** V1+ ★

 Start sitting and climb to edges on the low trailside arête.

___13. **Bertha** V0 ★★

 Starting from the deep crack and climb the small corner next to the trail on cool incuts. Way better than it first appears.

___14. **Smokestack Lightnin'** V2 ★★

 Climb the left side of the tall face, following edges in the left-leaning seam to a nine-foot-high jug. Make a big move to the lip, then gather your wits for the committing high-step finish. Sharp, but well worth the adventure.

___15. **Musashi** V9 ★★★

 A.K.A. **The Egg Part 2**. One of Leavenworth's best. Start on the obvious jug rail, bear-hug the wide slopers, and chuck to the perfect brick-shaped pinch on the corner. If you supuinate, you'll levitate… F.A. Cole Allen.

___16. **Hara-Kiri** V5 ★

 Start with two low underclings and slap to sidepulls in the dirty seam. Top out straight up the tall, dirty face.

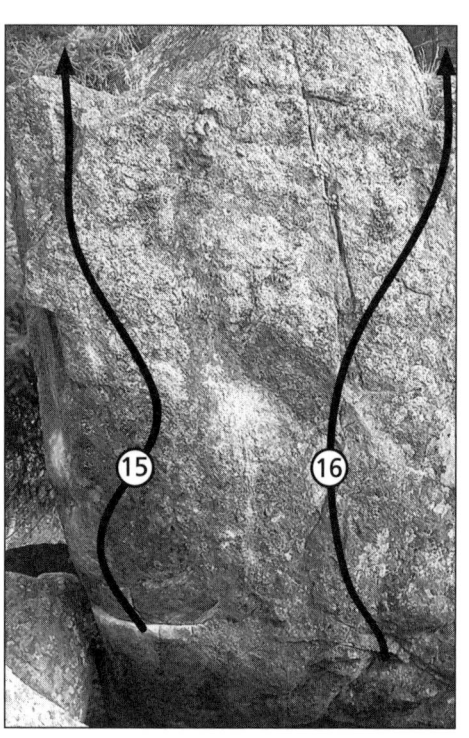

FUZZ WALL

Fuzz Wall is among the furthest developed bouldering areas in Icicle Canyon. The air is typically much crisper here than in town, and the rock in and around this tiny roadside area sees less traffic than most other Icicle spots. Home to the sweet pain of **Epoxy Flake** (V10) and a couple nice moderates, Fuzz Wall is a good place to check out when you think you've seen it all.

The boulders at the top of the hill just north of Fuzz Wall, on the way to Tin Man, also ought to yield some fun problems. This area of the canyon is a good launching point for more serious explorations; the canyon becomes much wider after Fuzz Wall, and the roadside less rocky, but there are plenty of boulders left to be discovered for those willing to hike!

Approach: Fuzz Wall lies on the north side of the road 9.2 miles from Icicle Junction. Park 40 yards down canyon from the boulder, in the eastern end of the rocky cul de sac where the road passes through an obvious roadcut. Fuzz Wall is the dark west-facing wall 10 yards above the road.

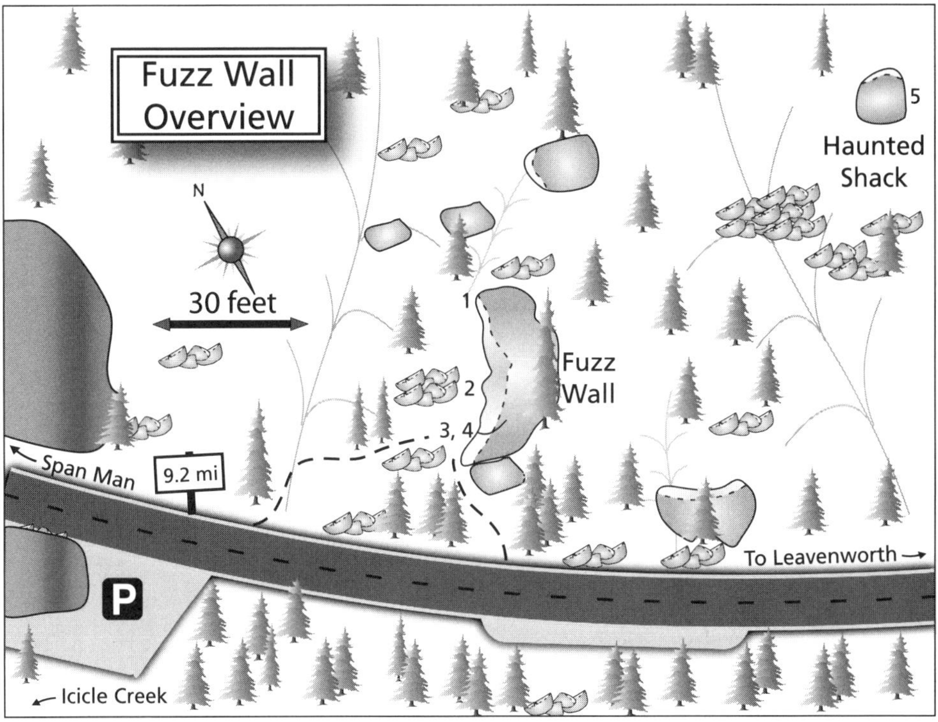

LEAVENWORTH : Icicle Canyon - Fuzz Wall

___1. **Peach Fuzz** V0 ★

Climb the short left arête of Fuzz Wall from a stand start. Dirty but solid.

___2. **Epoxy Flake** V10 ★★

 Start sitting in the center of the face with a lefthand sidepull in the seam and a very low right undercling. Stab to the reinforced flake, match, and climb up and left to sloping crimps and a juggy finish. The stand start on the flake is about the same difficulty—way tough! F.A. Chris Kirschbaum.

___3. **Pod Racer** V1+ ★

Climb the incut pods in the dirty crack a few feet right of **Epoxy Flake**, finishing with a cruxy mantel.

___4. **Busted** V3 ★★

Start in the crack as for **#3**, climbing up until the distant right arête comes within reach. Hug the grainy crack and arête in opposition as you finish straight up the corner. Heady!

___5. **Haunted Shack** V2 ★★

Find this little gem some 100 yards east of Fuzz Wall on top of a short rise. From two head-high crimps, climb the series of smooth edges up the east face to the juggy lip. The sit start on low, small edges on the right side of the face is a fun V3. F.A. Susan Mitchell

Icicle Canyon - Fuzz Wall **LEAVENWORTH**

SPAN MAN

Span Man is a roadside boulder roughly 0.1 miles further than Fuzz Wall. It is visible directly across the road from the far end of the short dirt loop. Hike up the short, steep hill to this streaked, motley boulder and find **Span Man** in the small cave on the west end.

6. Span Man V10 ★★★

Start inside the small cave with a low hueco in the roof and the right arête. Climb directly out the tube feature, performing several 'span moves' to reach the triangular jug on the face. Swing your heel around and climb up and right on grainy slopers to a cruxy finish. The grade is unconfirmed but the thing is hard. F.A. Kyle O'Meara.

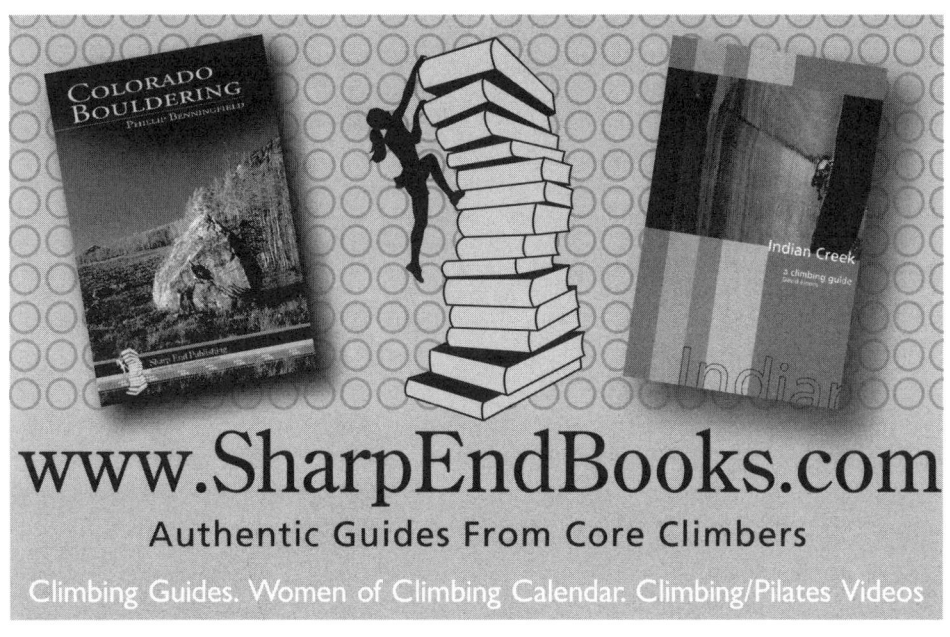

LEAVENWORTH : Icicle Canyon - Tin Man

TIN MAN

The spread-out Tin Man area is the furthest Icicle Canyon spot described in this guide. Poised on a flat plateau a few minutes' walk above Icicle Road, the boxcar-sized block that gives the area its name offers a handful of fun problems on sharp, textured granite. The delicate, reachy **Tin Man** (V6) alone is worth the visit, as is the pure movement of the **Slot Problem** (V4). Several variations can also be climbed on the boulder's featured east face, though it still needs some cleaning and traffic. The area surrounding Tin Man has potential for several easier problems, especially to the east and further uphill. Save this gem for a lazy afternoon when you think you've seen it all… you won't be disappointed.

Approach: The approach for Tin Man begins some 9.4 miles from Icicle Junction, roughly 0.1 miles down the road from the large pullout across from Span Man. Park in a small righthand pullout just after a small stream runs under the road, before the hillside becomes steep and rocky. Walk up and right through lush foliage past a short wall, then past a helpful log to the steep, sandy Pen 15 wall. For Tin Man, follow the drainage on either side of this wall, eventually topping out onto the flat plateau above. Tin Man lies straight ahead in the clearing. Not finding the stream and don't know where to park? Just try heading up the steep hillside at the beginning of the scraggly roadside cliffs. You'll find this big, square boulder lurking at the base of a steeper hillside.

____1. **Tonya Harding** V4/5 ★
Start on the big flake jug in front of the tree. Climb up and left to the incut pod, then traverse left on slopers to a high jug in the dark rock above and drop. The grade is reach-dependent.

____2. **Seams Dangerous** V6 ★★★
  Climb the tall, slightly overhanging face a few feet right of the tree on cool seam edges to a high crux. Finish up the high slab over the dangerously sloping landing. Most will opt for a toprope from the tree above, or at least preview the route on rappel.

____3. **Spanish Traverse** V2/3 ★
Start on big, sharp edges in the middle of the rail, climbing up and left to a balancey reach for the lip and an easy mantel.

____4. **The Slot Problem** V4 ★★
Start on two sharp edges on the right end of the crimp rail. Work your feet up and stab for a gaston pocket left of the ancient tree. Solid moves lead through the juggy slot to an easy mantel finish. Very good.

____5. **Tin Man** V6 ★★★
Climb the arête right of the tree from a high start on the left arête and a right-hand sidepull. Hit the odd pocket high on the face, slap the jug around the corner, and top out. Strange and beautiful. **Variation** (V7): Start crouched, your left hand cupping the triangular block in the low roof. Slap your way into the start of **Tin Man** using the arête and the sidepull rail on the face.

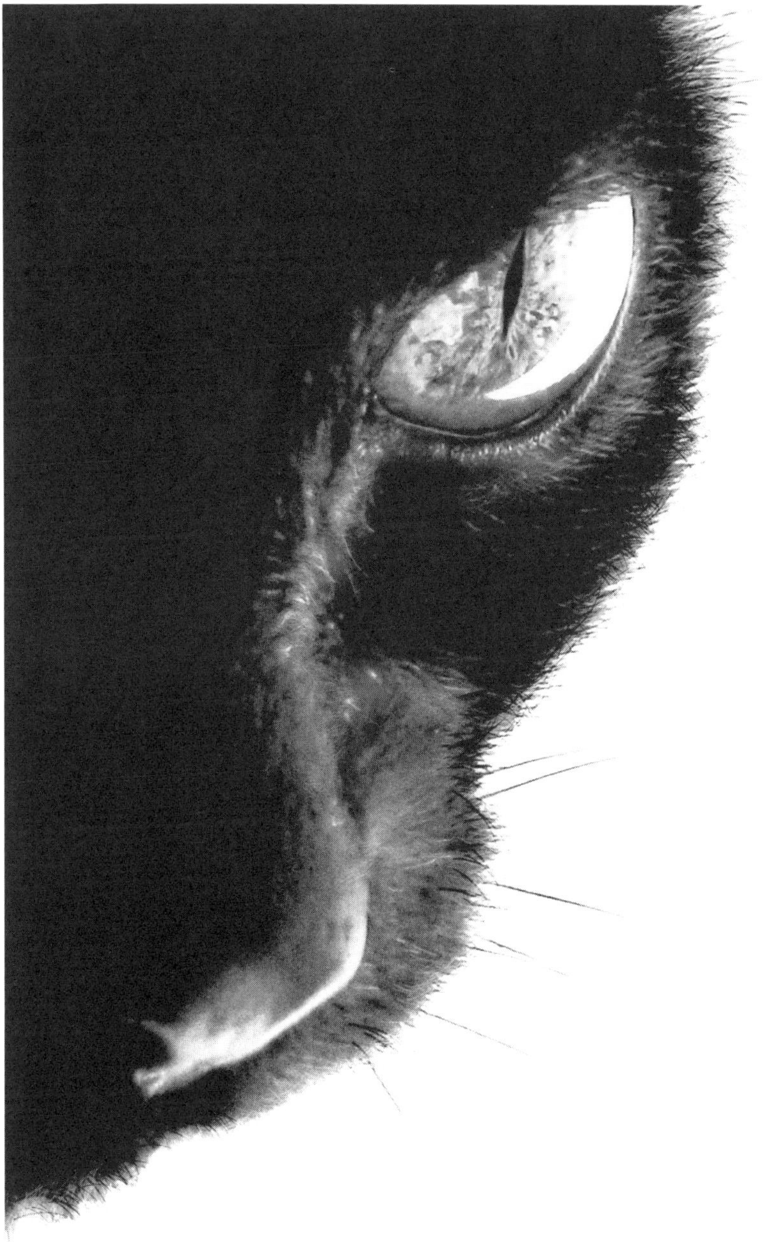

Icicle Canyon - Tin Man : **LEAVENWORTH**

www.stealthrubber.com

LEAVENWORTH : Icicle Canyon - Tin Man

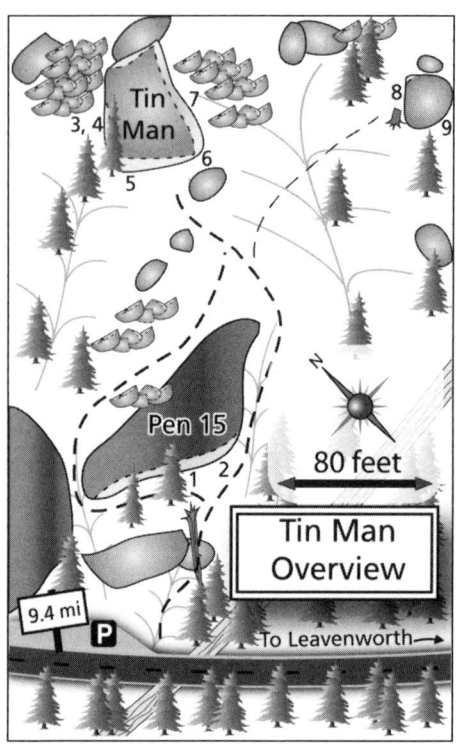

___6. **Joe's Nose** V4 ★

Start sitting on the low corner matched on the lip or with a low undercling jug. Slap up the blunt, low corner to a wide rockover move for an edge on the face. Very silly, and pretty fun too.

___7. **(Various)**

Several variations climb the featured face around the corner from **Tin Man**. You might want to give this one some brushwork, and be wary of bad rock.

___8. **Divided Sky** V3 ★★

Start with a high edge just right of the arête on this short face. Stab straight up on cool edges and ledges to the lip.

___9. **Faht** V0

Climb the juggy flake on the rear of this little cube. Might be a bit dirty...

Kyle O'Meara wide-eyed with the fear on Seams Dangerous (V6)

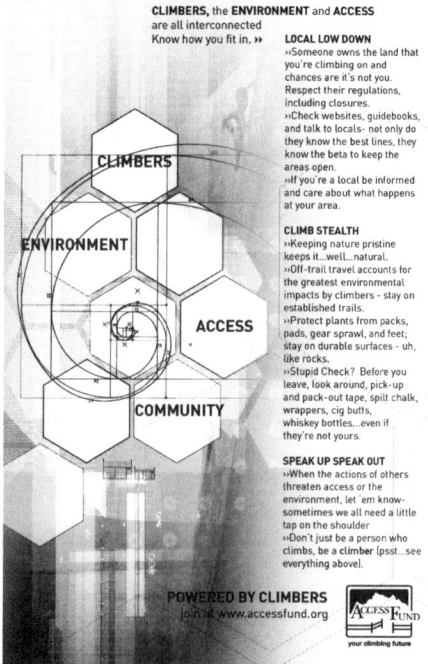

LEAVENWORTH-2
TUMWATER CANYON

Drew Schick contemplates the insecure finish of Slingblade (V6).

LEAVENWORTH : Tumwater - Torture Chamber

TUMWATER CANYON

Many visitors to Leavenworth first experience the grandeur of the Wenatchee Mountains as they wind their way through the narrow valleys of Tumwater Canyon on Rt. 2. Fittingly, many boulderers have their first experiences in Leavenworth at popular Tumwater venues like the Swiftwater Picnic Area and The Beach. While these two major spots get all the traffic, the canyon is home to several other areas offering small concentrations of superb problems. Dubbed "The Canyon of Granite" by Fred Beckey in ***Challenge of the North Cascades***, Tumwater Canyon's dramatic slopes are generously sprinkled with rocks of all shapes and sizes, from gigantic monoliths like Castle Rock to the top-heavy blobs that get us so psyched. Though the bouldering options on the steep hillsides and narrow floor of the Tumwater may be somewhat lacking in quantity compared to Icicle Canyon, the rock quality certainly makes up for it. Diversity is the theme here, from the Squamish-like stone of The Labyrinth area to the fine-grained slopers of Swiftwater North, the schist at Swiftwater South, and the river-polished cave at Jenny Craig. Potential for new problems is abundant in areas such as the Torture Chamber and The Labyrinth, and wherever the steep hillside gives way to small stone-filled plateaus.

The sheer slopes of the Tumwater Canyon keep it somewhat shadier during the summer months, and areas like The Beach remain tolerable on the warmest days even despite the canyon's low elevation. Cooler temperatures are a worthwhile trade-off for the intermittent hum of vehicles along Rt. 2, the Tumwater's only major drawback. Though Tumwater Canyon has very little private property, the volume of traffic through the canyon can make parking cruxy in some areas. Always park in a pullout, no matter how small, and park with all four tires outside of the white line. Keep an eye out for rattlesnakes on warmer days, and make plenty noise around sunrise and sunset to avoid startling the occasional bear. For camping, hit up the Tumwater Campground on the west end of the canyon, or head up the Icicle for some peace and quiet. Finally, it ought to be mentioned that Tumwater is home to several fine swimming holes, popular among locals for the mild temperatures as well as their location upstream of the raw sewage deposited at the popular Blackbird Island beach.

Approach: Tumwater Canyon stretches some 10 miles west of the town of Leavenworth on Rt. 2. The bouldering areas are described from east to west, ones closest to town first. As with Icicle Canyon, all mileages are given from the junction with Icicle Road just east of Leavenworth's famous welcome sign. Directions are given from Leavenworth, so a 'lefthand pullout' will be on the right if you're coming from the west. Those traveling from the west should reset their odometers at Swiftwater and use the chart to the right for navigation. For map-reading clarity, it should be noted that the Tumwater Canyon actually runs north-south after the Beach area parking, thus the Wenatchee River is to the west of Rt. 2 at most areas.

Tumwater Mileage Chart
A From Icicle Junction
B From Swiftwater
C From Previous Area

	A	B	C
Torture Chamber	0.5	6.3	NA
The Labyrinth	0.5	6.3	0.0
Range Boulders	0.9	5.9	0.4
Beach Parking	1.6	5.2	0.7
The Beach	1.6	5.2	0.0
Pitless Avocado	2.3	4.1	0.8
Driftwood	2.9	3.8	0.6
Jenny Craig	3.3	3.5	0.4
That Demon	5.5	1.2	2.3
Swiftwater	6.9	0.0	1.3

Tumwater - Torture Chamber   **LEAVENWORTH**

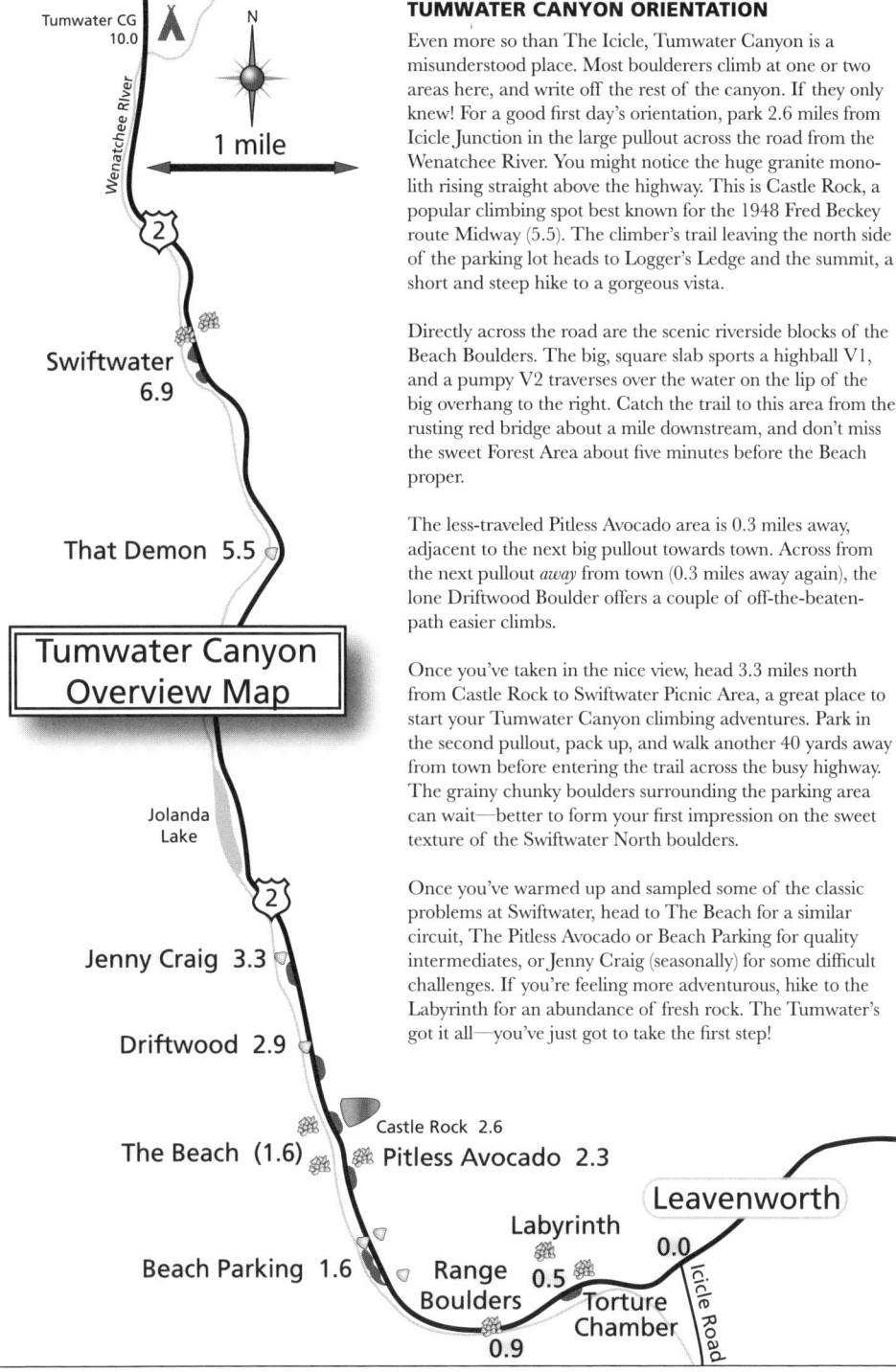

Tumwater Canyon Overview Map

TUMWATER CANYON ORIENTATION

Even more so than The Icicle, Tumwater Canyon is a misunderstood place. Most boulderers climb at one or two areas here, and write off the rest of the canyon. If they only knew! For a good first day's orientation, park 2.6 miles from Icicle Junction in the large pullout across the road from the Wenatchee River. You might notice the huge granite monolith rising straight above the highway. This is Castle Rock, a popular climbing spot best known for the 1948 Fred Beckey route Midway (5.5). The climber's trail leaving the north side of the parking lot heads to Logger's Ledge and the summit, a short and steep hike to a gorgeous vista.

Directly across the road are the scenic riverside blocks of the Beach Boulders. The big, square slab sports a highball V1, and a pumpy V2 traverses over the water on the lip of the big overhang to the right. Catch the trail to this area from the rusting red bridge about a mile downstream, and don't miss the sweet Forest Area about five minutes before the Beach proper.

The less-traveled Pitless Avocado area is 0.3 miles away, adjacent to the next big pullout towards town. Across from the next pullout *away* from town (0.3 miles away again), the lone Driftwood Boulder offers a couple of off-the-beaten-path easier climbs.

Once you've taken in the nice view, head 3.3 miles north from Castle Rock to Swiftwater Picnic Area, a great place to start your Tumwater Canyon climbing adventures. Park in the second pullout, pack up, and walk another 40 yards away from town before entering the trail across the busy highway. The grainy chunky boulders surrounding the parking area can wait—better to form your first impression on the sweet texture of the Swiftwater North boulders.

Once you've warmed up and sampled some of the classic problems at Swiftwater, head to The Beach for a similar circuit, The Pitless Avocado or Beach Parking for quality intermediates, or Jenny Craig (seasonally) for some difficult challenges. If you're feeling more adventurous, hike to the Labyrinth for an abundance of fresh rock. The Tumwater's got it all—you've just got to take the first step!

THE TORTURE CHAMBER

The Torture Chamber is a jumble of large boulders just inside the mouth of Tumwater Canyon. Visible above the road at the western end of Rt. 2's last big curve, the Torture Chamber is bound to catch your eye as you zip in to Leavenworth for the first time. Though only a few established problems can be found here, there is a good deal of potential, especially if you climb V13 and arêtes are your strong point. Needless to say, this isn't the first spot to visit in Leavenworth; head up here to try the burly squeeze-fest of **Chalksucker** (V10) or just check out the funky caves on an off day. The Torture Chamber stays relatively shady, and **Chalksucker** is sometimes clean and dry mid-winter.

Approach: From Leavenworth, drive 0.5 miles west from Icicle Junction on Rt. 2 and park in the small paved pullout on the left. Walk roughly 10 yards back along the road from the eastern end of the pullout, cross carefully, and follow the faint path up the short hill to the obvious boulders. The trail to the Labyrinth area departs from the west end of this pullout.

____1. **Water Torture** V3 ★★

This clean, whitish boulder is home to a fine problem that seems to have been reclaimed by the trees in recent years. If you can get in there, start standing with the right-facing rail and slap up to finish on better holds.

____2. **The Lobster** V4 ★★

Start standing matched on the flat shelf in the corridor. Climb left around the bulge on cool pinches to a powerful move for the lip and top out. **Variation** (V2): Lunge straight up from the rounded jug, finishing with a nice press on the flat ledges above.

____3. **Chalksucker** V10 ★★

Start in the dark corner with a good flat hold at head height. After a tough move to a miserable lefthand pinky-lock under the bulge, make an even tougher cross to the flat ledge of **The Lobster**. Finish straight up, or head left into **The Lobster** for a bit more climbing. Unconfirmed grade. F.A. Joel Campbell.

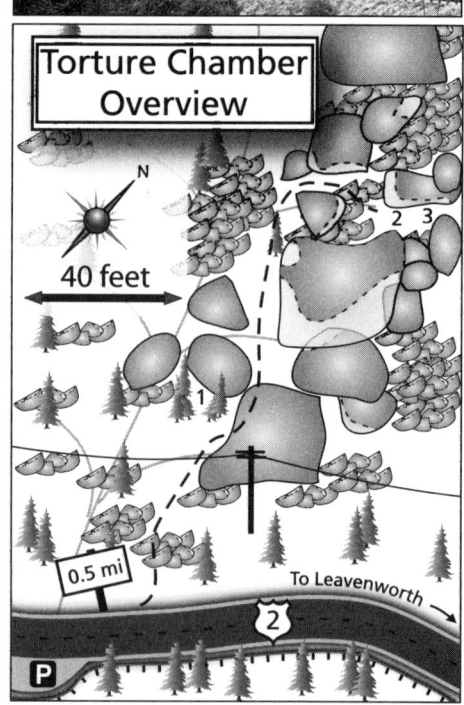

Jessica Campbell dances up Ballet (V3, Labyrinth Boulders)

LEAVENWORTH : Tumwater - Labyrinth

THE LABYRINTH

Just a half-mile from Leavenworth, the steep hillside below Clem's Holler crag is home to a bewildering mass of boulders in a steep forest setting. There are a handful of quality problems and much new route potential for those willing to tackle the sustained approach. While obvious boulders like the Warm Up have been climbed on for some time, the upper Labyrinth saw a rush of development during the spring of 2006. Instant classics like the striking **Beckey's Problem** (V7) and the exotic **Girlfunk** (V8) can really only hint at the potential. More problems can be found both on the way to these established problems and further uphill, so bring some brushes and several pads for the full experience. The Labyrinth is a good shady option on warm summer days.

Approach: This area is on the hillside just after the Torture Chamber boulders. Park in the second paved pullout on the left, 0.5 miles from Icicle Junction on Rt. 2. Walk to the west end of the pullout, then cross the road and head up the well-worn climbers' trail to Clem's Holler. The trail climbs straight up the hillside, staying atop a gentle ridge with a gully to the left. Roughly five minutes from the road, the trail makes a natural switchback formed by a trailside boulder. If you're not panting under the weight of your pad, you ought to reach the obvious Warm Up boulder in another five minutes. The Labyrinth area is much more intricate than the map indicates; prepare for an adventure!

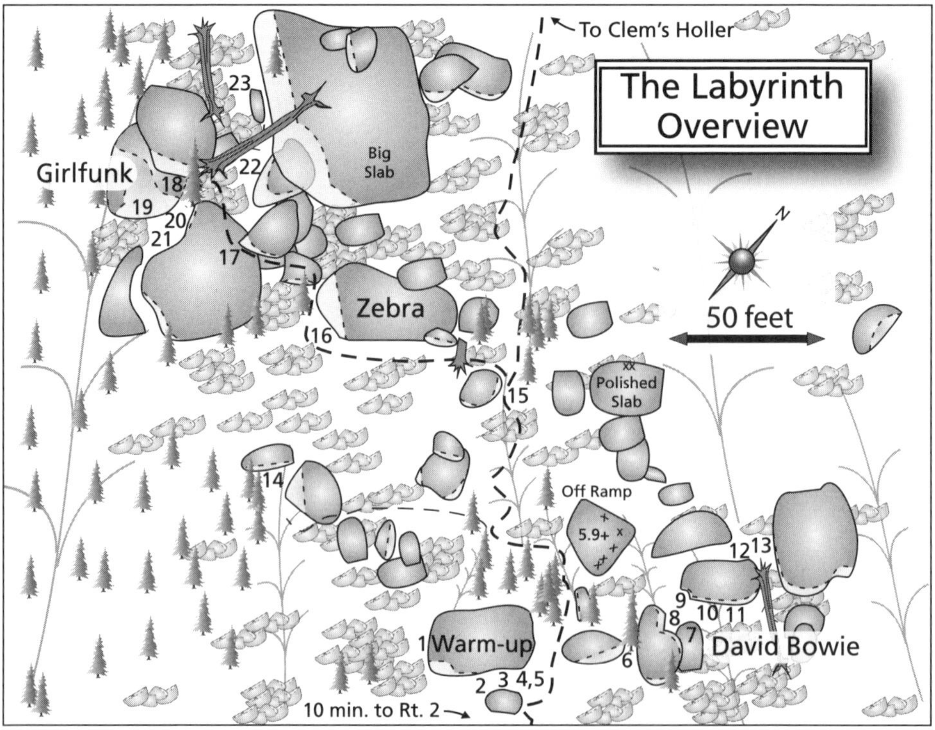

Tumwater - Labyrinth | **LEAVENWORTH**

___1. **Ryan's Other Problem** V3 ★★
Start in the center of the tall face with the guano-coated jug, stretch high for the prominent horizontal, then even higher for the lip and top out. Reachy and scary!

___2. **Ditch Witch** V0+ ★
Follow the mossy, juggy crack up and right, making a final tricky traverse to the right to top out.

___3. **Gymania** V0 ★★
Climb the classy line of crimps straight up the shallow scoop in the face to a nice mantel finish.

___4. **The Method Left** V2 ★★
Starting from two good head-high crimps, climb up and left on sharp crimpers into the finish of **Gymania**.

___5. **The Method Right** V1+ ★
Climb straight up and right from the head-high crimps to a tenuous rockover onto the slab.

___6. **GZA** V5 ★★
This tiny nugget climbs the far side of the short, steep boulder across the trail from the warmup. Start matched on the good shelf next to the tree, move left to a small crimp and punch for the stepped crimper above to gain the lip. Better than it looks, especially if you're short!

___7. **David Bowie** V2 ★★
Climb the white overhanging face from a lefthand sidepull and righthand arête hold. Move to a cool pinch, then crimps, finishing straight up with a cruxy press into the notch.

___8. **Jennifer Connoloy** V2 ★★
From a low incut slot, twist and stretch up the overhung corner to a neat square jug and top out.

___9. **Jazz Arete** (Project)
This beautiful, clean scoop will someday become a fantastic problem. There are starting holds…

LEAVENWORTH : Tumwater - Labyrinth

___10. **The Bone Collector** V6 ★★

Start in front of the pointed rock with two tiny crimpers and a good foothold. Climb up through perfect crimps to a big move for the lip and a real-deal mantel. It might help to be burly and fearless for this one.

___11. **Beckey's Problem** V7 ★★★

From good head-high edges, climb the right side of the tall overhanging face over bushes. A long bump move off a small sidepull gains the lip and a happy mantel finish.

___12. **Seussology** V3 ★

Start on slopers on the right arête and climb up and left on sweet holds to finish atop the corner.

___13. **Green Eggs and Ham** V0 ★

On the uphill end of this huge boulder, climb the slight scoop from a good edge and neat-o pocket. Finish up and left of the prominent sidepull, away from the scary gully.

___14. **Green Tea** V3 ★★

Find this hidden little climb by leaving the path a few yards uphill of the trailside sport climb **Off Ramp** and traversing west across some open talus. **Green Tea** climbs the smaller boulder over the seasonal streambed from the obvious rail in the middle of the face. The taller, overhung face next to **Green Tea** is still a project.

___15. **Stinkfoot** V2 ★

Climb the very low trailside bulge from a sit start with a flat knee-high ledge and your feet underneath, climbing up and right to finish with a dodgy high-step. Pretty silly, but fun.

122

Tumwater - Labyrinth : **LEAVENWORTH**

___16. **The Zebra** V4 ★

This beautiful streaked overhang used to have a perfect starting hold in the center of the roof—until we tried pulling on it. Now, try the stand start with the sloping rail at head height. Pull on and bust for the lip, then mantel into the scoop just right of the tree.

___17. **Cinderella Boy** V3 ★★

  Start sitting at the edge of the steep arête with opposing crimp slots. Fire to the incut crimp on the corner, then hit the sidepull jugs above to press it out and stand for the lip.

___18. **Sine of the Times** V5 ★★

Start matched on the left-leaning rail below the nicely curved lip. Climb up and left along the sloping shelf to the small fin on the left corner and press it out.

___19. **Girlfunk** V8 ★★★

  Start standing at the mouth of the cave with your right hand on the high flat edge in the roof. Jump to the tough-to-latch 'ear' hold, campus to the lip, and climb out right along the lip to mantel on crimps in the shallow dihedral. Strange and beautiful. F.A. Jessica Campbell. **Variation** (V5): Use the big rock on your left to get up to the lip, finishing out right with the mantel, and you've conquered **Girlfunk Light**. **Girlfunk** can also be finished directly over the bulge, which is a grade or two harder.

___20. **Tap** V1+ ★

Paw up the nice zigzag slopers on the short left end of the face, finishing up and left with the flat shelf on the slab. Might need some brushing…

___21. **Ballet** V3 ★★

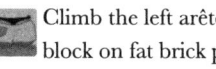 Climb the tallish wall from a big low rail the edge of the stepped landing. Head up through jugs to a slopey sidepull under the lip, finishing straight up with a perfect hidden crimp on the slab above.

___22. **The Africa Project** (Project)

Nestled inside the huge overhung 'room,' the left arête of this streaked prow will one day sport a heinous sloper problem finishing on high victory jugs. Mind-bogglingly cool.

___23. **The Tube** V0 ★

Climb the left arête of the small detached block on fat brick pinches to mantel on the sharp lip. If only it were twice as tall…or four times.

> "A few hours of mountain climbing turns a villain and a saint into two rather equal creatures. Exhaustion is the **shortest way to equality** and **fraternity**—and **liberty** is added eventually by sleep."
>
> *- Friedrich Nietzsche, Aphorism 263*

LEAVENWORTH : Tumwater - Range Boulders

THE RANGE BOULDERS

The Range Boulders is a a small, lesser-known area, and a last-minute addition to this guide. These few boulders can be found on a small island in the Wenatchee River, and are only accessible in the late summer and fall. Though you won't find any killer desperates here, a couple of fun climbs make a visit to the Range Boulders a nice once-a-year treat. **Washed Up** (V0) and **The Scorpion** (V2) make for classic warm-ups, complemented by a few moderate challenges like **Vaseline** (V4). The Range Boulders do get a bit of sun, but during the heat of summer, chances are you won't be able to get across the river anyway. The landings here are fine with just one pad, but bring a brush along as the Range doesn't see too much traffic.

Approach: The Range Boulders are 0.9 miles from Icicle Junction in the Tumwater Canyon. Park in the small lefthand pullout easily identified by the small white sign reading "Range Area, Watch Out for Livestock." Approaching from the west, a similar sign reading "Leaving Range Area" indicates the pullout. Follow the redneck party trail down the short, steep incline to the obvious Washed Up boulder on a narrow rocky shoal. The Scorpion boulder lies just beyond, on the larger, forested island. Getting across the river can be a bit cruxy even at its lowest, but this section can be reliably crossed during much of the fall season.

____1. **Washed Up** V0 ★★
From the curved flat hold just overhead, climb the tall east face through a vertical gaston rail to the high lip. Mantel using the rounded bucket up and right. Classic!

____2. **The Soap Dish** V1 ★
From a perfect head-high sidepull on the boulder's far corner, climb straight up the blunt arête to finish on the better holds around to the right.

____3. **The RZA** V6 ★
Start sitting, matched on the far right end of the sloping shelf. Climb the short corner on tiny crimpers to the blunt lip and finish up the arête.

____4. **Stinger** V2 ★
From a high edge on the corner left of **RZA**, climb up and left to a good sidepull under the point and mantel on the juggy lip.

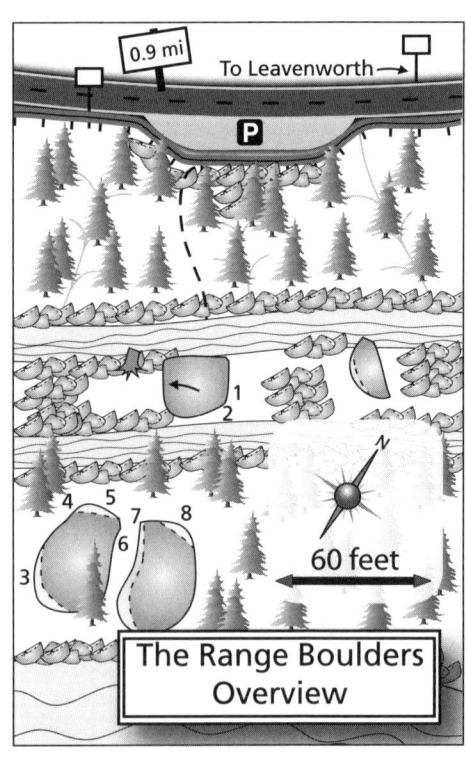

The Range Boulders Overview

___5. **The Scorpion** V2 ★★★
The area classic. From head-high edges on the left face, climb up and right using the arête and the good pinch under the point. Chuck to the juggy lip right of the apex and top out.

___6. **Pokin' The Pope** V0 ★
Climb the dirty slab on the right side of the corridor using right-facing sidepulls and a funky pocket. Might need some brushwork...

___7. **Vaseline** V4 ★★
Hop to a high incut on the left side of the corridor, working up and right on the blunt lip to an insecure mantel. Great moves, if not a bit dirty.

___8. **The Mole** V4 ★
Start crouched in the sandy hole with a low sidepull rail and a cool knob on the lip. A few awkward bumps on small lefthand edges lead to the jug on the corner and a thrutchy mantel. The sit-start might go; bring a shovel.

Erik Lambert flying through Han Solo's Lightsaber Tournament (V5)

LEAVENWORTH : Tumwater - Beach Parking

BEACH PARKING

With boulders scattered along most roads and approaches in Leavenworth's canyons, sometimes you don't end up where you meant to go. The boulders around the parking area for The Beach, one of Leavenworth's finest bouldering spots, are a fine example of this, and just might keep you from venturing across the river. While the classic dyno of **Han Solo's Lightsaber Tournament** (V5) is definitely worth the short walk, the confusing sloper problems on the Parking Lot boulder may even reel you in as you begin your walk to the bridge. Across the road, the shady Backseat boulder offers two off-the-beaten-path moderates with not-so-fun landings. Watch for poison ivy around the Parking Lot boulder.

Approach: The Beach parking area is located next to the Wenatchee River on the south side of Rt. 2 in Tumwater canyon, 1.6 miles from Icicle Junction. At the break in the guardrail, turn downhill and follow the short dirt driveway to the parking area. Though not signed, the Beach parking is the only parking area with an outhouse between Leavenworth and the Swiftwater picnic area. The Parking Lot boulder lies at the west end of the parking area, at the start of the trail to the Beach area. The Backseat boulder is directly across the road from the Parking Lot boulder, in a grove of trees set back from the road. **Han Solo** is on the large hilltop boulder roughly 50 yards east of the turnoff. Cross the road carefully, walk east past the small grove of trees, and head up the short hill to find this granite oddity.

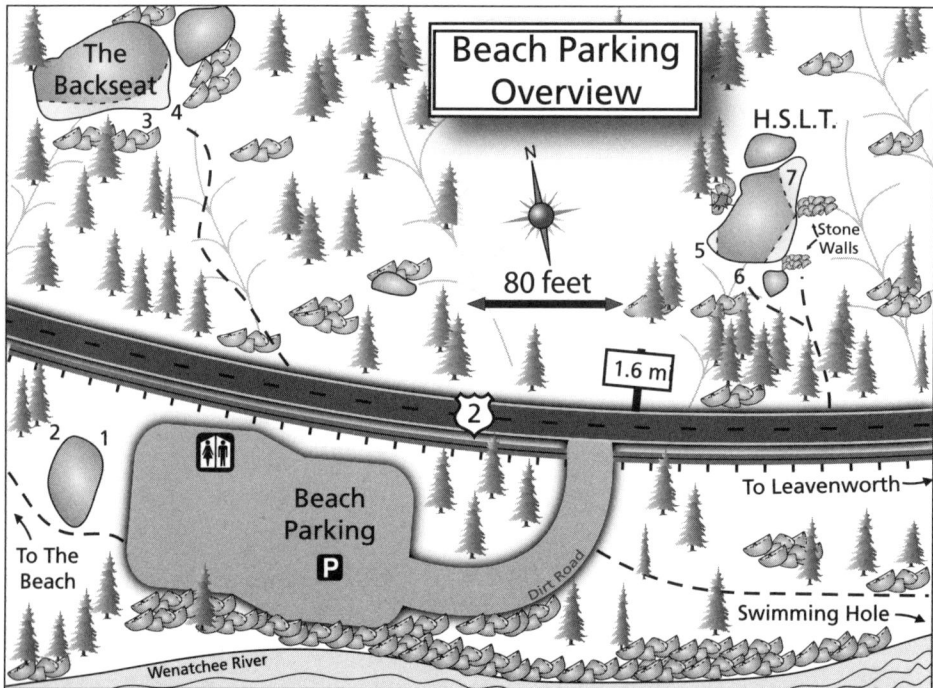

126

Tumwater - Beach Parking : **LEAVENWORTH**

___1. **Yeti** V6 ★
Start on a chest-high sloper, climbing up and right through technical slopers on the blunt arête. F.A. Ben Shrope.

___2. **One Stupid Problem** V6 ★
Climb the awkward, bulgy arête from a high start with a righthand sidepull on the face. We're as puzzled as you are...

___3. **Three-Armed Baby** V4 ★★
Start matched on the better (right) sloping rail in the middle of the gentle overhang. Throw your heel up and reach to an incut edge, then the lip, pressing out the crux mantel onto the dirty slab above. The similar line to the left is significantly more difficult. F.A. Ben Shrope

___4. **Gaze of the Grasshopper** V4 ★★★
On the arête right of **Three-Armed Baby**, start matched on the bubbly sloper at head height. Move right to a good sidepull, then climb the increasingly positive rails above to an eye-opening mantel. A beautiful line made better by the commitment factor of its jumbled landing.
Variation (V7): Start on the far left end of the sloping rail, heel hooking or campusing right through the start of **Three-Armed Baby** to finish as above. Feel like you're in Squamish yet?

___5. **The Executioner** V5 ★★
Climb up to two underclings on the tall west face of the boulder, finishing via crimpers on the left side of the mini-prow. Not all that hard, but insecure and really scary!

___6. **The Hobo** V0 ★
Climb the featured face on the downhill side of the tall boulder. This climb has some neat holds, but could use some traffic.

___7. **Han Solo's Lightsaber Tournament** V5 ★★★
Start with a cool righthand sidepull under the steep overhang. Pull on and chuck to the juggy lip. The vertically challenged can find static variations to tame the dyno while keeping roughly the same difficulty on this wildly steep line.

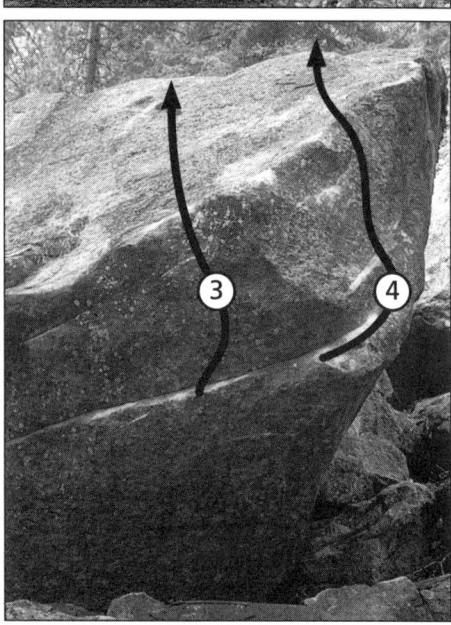

LEAVENWORTH : Tumwater - The Beach

THE BEACH

For seclusion and a wide variety of interesting problems on quality rock, the Beach can't be beat. The rock here is a finely textured granite similar to the Swiftwater North boulders, and is home to nearly as many slopers as crimps. The Beach is in fact two areas: one in the forest, and one actually on the beach.

The Forest area boulders are reached first. They stay relatively well-shaded throughout the day, and feature such quality moderates as **Brickwork** (V0) and the fun compression lesson of **The Fin** (V2). Those specializing in crimps will enjoy throwing themselves at the micro-edges of **Aggressive Reject** (V9) and the super-steep seam of **Goicoechea** (V9).

Tumwater - The Beach : LEAVENWORTH

A few minutes down the trail from the Forest area are the true Beach boulders, home to a mellow circuit of easier problems in a gorgeous setting next to the Wenatchee River, and a great place to catch some afternoon rays. Almost directly across from the monolithic Castle Rock, the daunting **Beach Slab** (V1) is definitely not to be missed. Enjoy the nice sandy landings on problems like the uncontrived **Dyno 101** (V3), hopefully avoiding the water landing on **Beach Arête** (V2).

Approach: Park for the Beach in the Beach Parking area, 1.6 miles from Icicle Junction in the Tumwater Canyon. This dirt parking area lies below the road on the river side of Rt. 2; the pullout is unmarked and easy to miss, but is the only one with an outhouse between Leavenworth and Swiftwater. Coming from the west, keep an eye out for the rusting red bridge just before the pullout. Park and follow the trail west and across the old red bridge. Follow the pipeline trail west along the south side of the river, crossing a recent landslide after roughly 10 minutes. After another five minutes, stay left at the fork and enter the forest 10 yards beyond, among the remnants of a small stone wall.

THE BEACH - FOREST AREA

___1. **Evil Petting Zoo** V4 ★★
A funky classic. Start standing on the corner adjacent to the trail with a decent right hand sidepull, mantel, and top out. Way harder than it looks!

___2. **Rocky** V2/3
Climb the short face around the corner left of #1 using the arête and poor holds on the slab.

___3. **Bullwinkle** V0
Climb the mossy finger crack and/or the face around it. Pretty dirty.

___4. **Ledges** V0 ★★
Climb the short face right of the large tree using edges and ledges. This is also the boulder's downclimb—might want to climb up it first.

___5. **Aggressive Reject** V9 ★★★
Start sitting matched on the small, incut crimper two feet left of the tree and make savage moves up the short arête. The stand start on head-high crimps clocks in around V2. F.A. Leif Palmer

___6. **Tweaker** V4 ★
Climb the center of the face on small, tweaky crimps. Could use some cleaning.

___7. **Veltex** V6 ★★
Start standing on the left side of the face with a small righthand sidepull and a high lefthand sloper on the arête. Climb up and right on the sloping lip and crimps below to an awkward mantel on better holds out right.

___8. **Walk The Line** V3 ★★
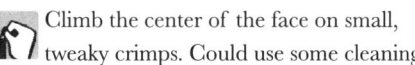
Climb the tallish corner on flat, flexing holds from head-high slopers down and left. A bit inobvious and dirty near the top, but still good climbing.

___9. **Mossline** V1 ★
Climb the left-facing rail on the right side of the face. Needs some cleaning.

___10. **Swamp Thing** V0+
Climb the left side of the face on small edges. Probably needs even more cleaning.

LEAVENWORTH : Tumwater - The Beach

___11. **Alpine Cow** V0- ★
Start on a sloper on the left arête of the smallish boulder. Mantel, walk up the slab, and finish on better holds out right. A great beginner's climb.

___12. **Off-Kilter** V0 ★
Climb the off-vertical face from cool sidepulls. Top out straight up with a nice high-step.

___13. **Fountain Blues** V0 ★★
Start crouched on the corner with chest-high slopers and slap up and right to incuts. Very groovy.

___14. **Get Shorty** V0- ★
Climb the short face on good holds. Lots of fun variations.

___15. **The Backstroke** V2 ★
Climb the short slab around the back of the boulder without using either arête. Or use them, if you want; contrived but fun.

___16. **Bofunk** V2 ★
Strange is as strange does. Lie down between two trees on the back of the short boulder and mantel on the sloping shelf to top out.

___17. **Nosy** V1 ★
Mantel the small 'nose' feature on the right side of this squat boulder and finish up the low-angle arête.

___18. **Presto Change-O** V3 ★
Mantel on small edges on the undercut lip of the smallish boulder, finishing up the short slab.

___19. **The Hardest Problem In The Universe** V0- ★
The rear arête of this boulder on nice big holds.

___20. **The Fin** V2 ★★★
The obvious short fin, finishing straight up on blocky jugs. Great moves; a nice introduction to the world of steep bouldering.

___21. **The Savage Act** V5 ★
Start as for **#20** but climb the face on the right side of the fin using a small righthand sidepull. Just one hard move, but pretty darn cool.

___22. **Spooner** V0 ★★
Climb the scoop left of the fin from a stand start. Use them feet!

___23. **Jumper** V3 ★★
Start low in the finger crack on the right of the tall face and climb to a good flat edge above head height. Lunge to the sloping lip and press it out.

___24. **The Terrible** V7 ★★
From the low flake on the left corner, climb up and right past a poor sloper to a small edge. Rock to a crimp below the lip, and finish nearly straight up from the start.

25. U2 V3 ★★★
Climb the arête from the same start as **#24**. A strenuous undercling move near the start leads to poor crimps below the lip. Classic!

26. The Crystal Method V3 ★★
Start as above, but climb left to the right side of the white crystal plate. Finish straight up on painful sidepulls at the edge of the dyke. Sharp but good.

27. F*ck The Crystal V3 ★★
Start on the blocky jugs near the left end of the face and climb up and right to a flexing flake on the left side of the sharp crystal dyke. Starting from two underclings at the bottom of the dyke adds a few grades.

28. Brickwork V0 ★★★
Start on the blocky jugs on the left end of the face, climbing up and left through inobvious incuts to top out slightly right.

29. Get Up, Stand Up V5 ★★
Start sitting with a low jug around the corner and over the boulder from **#28**. Climb up and right with the slab at your back to a tall move for a jug on the arête. Finish straight up the corner. It's big, yo!

30. Flex V1
Climb the tall face left of **#29** on less-than-solid flakes. Could use some cleaning.

31. Top Foot on the Good Foot V2 ★★
Climb the steep right arête of the friable uphill face from two opposing crimpers at chest-height. Big moves on big holds lead to a delicate high-step and top-out. Scary! The face to the left is equipped with toprope anchors.

32. Goicoechea V9 ★★★
On top of the slab right of **#29** is one of Leavenworth's most classic hard lines. Start matched on a rounded crimp rail at the bottom of the seam in the roof, move left to crimps and lunge to better holds on the lip. "About as mellow a landing as you could want, so go for it!" F.A. Jonny Goicoechea.

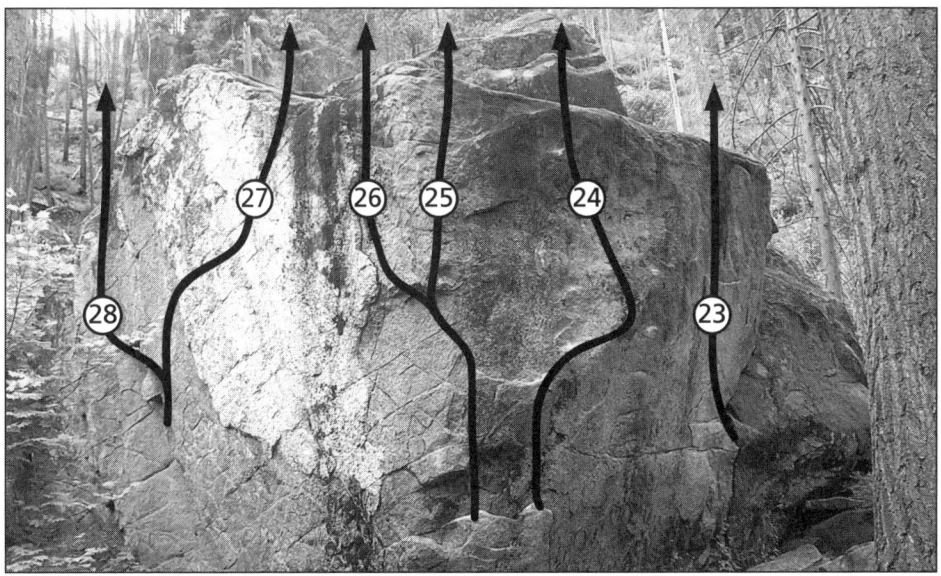

LEAVENWORTH : Tumwater - The Beach

THE BEACH – BEACH AREA

The Beach area is another 10 minutes down the trail from the Forest area. The boulders become apparent to the right of the trail several minutes after passing a small black boulder in a bit of talus on the right. Several faint paths lead to the beach from the pipeline trail—it's easiest to keep going until the **Beach Arête** is visible from an open clearing at the north end of the cluster. If you pass a low spraypainted boulder on the left, it's time to turn around. The beach boulders stay partially submerged until well after the spring thaw, but make a fantastic swimming hole in the late summer.

___1. **The Wave** V1 ★★★
Climb the tallish bulge over a sandy landing, exiting either straight up in the notch or slightly to the left for a bit more of a challenge. Great fun.

___2. **Beach Slab** V1 ★★★
Follow the edges of least resistance up the left side of the tall slab, beginning either on the arête or slightly right on the face. Fantastic!

___3. **Beached Whale** V2 ★★
Several variations climb the middle of the big slab, wandering over the sea of small edges to the dirty lip. We'll understand if you sacrifice some style points on the topout of this one…

___4. **Flotsam** V1
Climb the low arête from decent holds on either side, following the arête up and left to finish.

___5. **Jetsam** V0+ ★
Start standing with a high jug and small crimp, get your feet set and bust for the top.

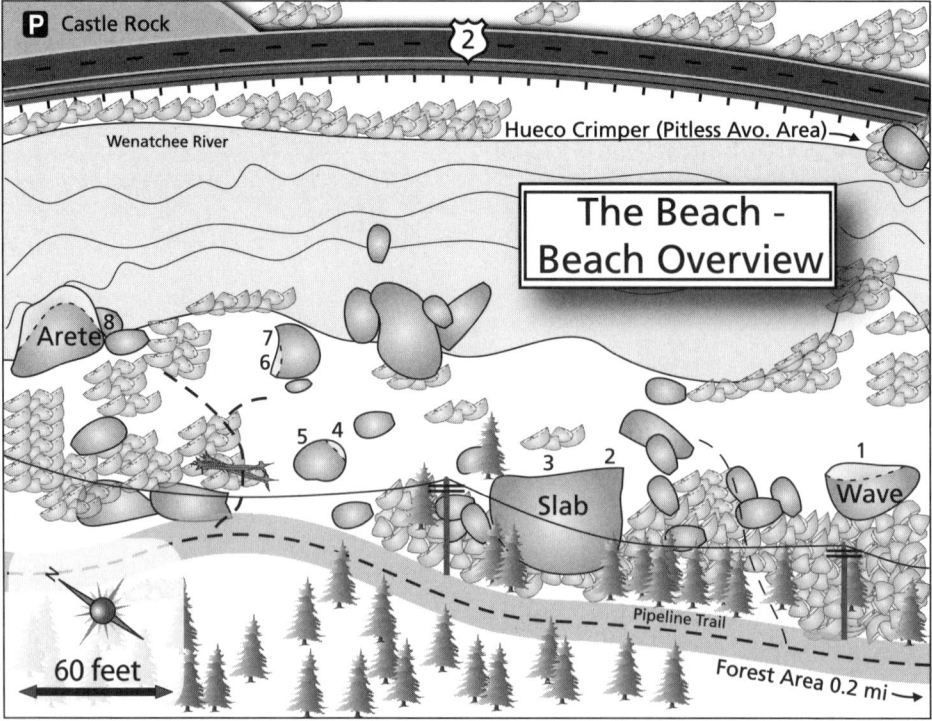

Tumwater - The Beach : **LEAVENWORTH**

Kyle O'Meara fights the pump on the sloping finish of The Beach Arête (V2)

LEAVENWORTH : Tumwater - The Beach

The Beach Area from Castle Rock Parking

___6. **Dyno 101** V3 ★★★

Climb the center of the upstream side of this squat, cube-shaped boulder. The beta? Grab the rail and jump for the top! A nice introduction to big dynos.

___7. **Rocks For Jocks** V1 ★★

Climb the left side of the square boulder slapping between the left arête and sidepulls on the face.

___8. **Beach Arête** V2 ★★★

This super-cool problem climbs the big, blunt lip 15 yards upstream of **Dyno 101**. Lean out over the water to grab the starting hold, throw that heel up, and it's summit or soak. Not a spring problem—try this one when the current is too strong and you'll be joining the boaters headed towards town!

Returning from the Beach Boulders, Tumwater Canyon   Photo: Brian Sweeney

"The best climber in the world is the one having the most fun."
- *Alex Lowe*

Tumwater - Pitless Avocado : **LEAVENWORTH**

THE PITLESS AVOCADO

The Pitless Avocado area is a grand addition to the Tumwater's small collection of quality areas. Visible from the road, these large, fine-grained granite boulders host some of Leavenworth's best moderate problems. The rock quality is impeccable, the approach is short, and there isn't a bad problem here. Kyle O'Meara's **Pitless Avocado** (V5) is a serious highball challenge for any visiting hardman, while **Slingblade** (V6) may be the best problem of its grade in the Leavenworth area. This is probably the most exciting of the *new* areas in this book—take it out the box yo! The Pitless Avocado isn't a very good place to warm up, but it is a great place to find summer shade, as most of the problems are nestled in amongst the pines. Be sure to check out the swimming hole across from Slingblade for a midday cool-down and some fun climbing on the boulder in the middle of the river.

Approach: The Pitless Avocado area is located just over 2.3 miles from Icicle Junction in the Tumwater Canyon. Park on the north side of Rt. 2 in a large pullout identifiable from either direction by a sign with an arrow indicating curves ahead. Walk west along the road for roughly 50 yards before turning onto a faint trail up the short steep hill towards the looming Slingblade boulder. Bring plenty of pads and an appreciation for the fresh stone.

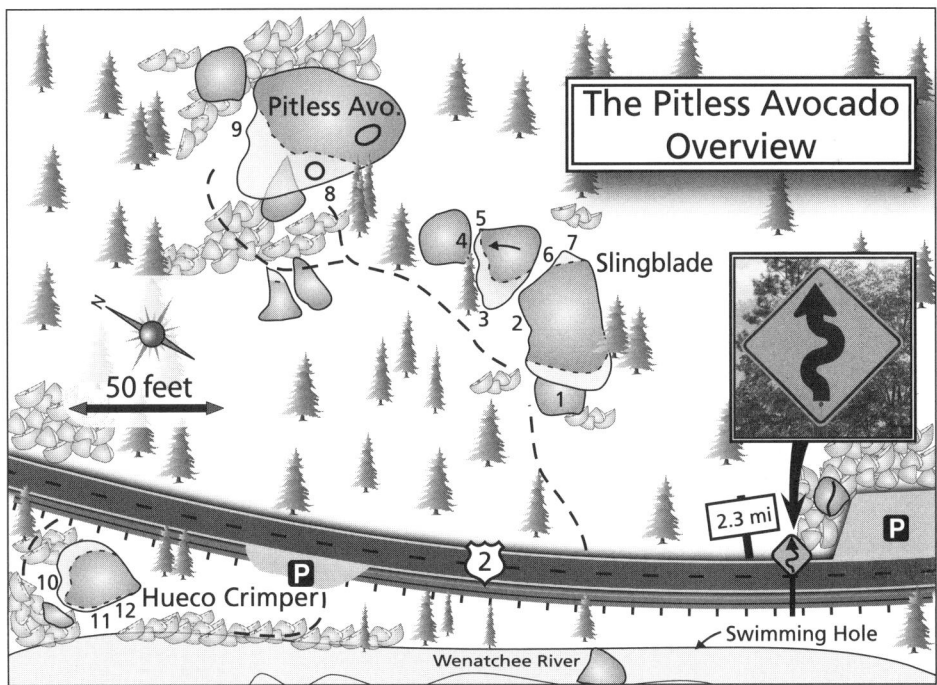

LEAVENWORTH : Tumwater - Pitless Avocado

___1. **Slingblade** V6 ★★★

Start standing on the angled platform with a good righthand sidepull and a sloping lefthand crimp. Pull on and 'sling' your left hand to the good jug at the eight-foot level. Hold it together for the committing finish up the tall corner. Classic! F.A. Kyle O'Meara.

___2. **IHOP** V1 ★★

Climb the tall slab on the right side of the corner from a waist-high crimp. Finish left of the jug in the brush-filled notch or proceed directly up the slab for bit more climbing.

___3. **Between The Legs** V6 ★★

Climb the tall arête next to the tree from a short hop to a high lefthand sloper. Squeeze and crimp up the right face to a direct finish high on the arête. F.A. Kyle O.

___4. **Salem Slab** V0

Climb the tall, dirty slab from the top of the short boulder. To descend the boulder, downclimb this route or shuffle down the tree.

___5. **Skittles** V3

Climb the dirty arête from high slopers. Scary and overgrown!

___6. **Solar Arête** V4 ★

Start crouched on slopers on the right arête, climbing up and left along the lip to the horn. Finish direct.

___7. **The Layman** V5 ★★

Start on sloping edges at the bottom of the left-facing corner and climb straight up on slopers and sidepulls. Fun and technical. F.A. Joel Campbell.

___8. **The Pitless Avocado** V5 ★★★

Jump to the huge hueco in the middle of the roof and establish with hands and feet. Make committing moves over the lip and onto the featured face of the enormous boulder. Top out up and right of the huecos on looser rock. Scared? The first ascent was done in the middle of the night! The low start, beginning 10 feet back in the recessed cave, is an obvious project requiring a six-foot dyno!

____9. **The Kiwi** V5/6 ★★

Start on the unique wedge-shaped pinch in the middle of the overhanging scoop. Climb right, up, and back left on increasingly friendly holds. A harder variation or two can also be done.

THE HUECO CRIMPER

Problems **#10**–**#12** can be found on the large riverside boulder another 50 yards past the Pitless Avocado area. Walk past a small pullout on the south side of the road and the boulder will be visible at the upstream edge of the forested patch.

____10. **The Hueco Crimper** V6 ★★

Start crouched on the right side of the low overhang with a right hand-heel match and a good lefthand edge on the lip. Climb straight up the right side of the bulge using strange pinches and slopes to a tenuous rock-over finish. Sweet. **Variation (V9):** Start matched with hands and heel in the low right slot.

____11. **Missin' Nugget** V2 ★

Begin on the left side of the tall wall with a good righthand gaston and a high left pocket. Climb straight up through one small crimper to a juggy finish.

____12. **Claim Jumper** V4 ★★

Start in the middle of the face with a head-high righthand sidepull and a high lefthand crimp. Pull on and slap to the detached block, then fight your way through footless gaston moves to top out on good shelves.

LEAVENWORTH : Tumwater - Driftwood

THE DRIFTWOOD BOULDER

The Driftwood boulder is a small riverside block just west of Castle Rock in Tumwater Canyon. There aren't a lot of climbs here, but a couple fun moderates make this a good place to break away from the typical areas for a bit. The off-vertical climbs on the west side of the Driftwood boulder are on a slicker, more polished rock, while the riverside **Driftwood** (V2) offers good, rough grain on an easier steep climb. Whichever your preference, be prepared to do a little brushing, as these climbs don't see much traffic. The Driftwood boulder is a nice hangout with decent winter sun coverage, but not a primo destination by any means.

Approach: The Driftwood boulder can be found 3.0 miles from Icicle Junction in the Tumwater Canyon. Park in the large righthand pullout (non-river side); it is the first pullout west of the Castle Rock pullout, and the second one past the Pitless Avocado area. This particular pullout is also marked on either side by a triangular sign reading "rocks." Thanks guys. Cross the road and the guardrail, walking north along the road for roughly 20 yards before descending to the obvious boulder above the Wenatchee River.

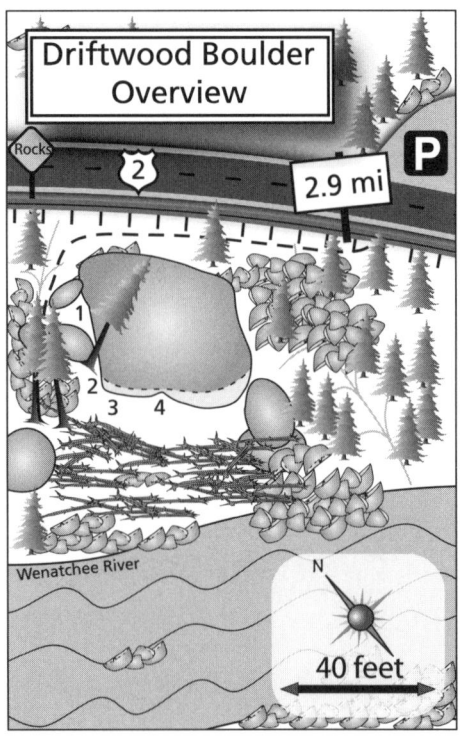

___1. **Bubbleslab** V4 ★★
Start standing in the hole made by the boulders, arms spread between two small edges. Climb the tall slab through long moves on bubbly crimp pockets, eventually heading slightly right to the lip. Scary!

___2. **Gooseneck** V1 ★
Start sitting just right of the tree with two really low sidepulls. Climb straight up on crimps and squeeze under the branches to finish. May need some cleaning.

___3. **Clipped Wings** V0
From questionable jugs on the upstream corner, climb up a few moves before mantling and finishing in the dirty corner among branches. Sound like fun? It actually kind of is.

Tumwater - Driftwood : **LEAVENWORTH**

___4. **Driftwood** V2 ★★

Climb up and left from the low jug in the center of the overhang, moving through sharp crimpers to better holds above. Top out up the dirty face. Climbing right and somehow up is a project.

> "Bouldering was and is about the effect on consciousness the mountains have. To climb seemed to expand the space I occupied, space filled with my consciousness and with the **living phenomena of nature**. An element of mystery existed even in walking or sitting in stillness among the boulders. Those days had great depth of feeling. I never will forget moments I seemed to slip from the usual world and engage in a beautiful, personal form of climbing."
>
> – Pat Ament, *The Poetry of Mountaineering*

LEAVENWORTH : Tumwater - Jenny Craig

JENNY CRAIG

Jenny Craig is unique. Two riverside boulders have settled against each other here to form a sheltered corridor echoing the sounds of the Wenatchee River. The Jenny Craig cave is partially submerged during the spring months, but a small selection of challenging boulder problems can be found here during the remainder of the year. The strange and bizarre **Jenny Craig** requires the boulderer to top out through a narrow slot a la Hueco Tanks' Birth Simulator, while the full-value Whirlpool (V9) threatens to soak those who fall from the crux. The spring floods of 2006 deposited several feet of driftwood on the upstream side of the boulders, burying problems **#2** and **#3**; a tangible example of seasonal change acting upon a Leavenworth bouldering spot. Jenny Craig is a miniature area without much to warm up on, but well worth the non-approach for its unique ambience and awesome tough problems.

Approach: Jenny Craig is in Tumwater Canyon, located at the water's edge 3.3 miles from Icicle Junction. Park in the large lefthand pullout and follow one of several trails to the large boulders by the river. At the time of this writing, the logjam blocks access to Jenny Craig via the west side, forcing a sometimes-dicey step across to enter the east side of the cave.

___1. **Kim + Randy** (Project)
Climb the tall, slightly overhanging face on small edges. Good thing the landing is seasonally sandy—you'll be visiting it quite a lot. If you ever find yourself in New England, check out the Egg Boulder's **Norma + Rico** project in Lincoln Woods, RI for some serious déjà vu…

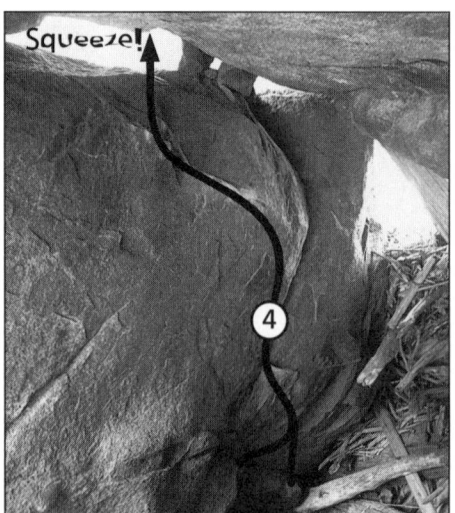

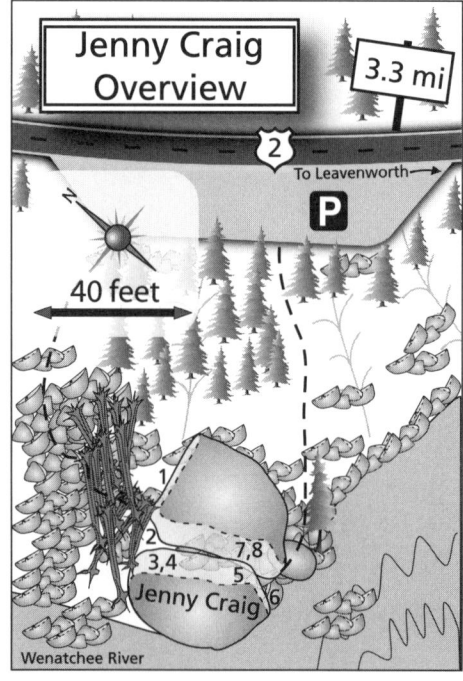

___2. **The Logmonster** V5 ★★

This problem used to begin sitting atop the logjam, but is now buried. From a strangely solid incut sidepull at the (now) six-inch level, move right to an incut gaston. Finish up and right with a technical mantel over what was formerly the **Hole of Doom**. F.A. Cole Allen.

___3. **White Fang** V3 ★

Start matched on the low sloping rail on the river side of the cave, next to the logs. Climb up, then right on crimps up the arête. Along with **#2**, now totally inaccessible.

___4. **Jenny Craig** VBlahblahblah ★★★

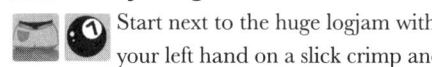
Start next to the huge logjam with your left hand on a slick crimp and your right on the sloping rail of **#3**. Climb up and left past a flat jug at head level, a slippery pinch in the seam, and out left to slopers below the lip. Finish through the hole, using anything you can grab. You may want to go on a diet for this one… F.A. Joel Campbell.

___5. **Anorexia** V4 ★

Begin matched on a good undercling on the left side of the face. Move up to crimps, then the lip. Drop from here or traverse either direction if you're dead-set on topping out.

___6. **Finished Product** V9 ★★★

Climb the dark face on perfect little crimpers from flat jugs at the water's edge. A nice sloper on the lip leads to an easier topout in dodgy territory. The landing of this beautiful testpiece is seasonally wet. F.A. Joel Zerr.

___7. **Head and Shoulders** V4 ★★

From the right end of the juggy shelf, climb up and left along the incut seam. When the holds run out, stab backwards to the jug on Jenny Craig, switch walls and finish through the slot.

___8. **The Whirlpool** V9 ★★★

From the juggy shelf on the steeper wall of the cave, climb right through the roof on incuts to a tough match and cruxy lip encounter. Finish on the slab high above. A fall past the middle of the climb will send you tumbling backwards into the river. F.A. Kyle O'Meara.

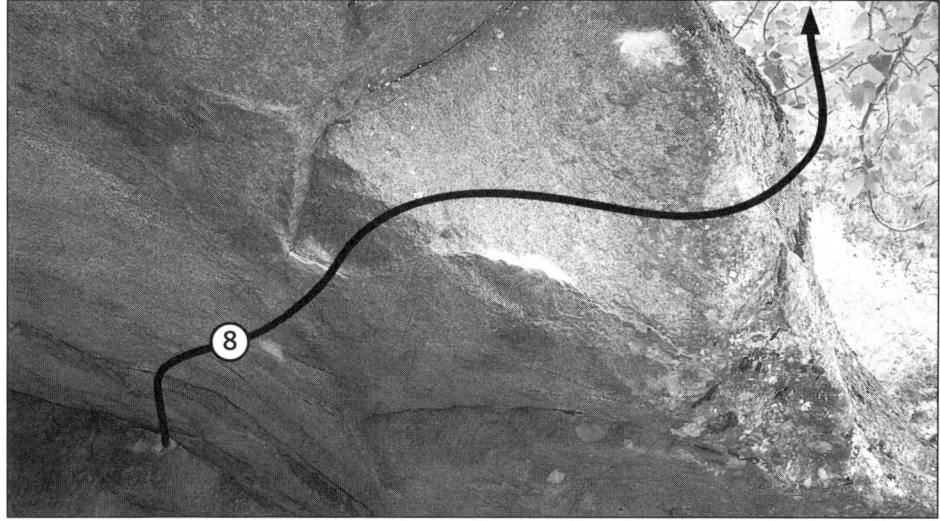

LEAVENWORTH : Tumwater - That Demon

THAT DEMON

That Demon is yet another seasonal riverside boulder in Tumwater Canyon. Easily visible on a large sandbar at the edge of the Wenatchee River, That Demon is typically only climbable in the late summer and fall. The small handful of problems to be found here are well worth the wait though, from the beautiful rail of **The Skuke** (V3) to the tendon-busting one-mover **The Virgin** (V8/9). The ambience of climbing in the middle of the river isn't bad either, especially if you can ignore the gawking motorists and the perilous half-water landings. Bring a friend to spot and a sense of adventure, and you'll rest happily knowing you've put this eye-catching 'demon' to rest.

Approach: That Demon is 5.7 miles from Icicle Junction on Rt. 2. Park in the large lefthand pull-out at 5.5 miles and descend to the riverbank. Walk upstream through bushes and small rocks on the wide sandbar to this round, dark boulder. That Demon is a highly seasonal area; wait until the landing is partially dry to throw yourself at this one... and bring an extra pair of shoes and a towel if you're feeling shaky.

___1. **The Skuke** V3 ★★

Start crouched with the obvious square-cut jug on the right end of the face. Climb left through small edges to the striking curved rail. Traverse up and left until you can rock up to the lip and top out.

___2. **That Demon** V5 ★★

From the flat jug of **The Skuke**, climb left to edges, then straight up on more edges. Finish in the flat, scooped ledge on the lip. Awesome!

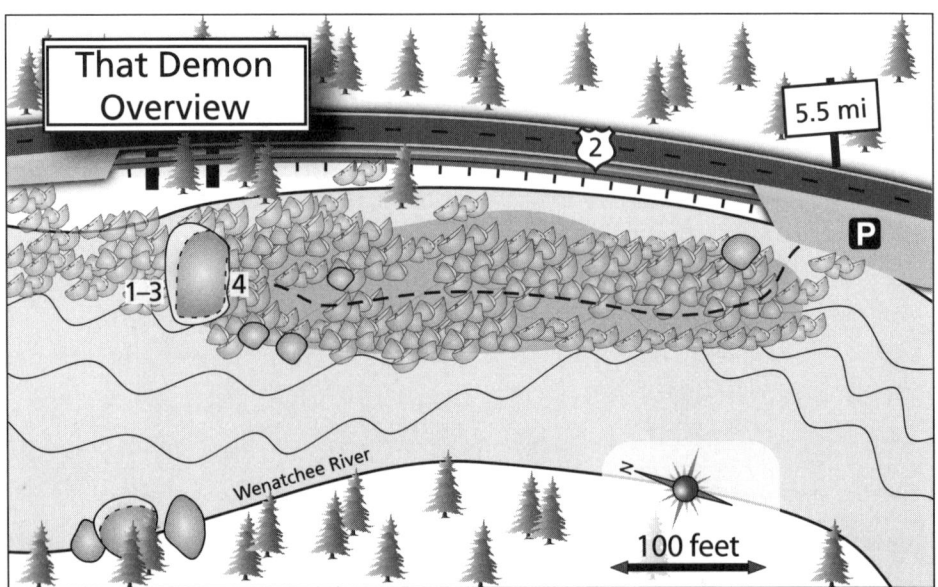

Tumwater - That Demon | **LEAVENWORTH**

___3. **Damian's Thoughts** V7 ★★
From the same start as the previous two climbs, move straight up to a sloper and better holds below the lip. Unconfirmed grade.

___4. **The Virgin** V8/9 ★★
On the boulder's less-steep south side, this heinous finger-wrencher begins with a high mono pocket and a poor undercling at head height. Pull on and bust for the lip. Yowie! F.A. Johnny Goicoechea.

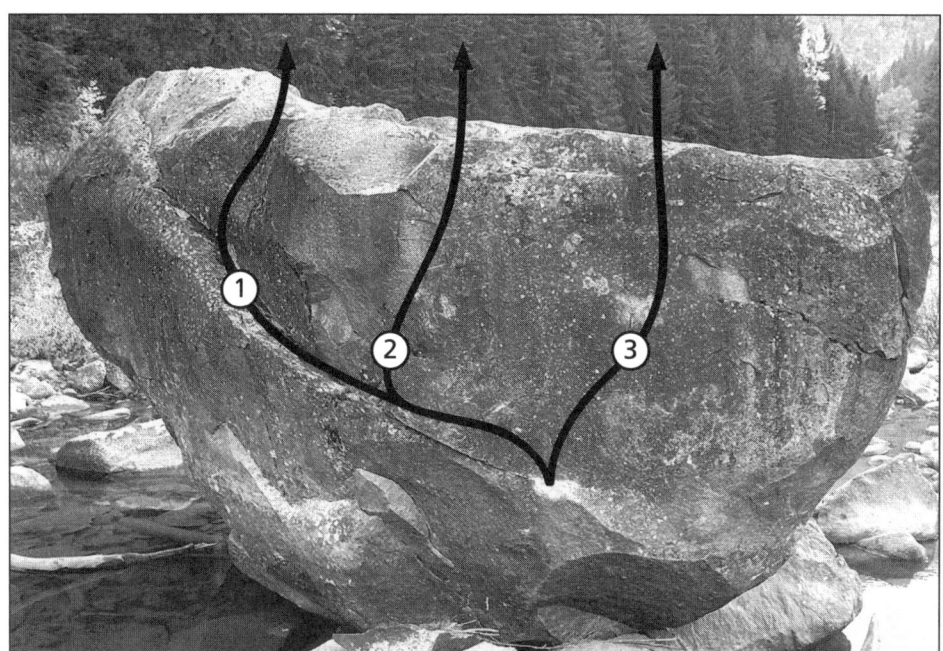

Johnny Goicochea projecting at Swiftwater   Photo: Brian Sweeney

LEAVENWORTH : Tumwater - Swiftwater

SWIFTWATER

Swiftwater is one of Leavenworth's most popular and historic bouldering circuits. This area boasts a good variety of problems in all ranges of difficulty, with plenty of moderates. As with the difficulty, the rock quality is also varied, with schist, the large-grain granite of Hate Rock, and fine sandpaper texture on the north side of the highway. Swiftwater has virtually all flat landings and summer shade.

Swiftwater's south side is home to a good small circuit, replete with plenty of historic oddities like the lowball classics on Heel Hook Rock. However, please don't judge all of Leavenworth on the Swiftwater South boulders, as many visitors do… Instead, venture north into the woods just across the road to a concentrated assortment of intermediate challenges, from the Fontainbleau slopers of **Premium Coffee** (V7) to the famous roof crack **Royal Flush** (V2). Be sure to follow the trail to the end of the cluster, where you'll find one of Leavenworth's biggest featured overhangs, home to the classic **Footless Traverse** (V5).

Approach: Swiftwater is located 6.9 miles from Icicle Junction. Park in the western of the two well-signed parking areas, the second as you approach from Leavenworth. Hate Rock is just east of the parking area; follow the trail on the west side of the lot to Heel Hook Rock and the tall schist overhang. To find the boulders on the north side of the road, walk west along Rt. 2 for roughly 50 yards, cross the road, and follow the short path to **Premium Coffee**. Continuing on, the trail runs parallel to the road through a vegetated burn area to the next cluster of boulders. Use the traffic noise from the highway as a reminder to walk well off the road, and please use extreme caution when crossing.

Cole Allen on The Footless Traverse (V5). Photo: Brian Sweeney

Tumwater - Swiftwater : **LEAVENWORTH**

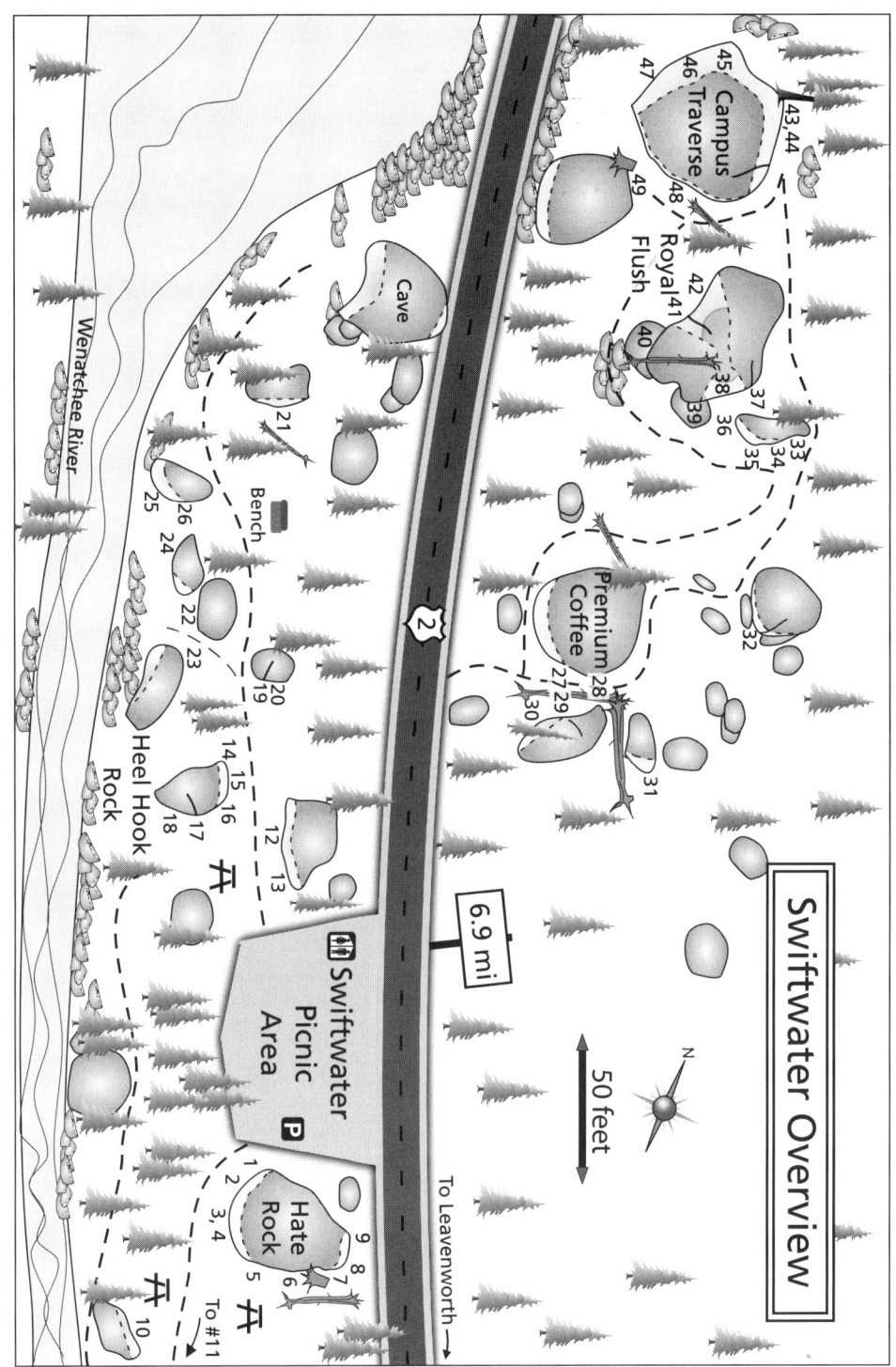

LEAVENWORTH : Tumwater - Swiftwater

___1. **Cramps** V2 ★

Start with head-high edges just right of the arête, crimping up and right to top out.

___2. **Hate Monger** V3 ★★

Start sitting, matched on the obvious flake jug on the left end of the boulder. Move right to the grainy Vulcan grip, finishing up and left on better holds. Good climbing on not-so-pleasant stone.

___3. **Slap and Dangle** V3 ★★

Jump start to a flat shelf at the nine-foot level, roughly two feet right of the small left-facing corner. Campus up and left to press out an awkward mantel on slopers.

___4. **Shock and Awe** V3+ ★★

Jump to the flat edge as for **#3**, but campus and heel hook rightwards to top out on better holds. Gritty but good.

___5. **Raven** V9 ★★★

Somebody's climbed that??? Just right of the overhang, jump to a small crimp pocket at the 12-foot level above the 'DJ Merced' grafitti. Climb up and left to a crimp and mantel onto the near-vertical wall above to reach the lip. Use a couple cheater stones if you need to—the first ascent was done using two crash pads and a spare tire! F.A. Joel Campbell.

___6. **Snake Eyes (project)**

Starting from the tree stump, climb the tall slab to two identical pockets a few feet below the lip.

___7. **14 Years** V6 ★★

Start sitting on the corner with a small righthand sidepull and a left sloper. Slap up to better holds on the arete, finishing slightly left on easier ground.

Colorado's Hermanator glides through the immaculate slopers of Premium Coffee (V7). Photo: Jackie Hueftle

LEAVENWORTH : Tumwater - Swiftwater

___8. **Lip Gloss** V2 ★
Start standing with a good hold on the left arête of the short roadside face. Climb up and right on the arête to finish on the corner. Can also be done as a dynamic throw to the right arête.

___9. **The Transverse** V1 ★
Start crouched with slopers on the right arête and traverse up and left on better holds to top out on the point.

___10. **The Devonian Fish** V0 ★
This baby boulder offers countless varitions, all of which are pretty darn easy. A nice option for those of us who prefer really easy warm-ups.

___11. **Caveman Cole** V9 ★★
This rarely-attempted one-mover lies roughly 20 yards past the **Devonian**; a side-trail leads to the summit of this riverside boulder. Start matched on the small crimper in the overhang, moving to the sloper above then wildly chucking for the jug on the lip. F.A. Cole Allen.

___12. **Schisthead** V2 ★★★
Climb the center of the overhanging face to a big reach for a hard-to-spot jug. **Variation** (V3): Start on the left side of the face, climbing right into the topout of **Schisthead**.

___13. **The Prey** V0 ★★
Climb the shorter right side of the face on increasingly large holds. Many variations, as well as high, low, and complete traverses of the boulder have been done at around V1 and up.

___14. **Heel Hook Right** V2+ ★
I'm not even going to try and name these ones... From a low incut on the right end of the tiny overhang, move up to a flat sidepull and finish up and left on slippery slopers.

___15. **Heel Hook Center** V2 ★★
Start sitting under the overhang with a smallish crimp pocket and a decent low foot. Move up to the wide crimp, then the lip and top out. Good fun.

___16. **Heel Hook Left** V1+ ★★
Start sitting on the left side of the small overhang with good slopers on the lip. Move up and right on slopers to the topout of **#15**.

___17. **Minnie** V1
Climb the ultra-short finger crack.

___18. **Mickey** V0 ★
From a crouch, with both hands in the low seam, climb up and right to good holds on the lip and a beginner's mantel topout.

___19. **No Pitons Here** V0 ★
Climb the widening crack on the miniature boulder. A good place to experiment with those bizarre crack climbing techniques... Hand jam? What's that???

Tumwater - Swiftwater | LEAVENWORTH

____20. **Bubbles** V0- ★

Just right of **#19**, climb the short face on super-cool bubbles and grooves. Fun for the whole family!

____21. **Bam** V2 ★★

Hop to the good sloper just above head height, and finish straight up with a nice mantel. A fun short problem on fantastic rock.

____22. **Oceanfront** V1

Traverse the riverside lip of this squat boulder either way.

____23. **The Ripple Effect** V1 ★

On the short uphill side of this large boulder, climb the wavy slab over a slanted landing.

____24. **Joel's Traverse** V6 ★

 On the boulder just below **#22**, traverse the low lip up and right on neat slopers.

____25. **Chicken Man** V8 ★★

Jump from the edge of the flat rock to slap two high, opposing slopers on this semi-hidden boulder, finishing straight up via a small crimp and tenuous mantel. The difficulty can vary from year to year with the ground level. F.A. Cole Allen.

____26. **Goat Boy** V7 ★

Start matched on a small undercling and balancing on a big foot ledge right of **Chicken Man**. Your simple goal here is to reach the flat crimp just in sight above… alas, simple but for the effects of gravity… Grade unconfirmed.

____27. **Premium Coffee** V7 ★★★

 A.K.A. **Heavy Petting Zoo**. One of Leavenworth's most beautiful and unique problems. Upon entering the woods on the north side of the road, your eyes may be immediately drawn to this obvious smooth line extending from a low bulb on the left. Start matched on the lowest sloper with a tricky ramp foothold, slap up and left on fine-grained slopers, then rock up and swing for the jug. Pretty temperature dependent—prepare for a good sandbag in the summer.

____28. **Percolator** V1 ★

Climb the arête right of **Premium Coffee** from a bubbly head-high jug to a scary top-out.

____29. **Unobvious** V2/3 ★

Follow weird sidepulls and finger locks up the obvious seam on the left side of the boulder facing **Premium Coffee**. The grade depends on whether you start from the rock or the ground.

____30. **The Barista** V1 ★★

Climb the bulge just left of the tree to a good left-facing flake, then layback to the top and press the dirty mantel. Awesome!

____31. **The Squatter** V3 ★★

Find this short, blunt arête behind the corner left of **#29**. From the loaf hold at chest height, hug and slap your way to better holds in the vegetated seam.

____32. **Lowe Rider** V1 ★

Climb the wide crack from a sitdown start in the small alcove, finishing on top of the detached flake. Enjoy!

LEAVENWORTH : Tumwater - Swiftwater

___33. **Pod Racer** V1 ★
The first problem reached if hiking from the Premium Coffee area. Start matched in the pod above the small boulder and traverse left to follow decent holds up the arête, a fun V0 in its own right.

___34. **Tentacles** V0 ★★
Layback up the short flake to a jug and the strange fin feature above—but don't pull it off!

___35. **Bangladore Torpedo** V8
On the left end of the face, find two small right-facing sidepulls at waist height. Pull on with a crap low foot and stab up through crimps to finish slightly left.

___36. **Lead Pants** V3 ★★
Start sitting on the left corner of the small prow with a lefthand sloper and a poor right undercling. Move to the good sloper rail and finish straight up, or for an extra grade and unimaginable personal satisfaction, continue right on crimps to a more powerful finish.

___37. **Raging Cow** V1 ★
Climb the wideish crack on the right end of the short overhang, from a sitdown start.

___38. **Sitting Bull** V3 ★★
Start in the mini-roof with good holds in the crack. Move right to jugs on the low lip, then face forward and climb the sidepulls to a cruxy slap. Very nice.

___39. **Hormonal Monkey** V8
Start sitting on the rock a few feet left of #38 with two pinches near the edge of the roof. Somehow utilizing the good but low foothold, pull on and slap the juggy lip above. Why? Don't ask me. Heel hooks spoil the fun and the grade

___40. **Jack of Spades** V6 ★
A few feet right of the prominent **Royal Flush** crack, climb the undercut corner from a low righthand crimp and the lowest sloper on the lip. Stuff your foot in the crack, slap your left hand to the pinch, and stab right and up on crimps to finish.

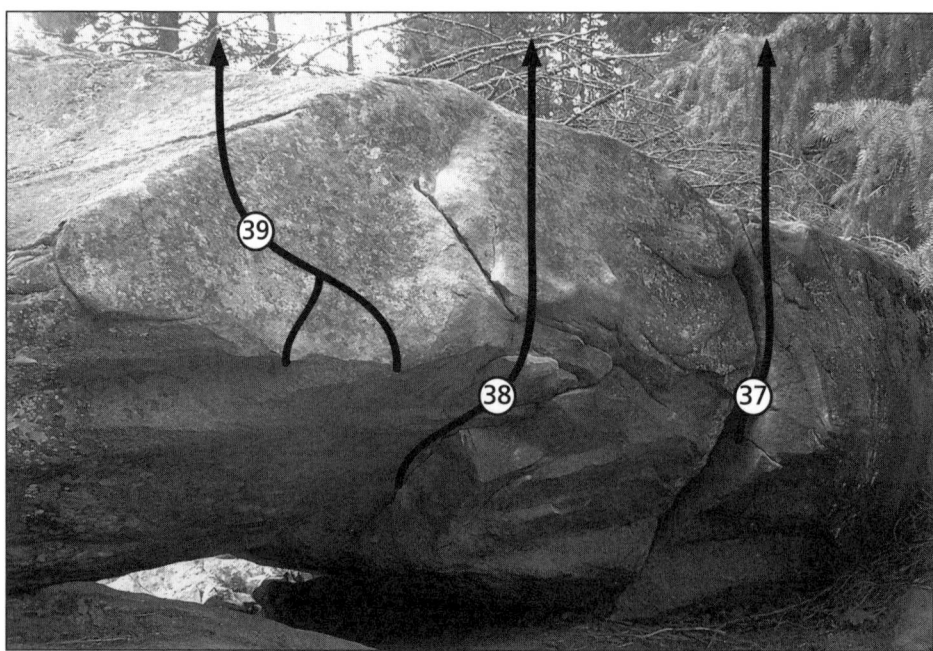

Tumwater - Swiftwater : **LEAVENWORTH**

___41. **Royal Flush** V2 ★★★

The famous roof crack. Start in the deepest part of the cave and climb the horizontal fist crack to finish high on the slab above. Not your typical tick-marked gymbo crimpfest—unless you can't hand jam! "It's so good that even French climbers have been known to look at it."

___42. **Sleeve Ace** V3 ★★★

From the lowest jug at the edge of the roof left of **Royal Flush**, climb over the bulge on flat holds 'till you can rock up on your foot. Use that power! And your brain!

___43. **Dark Days** V2 ★★

Starting from the incut crack jug by the tree, traverse left along the sloping shelf to finish up the wide crack on the left end of the boulder. Climbing just the crack is a fun V0.

___44. **The Backscratcher** V6 ★

At the left end of the steepest part of the overhang, climb straight up from an incut jug in the crack to an edge just behind the tree, then lunge for the lip and top out. A fall inevitably leads to a painful raspberry from the tree behind you. F.A. Cole Allen.

___45. **Raging Bull** V7 ★★

Start sitting under the low bulge with an angular left crimp and a sloping righthand edge. Squeeze and heel hook to two good slopers on the lip, finishing up and slightly right by mantling onto the shelf.

___46. **Big Booty Bitch Slap** V10 ★★

A.K.A. **Heaviness of the Load**. Start in the rightmost part of the overhang, matched on a wide low undercling with the bulge in your face. Kick your right foot on and slap to the crack, finishing left around the corner on the ramp of **#45**, or for full value, continuing straight up from the start to top out.

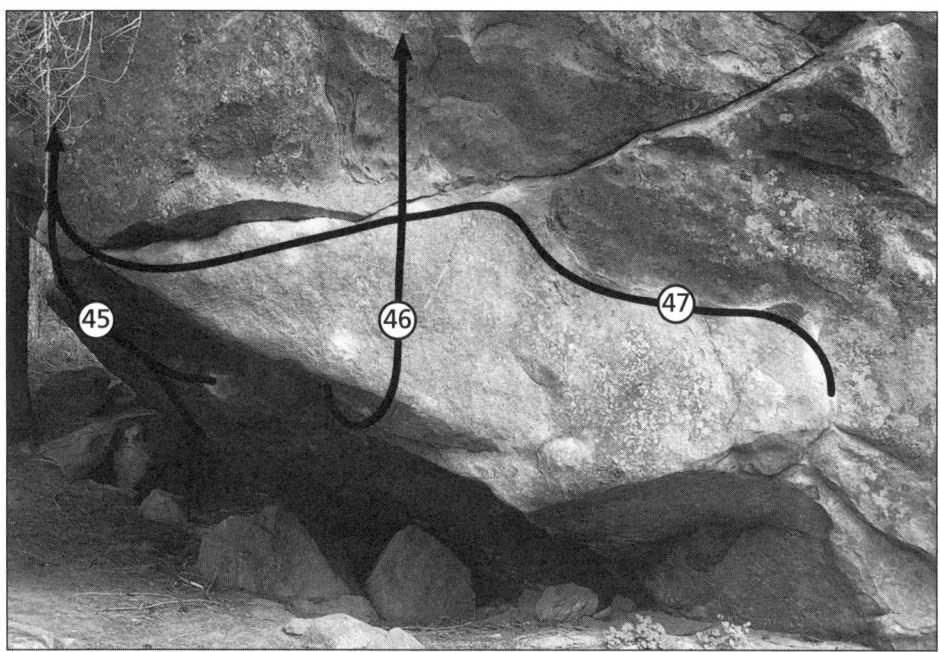

151

LEAVENWORTH : Tumwater - Swiftwater

___47. **The Footless Traverse** V5 ★★★
Start in the middle of the tall face with jugs in the right end of the obvious crack. Traverse left in the crack to the loaf hold at the edge of the steep roof, finishing up and left on the ramp as for **#45**. Continue left to the crack finish of **#43** for an extra pump. Climbing straight up from the start of the **Footless Traverse** is a quality highball with a full-value mantel that's roughly the same difficulty as the traverse.

___48. **(project)**
Climb the shallow dihedral feature just left of the suspiciously fallen tree. Tough, but doable.

___49. **Balance Slap** V4 ★★
Climb the slabby face left of the stump to, well, a balancey slap for the top. Starting off of the stump and using the arête makes the climbing easier, but the landing sketchier.

Bobby Hardage slapping Sitting Bull (V3)

There is another climb at Swiftwater, not indicated on the map. To the east of the first pullout, some 6.7 miles from Icicle Junction, there is a funky arête on the beach (V2) that is well worth the quick visit.

"We have a lot of **fun** together, going out bouldering and monkeying around, and we always have... and that's the important thing, you know? It doesn't matter how good a climber is, if you can't go out and have fun with him climbing then it's **not** really that **much use**, is it?"

- *Jerry Moffatt, The Real Thing*

LEAVENWORTH-3
MOUNTAIN HOME ROAD BOULDERS

Jessica Campbell homing in on the crisp edge of The Cattleguard Arête (V8)

MOUNTAIN HOME ROAD

Perched high on the hillside of Boundary Butte at the mouth of Icicle Canyon, the boulders of Mountain Home Road are Leavenworth's Druid Stones; a dense collection of quality stone set aside from the rest, the satellite area that can be more enjoyable than the main thoroughfare. The white, compact granite and flat, grassy landings at Mountain Home are a pleasant addition to Leavenworth's wide array of rock types and landscapes. And unlike the Druid Stones, one is able to drive to the top of the steep hillside and actually walk down to go climbing. Save the hiking for the sunset.

The setting at Mountain Home is comparable to Gold Bar's Clearcut area, both victims of the wide-scale logging operations which bring the boulderer such mixed blessings. A wide variety of climbs can be found at Mountain Home, with something to satisfy everyone. The open hillside here typically receives all-day sun and makes for a great evening spot. Mountain Home would also offer prime winter conditions for the gung-ho climber willing to snowshoe or ski up the unplowed road. During the rest of the year, the approach is mellow and the scenery fantastic. As at most Leavenworth areas, keep an eye out for rattlesnakes on warm summer days. Finally, please help to keep this magical spot free from the litter and cigarette butts that characterize lesser climbing areas.

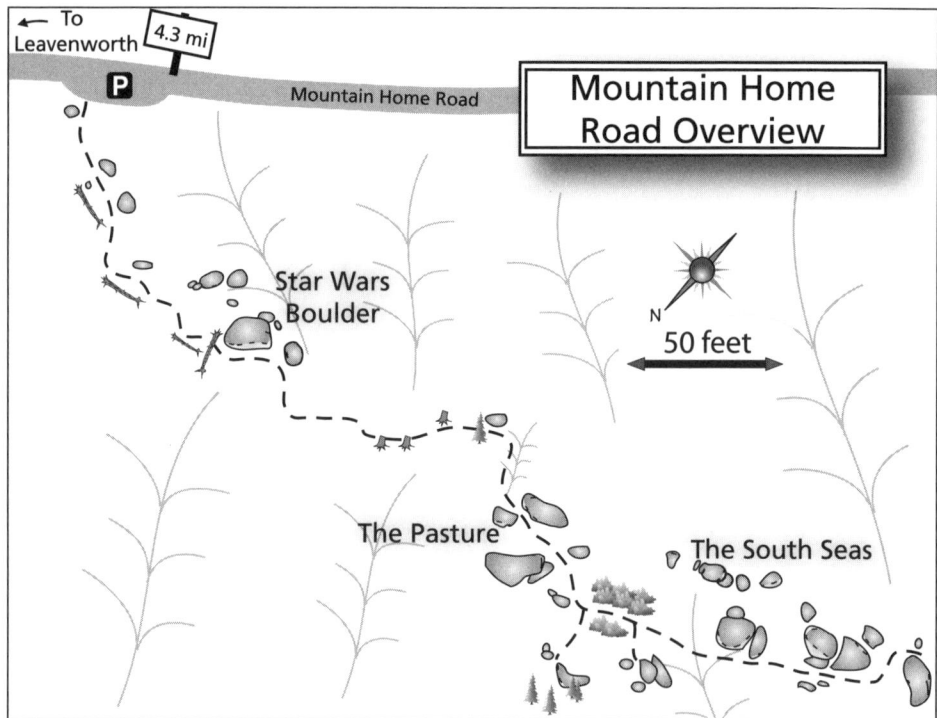

Mountain Home - Introduction   **LEAVENWORTH**

Approach: Getting to the Mountain Home Road bouldering spots is easy. All of the climbing is accessed from the small pullout 4.3 miles from E. Leavenworth Road, across from a large white slab marked by a dark, round 'eye.' See individual area sections for directions. Unclimbed boulders still abound at Mountain Home, though most of the potential is a serious bushwhack away. While the hilltop vista of Mountain Home may seem like the middle of nowhere it gets more visitors than one may think, including patrols by the county sheriff. Don't camp here, instead, drive down the hill and turn left onto East Leavenworth Road to zip up Icicle Canyon for the evening.

Mountain Home Road from the Leavenworth National Fish Hatchery

LEAVENWORTH : Mountain Home - Star Wars

THE STAR WARS BOULDER

The Star Wars Boulder is Mountain Home's premier block, home to some of Leavenworth's most striking problems. Discovered by Jeff Hashimoto and Damian Potts in the summer of 1999, the Star Wars has a grittier stone than other Mountain Home areas, often providing a week's worth of skin removal in just a few hours. The side-by-side classics **Yoda** (V9) and **Obi-Wan** (V9) are both uber-proud ticks, while the beautiful traverse **Darth Maul** (V4) is definitely a burly classic in its own right. Along with the rest of the Mountain Home Road bouldering, the Star Wars boulder bakes in the sun during the better part of summer days. In winter, the road remains unplowed; for the best sending temps try hitting the Star Wars on a cool spring or fall evening.

Approach: To reach the Star Wars boulder and all Mountain Home bouldering areas from Rt. 2, turn onto East Leavenworth road just after the Wenatchee River bridge on the east end of town. Once on East Leavenworth road, immediately turn left onto Mountain Home road. The road passes a few homes, turning to dirt after 0.3 miles and heading up a steep hill. Reach the large clearing at 4.0 miles and eventually park directly downhill from a large white slab 4.3 miles from East Leavenworth Road. A well-traveled trail heads down the hill and to the left; the downhill-facing overhang of the Star Wars boulder is the first large boulder encountered, roughly five minutes from the road.

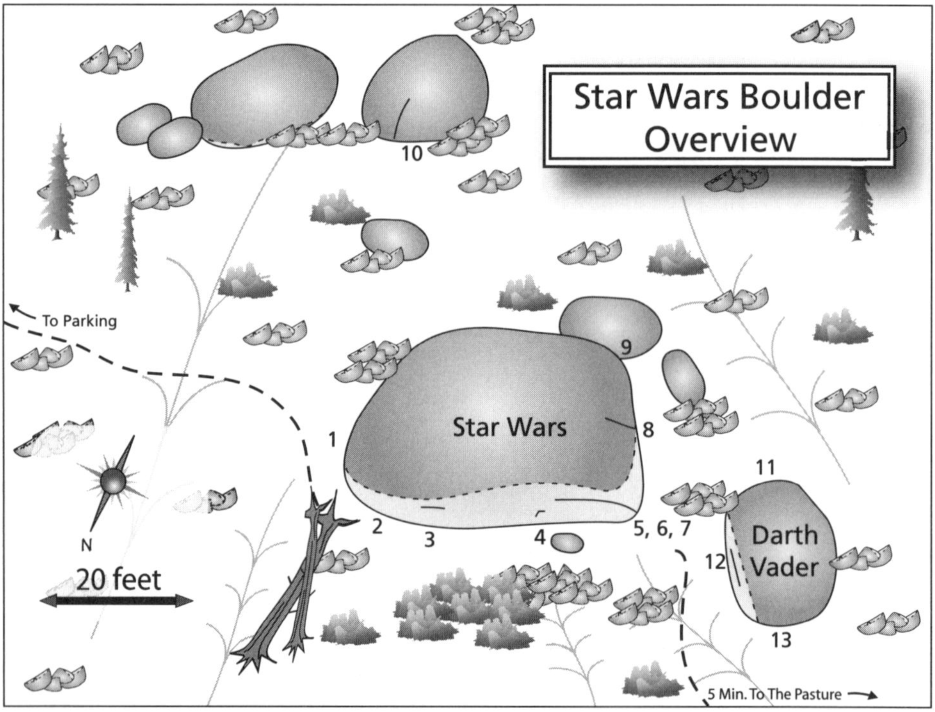

Mountain Home - Star Wars — LEAVENWORTH

___1. **Padmi Trainer** V1 ★

Climb the left side of the first face reached on the boulder, starting from two crimps. A nice but oft-overlooked option for warming up here. **Variation** (V3): Starting from crimps in the middle of the face, move right to a small crimp/pinch, finishing up and right.

___2. **Han Solo** V3 ★

On the left end of the overhang, jump start to opposing slopers on the lip of the bulge. Smear your feet high and pop to the lip.

___3. **Yoda** V9 ★★

Start on the chest-high rounded crimp rail on the left side of the overhang. Pull on and dyno to the sharp, incut pocket on the lip, finishing up and right with friendlier holds. The force must be strong in you for this one.

___4. **Obi-Wan** V9 ★★★

Start sitting on a small boulder with an angular crimp in the steepest part of the overhang. Slap up and right to a crapola sloper, then follow the seam left to a lunge for the lip and a tricky mantel. F.A. Johnny Goicoechea.

___5. **Darth Maul** V4 ★★★

Starting from a low jug on the right corner of the overhang, follow the obvious seam up and left 'til the crimps run out. Make a committing lunge for the lip and hold it together for the cruxy mantel. Classic!

___6. **Nice Men** V2 ★★

Start sitting on the arête as for **#5**, climbing straight up on jugs to a more delicate finish.

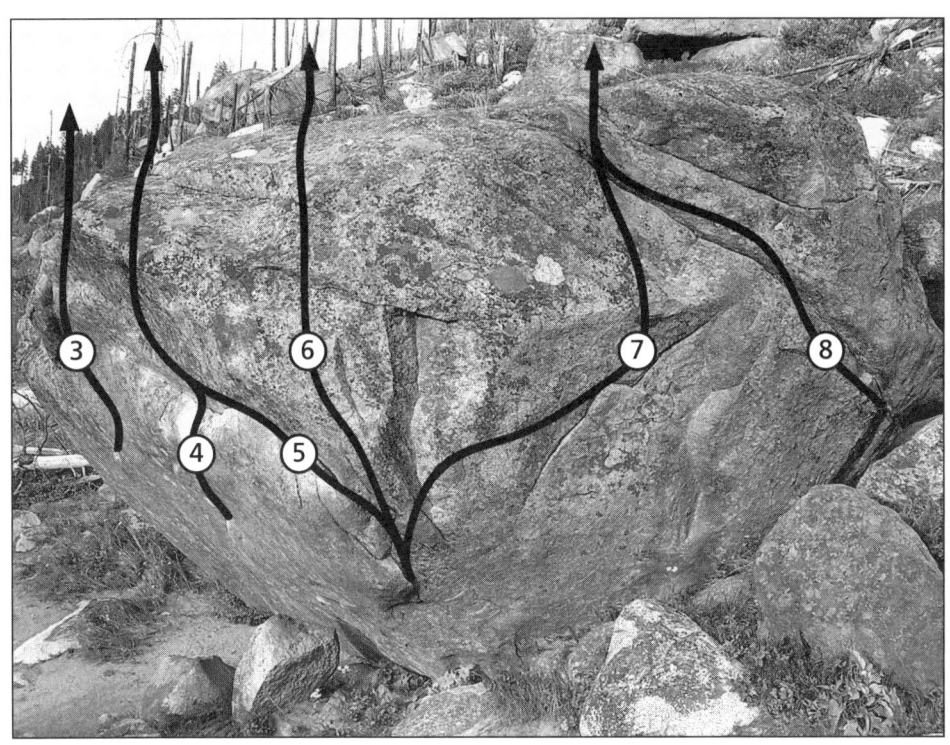

157

____7. **Emperor's Lightning** V7 ★★

Start on the jug as above, but climb up and right through the lightning-bolt seam to the lip and crack. Finish straight up with the left-facing flakes on the lip. Any resemblance to the deep-south classic **Skywalker** is purely coincidental… F.A. Jeff Hashimoto.

____8. **Wookie Crack** V1 ★

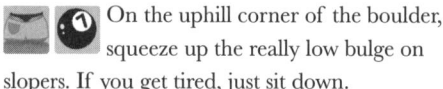

Climb the grainy hand crack on the right side of the face. The holds are good but the landing gets a bit hairier as you go.

____9. **Rich's Non-Star-Wars-Named Climb** V3

On the uphill corner of the boulder, squeeze up the really low bulge on slopers. If you get tired, just sit down.

____10. **Jabba The Slab** V0 ★

Follow the seam up the center of the clean slab thirty yards above the Star Wars boulder.

Kelly Sheridan working Darth Vader (V10)
Photo: Kyle O'Meara

____11. **Castle Run (In 12 Parsecs)** V0

This somewhat cramped problem climbs the uphill side of the Darth Vader boulder. Start low in the small corner, avoiding the dab on your short journey to the summit.

____12. **Darth Vader** V10 ★★★

Climb the overhanging face of the boulder just below the Star Wars boulder. Start on bad chest-high underclings in the seam, slap to the sloping lip, and grovel over with some tenuous compression and lots of poor slopers. Very tough. F.A. Joel Campbell.

____13. **Moon of Endor** V2 ★

On the downhill side of the Darth Vader boulder, climb the left-leaning ramp from high crimps in the seam. Finish up and left.

THE PASTURE

Along with the adjacent South Seas, the Pasture area at Mountain Home Road boasts some of the best rock quality in Leavenworth. Developed along with the Star Wars Boulder during the summer of 1999, these boulders scattered along the side of Boundary Butte appear to be glacially deposited chunks of granite from higher in the Alpine Lakes region. The stone is slick 'salt and pepper' granite, and the lines are typically proud and independent. The clean arête of **The Barn Door** (V3) and the sandbagger's bulge on **Fairly Desperate** (V4) are not to be missed, nor is the striking classic **Cattleguard Arête** (V8). Most problems in The Pasture have flat, grassy landings and see less traffic than other Leavenworth areas. The open setting of the Pasture can be quite warm in the summer, but makes for a great evening spot even after hot sunny days.

Approach: The Pasture is located roughly five minutes downhill from the Star Wars boulder, some 10 minutes from Mountain Home Road. From the Star Wars, follow the trail downhill, then directly left, traversing roughly 100 yards along flat ground before eventually dropping through a small grove of trees to the cluster of boulders. When you've had your fill of this quaint spot, head downhill and left to the neighboring South Seas area.

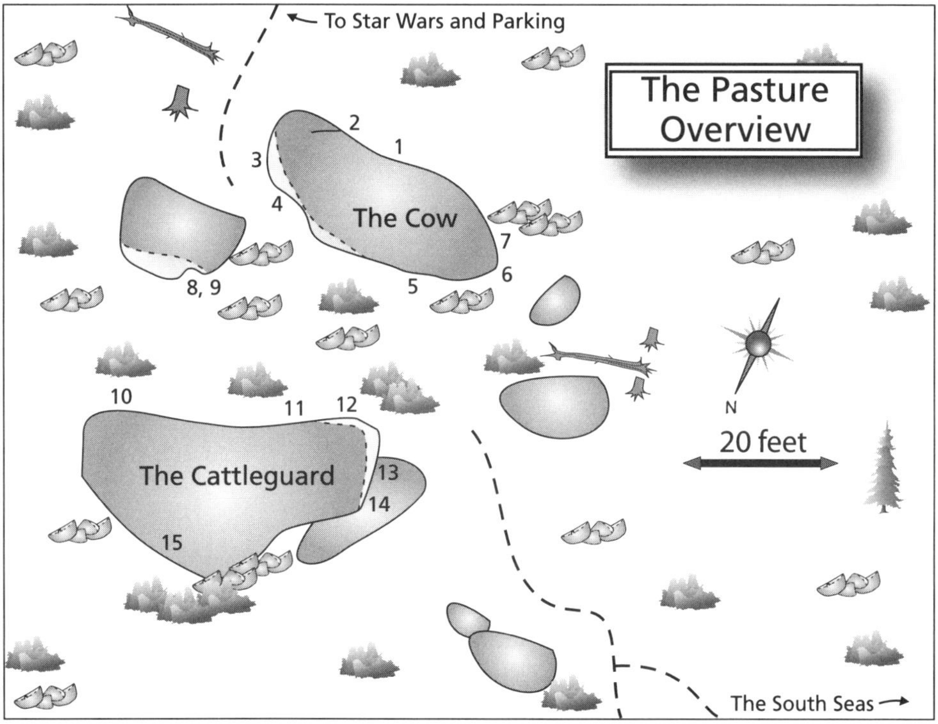

LEAVENWORTH : Mountain Home - The Pasture

___1. **Slab Cow** V1 ★

Climb the one-move slab on the uphill side of the Cow boulder. Subtract major style points if you skip the tiny edges and just hop to the lip…

___2. **Cud Crack** V1

Follow tiny edges up the short off-vertical seam on the uphill corner of the Cow.

___3. **Feche la Vache** V3 ★★

Start sitting on the trailside corner of the Cow with a hidden undercling jug. Haul your butt off the ground and make a couple strenuous moves to finish on the right side of the arête. Cooler than it looks!

___4. **Cattle Terrace** V1 ★

Hop, skip, or jump to the good rounded ledge at the eight-foot level, trusting slippery footholds as you finish up and left.

___5. **Goodnight Moon** V8 ★★

The tall downhill face of the Cow. Leap roughly 50 feet to the decent handhold in the center of the face, then finish up and right via some tricky crimpers. F.A. Joel Campbell.

___6. **BSE** V3 ★★

Climb the tall arête on the right side of the face, eventually moving slightly left into the finish of #5. Great fun.

___7. **Hoofin' It** V0 ★

Climb the tallish slabby face just right of **BSE** on nice edges. Definitely not a lowball; makes a rewarding beginner climb.

___8. **Slaughterhouse** V5 ★

Start sitting on the right side of the small bulge with an undercling flake. Climb up and left just under the lip of the boulder, finishing with a tough mantel on the left side of the bulge.

With Icicle Canyon in the background, Kyle O'Meara grapples with the Cattleguard Arête (V8).

____9. **Fairly Desperate** V4 ★★

Start sitting as for **#8**, climbing straight up the dihedral on confusing features. A little harder than it looks, to say the least.

____10. **Andy's Arête** V5 ★★★

Traverse up and left along the obvious lip of the Cattleguard boulder. Keep an eye on your feet as you work past slick slopers to press it out just below the apex of the arête. If that didn't tire you out, following the lip all the way to the top adds a definite challenge.

____11. **Cattleguard Dyno** V8 ★★

This tough dynamic problem starts roughly five feet right of the blunt arête. Grab a tiny lefthand sidepull and even smaller righthand edge, paste your feet on more small edges, and huck to the flat crimp three feet below the top. Not very finger-friendly!

____12. **The Cattleguard Arête** V8 ★★★

The area classic… Start in the bushes, hugging the blunt arête with your right hand on a small chest-high sidepull and your left on a high pinch. Reach for the sloping crimp, match, and campus up to better holds to finish. Fantastic!

____13. **Cow Jumped Over The Moon** V1 ★

Starting from the flat rock, hop to the juggy lip and press out the mantel. Why not???

____14. **The Barn Door** V4 ★★

Start sitting on the left end of the small overhung corner. Fight the swing as you follow clean slopers up the striking lip to mantel on the flat ledge. F.A. Jeff Hashimoto.

____15. **Air Is Air** V0 ★★

Several variations climb the wide low-angle slab on the back of the Cattleguard, all of which are enjoyable.

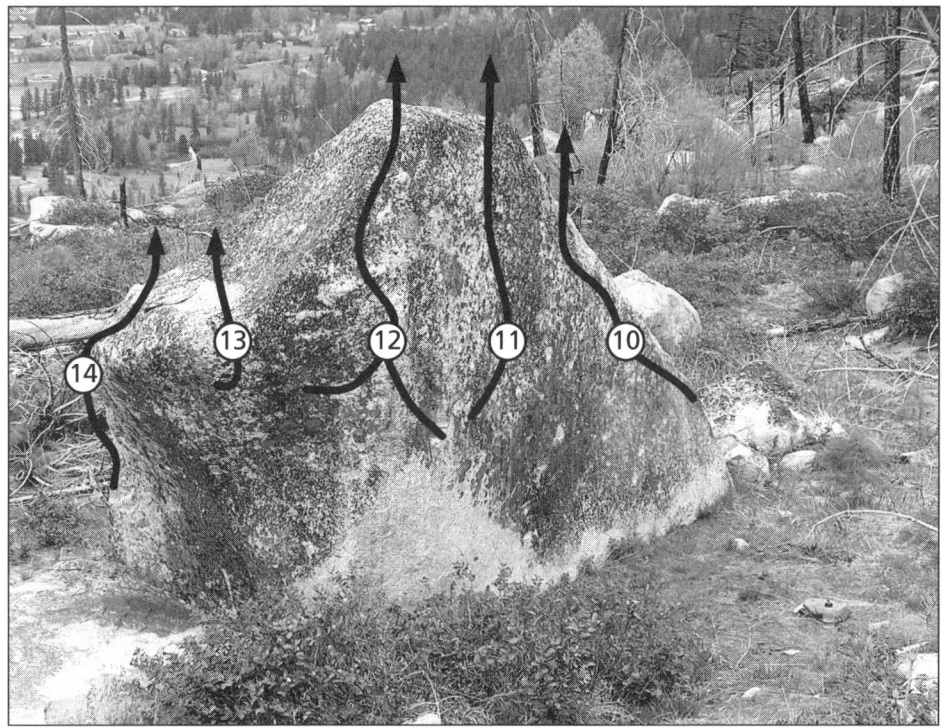

LEAVENWORTH : Mountain Home - The South Seas

THE SOUTH SEAS

This is it folks—the end of the line. Located just downhill from the Pasture area, The South Seas is one of Leavenworth's more remote bouldering spots, possessing something of an otherworldly feel under the right conditions. The stone is immaculate and the view breathtaking, with climbing to match. Check out the intermediate classics **Tall People Suck** (V4) and **Double Vision** (V4), then kick back and enjoy the bevy of easier climbs to be found here. Along with the rest of the Mountain Home bouldering, the South Seas gets plenty of sun, making for great evening sessions in the slow-dying light. The landings are generally decent, and the climbs inviting… What more can I say?

Approach: The South Seas area is somewhat nebulous, extending slightly downhill and mostly west of the Pasture area. Head straight downhill from the Cattleguard Boulder to find Tall People Suck, or traverse the faint trail left through bushes to reach the Vision boulder and the bulk of the South Seas bouldering. Some more fun sneaker climbs can be found in the shallow gully just past **Punk Ass Kid**.

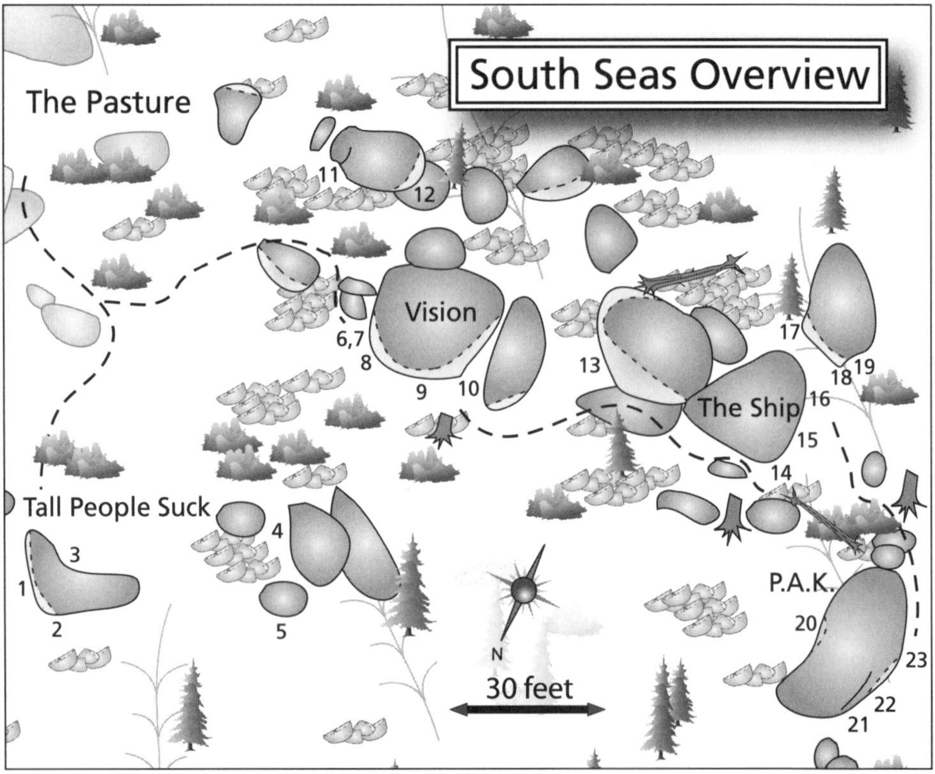

Mountain Home - The South Seas   **LEAVENWORTH**

___1. **Tall People Suck** V4 ★★★
Climb the blank face from a high start on a lefthand sidepull and neat-o righthand pinch, heading left at the lip to top out. Do I even have to say it's height dependent? A tough crouch-start (V7) can also be done on thin left-facing edges.

___2. **Piano Trainer** V2 ★
Mantel onto the low arête from a stand start with a small incut. Finish up the slab. Harder than it looks!

___3. **Polish Bob's Slab** V0 ★
Climb the scooped slab on the uphill side of the boulder. Many eliminates (up to V14) can be done to up the challenge…

___4. **Palm Down** V9 ★★
Climb the steep, undercut slab from a stand start in the middle of the face. Palm down, press up, cross to the arête, and work your feet up. Bizarre. F.A. Joel Campbell.

___5. **Probletunity** V2 ★
Climb the nice clean slab near the right arête over a somewhat intimidating landing.

___6. **Blurred Vision** V5
Starting on a flat sloping ledge below the smallish dihedral, climb left along the low seam to finish up the arête.

___7. **Neanderthal** V1 ★
Climb the short, wide crack from the low, flat hold of **#6**.

___8. **Television** V4 ★
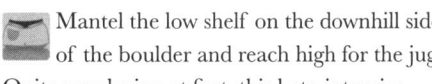Start on the corner just right of **#7** with a low kneebar. Climb the arête. If you can.

___9. **The Vision** V2 ★★
Mantel the low shelf on the downhill side of the boulder and reach high for the jug. Quite perplexing at first, this beta-intensive route can even been climbed in sneakers, without the sidepull flake.

163

LEAVENWORTH : Mountain Home - The South Seas

___10. **Double Vision** V4 ★★★
Start sitting matched on a low jug at the edge of the corridor. Climb up and left on tough crimps to top out straight up the blunt corner. Not the tallest climb around, but pretty darn good.

___11. **Pair of Deuces** V1
A few yards uphill from the Vision boulder, climb the wide crack from a sit-start. Swiftwater is definitely winning this crack climb poker game…

___12. **Full Metal Hairbrush** V3 ★
Start crouched on the flat rock, hugging the low double arêtes. Climbing a few stout moves up the corner to finish up and right on the lip. Or, start matched on a crumbling crimp on the left face and climb rightwards to finish up the arête, and you've just sent **Full Metal Toothbrush** (V4).

___13. **Abandon Ship (Project)**
Climb the very thin overhanging face to the sloping lip. The face moves are hard; the mantel harder.

___14. **Jolly Roger** V2 ★★
Climb the left arête of the tall, clean slab to a big move for a crimp. Shuffle up and right on the big ledge to finish.

___15. **Ship of Fools** V1 ★
Mantel the mini-bulge in the center of the face, finishing as for **#14**.

___16. **Shiver Me Timbers** V1 ★★

On the right side of the big slab, make a tricky mantel on small edges, finishing up the daunting face above. "…but it's a real 5.7 slab."

___17. **Walk The Plank** V2
Climb the short uphill arête from a stand start. Mind the tree, fear the talus.

____18. **South Seas Arête** V0+ ★★★

Climb the tall downhill arête with big holds beautiful stone. Classic!

____19. **Long John Silver** V1 ★★

Climb the face and arête just around the downhill corner of **#18**.

____20. **Shoeless Joe** V0 ★★
Great fun. Just downhill from The Ship, mantel the flat ledge on the uphill side of the big lumpy boulder, traversing left on the lip to finish. For full value, this one ought to be climbed in sneakers. "The first ascent was done in Airwalks, in the rain…"

____21. **Punk Ass Kid** V6 ★★★
Traverse right along the obvious seam from chest-high crimps near the left end. At the big sloping dish, mantel and shuffle right along the dirty shelf to top out. Pretty line.

____22. **Thumper** V3 ★★
Hop to the dish in the center of the face, mantel, and finish with the heady foot traverse of **#21**.

____23. **The Desert Of The Real** (project)
As far as anyone knows, the steeper slab to the right of **#22** has yet to be climbed…

That rock we were camped against was a marvel. It was thirty feet high and thirty feet at base, a perfect square almost, and twisted trees arched over it and peeked down on us. From the base it went outward, forming a concave, so if rain came we'd be partially covered. "How did this immense sonumbitch ever get here?"

"It probably was left here by the retreating glacier. See over there that field of snow?"

"Yeah."

"That's the glacier what's left of it. Either that or this rock tumbled here from inconceivable prehistoric mountains we can't understand, or maybe it just landed here when the friggin mountain range itself burst out of the ground in the Jurassic upheaval. Ray when you're up here you're not sittin in a Berkeley tea room. This is the beginning and the end of the world right here. Look at all those patient Buddhas lookin at us sayin nothing."

"And you come out here by yourself…"

"For weeks on end, just like John Muir, climb around all by myself following quartzite veins or making posies of flowers for my camp, or just walking around naked singing, and cook my supper and laugh."

- *Jack Kerouac, Dharma Bums*

LEAVENWORTH : Mountain Home - The South Seas

Drew Schick surfing the South Seas granite of Punk Ass Kid (V6)

2 Gold Bar

Todd Mannherz working the wide-open tension moves of **Ebriosity** (V11)

GOLD BAR : Introduction

GOLD BAR

The quiet town of Gold Bar, located roughly an hour from Seattle at the outset of the winding, forested Rt. 2 corridor, received its unusual name at the hands of optimistic prospectors who settled the area in the mid-1800s. Except for the thriving 4x4 culture, it may not seem to the casual visitor that all that much is happening in town. The chance of bumping into fellow rock climbers in Gold Bar, elevation 200, seems about as likely as on the outskirts of El Paso. Okay, bad example, but you get my drift. Unlike the Town Walls of neighboring Index, Gold Bar's Zeke's Wall lies high on a hilltop and doesn't see much traffic these days. Most west-side craggers head to Index, Leavenworth, or the exits along I-90 for their roped fix. What's really exciting about Gold Bar these days, for the rock climber at least, is the bouldering. The steep granite of Zeke's Wall has shed thousands of fine-grained white boulders onto the hillside below, creating a first-class playground for the cordless climber.

The Clearcut area, visible to the north of Rt. 2, and the Forest and Sanctuary areas just uphill, compose the bulk of Gold Bar's bouldering. This concentrated array of angular blocks houses many difficult and beautiful problems, though the dense bounty of the forest's bouldering has really yet to be tapped. The Five Star Boulder sits alone at the bottom of the hill, a majestic giant set aside from the rabble above, home to a dozen of the best problems on the planet. And across the valley, the Beach and Camp Serene boulders flank Rt. 2, each home to three-star moderates on impeccable stone. There is enough established bouldering in Gold Bar to make it a worthwhile destination for anyone—and there is much more left to do. This chapter is presented less as a comprehensive reference to Gold Bar bouldering than as a guide to the area's established classics. With a little work, any visiting climber can still leave their mark on Gold Bar… all you've got to do is hike uphill a bit.

Getting There: Like Leavenworth, the town of Gold Bar lies on US Highway 2. Gold Bar is about one hour northeast of Seattle, and one hour directly west of Leavenworth.

From Seattle and other points south, take I-405 north to exit 23 onto WA-522. WA-522 intersects Rt. 2. after 15 minutes; Gold Bar is some 14 miles to the east.
• From points north of Seattle, take I-5 to Everett and hook up with Rt. 2 there.

From Spokane and points east, you'll be traveling west on I-90. Take exit 151 onto WA-281 north and follow it for almost 10 miles. Then turn left onto WA-28 and follow it for 34 miles to Rt. 2. Gold Bar lies another 75 miles west through Leavenworth and over Steven's Pass. Some say it's fastest to take Rt. 2 the entire way — your call.

From I-82, I-84, and other points south, hook up with Rt. 97 north in Ellensburg and follow it to Rt. 2, where you'll be some 75 miles east of Gold Bar.

Introduction : **GOLD BAR**

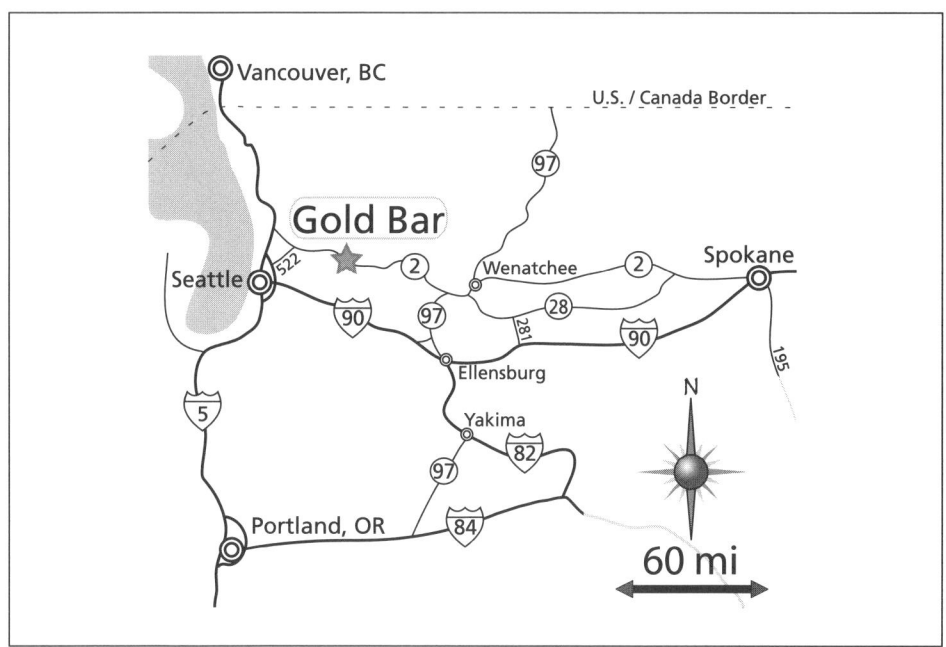

Zeke's Wall looms over the boulders of the clearcut

GOLD BAR : Introduction

GOLD BAR AMENITIES

The town of Gold Bar doesn't offer too many amenities to visiting climbers, but there's enough to get by. If you're looking for shopping or food beyond the modest options available here, your best bet is the town of Monroe, perhaps 20 minutes west. Fun rest day activities in the area include the trip to Eagle Falls, an interesting rocky corridor just below the wide pullout 3.4 miles east of Index on Rt. 2, or the hike to Bridalveil Falls and Lake Serene from Mt. Index road between Index and Gold Bar. Better yet, find yourself a dirt bike and get 'er done.

LODGING

Hotels: For a shower and a clean bed, the Steven's Pass Motel on Croft Ave, just off of Rt. 2 has rooms for 40 bucks and up. Call ahead on weekends to ensure a spot: (360) 793-6633.

Camping: For its utter lack of plush Bavarian hotels, Gold Bar does have some pretty good free camping. It's a good idea to get a little distance from the strange goings-on of Reiter Road, and the best spots are near the boulders. Try any of the three Clearcut pullouts at the top of the hill (see chapter for beta), or even the rutted-out hollows by the powerlines for true local flavor. Decent pullouts can also be found further along Reiter Road towards Index, though it would be wise to keep a low profile here, including the popular Index Town Wall camping. To shell out for a Forest Service campsite, drive east of Gold Bar on Rt. 2 to the turn for Index, take it, but continue past the bridge on Index-Galena Road along the North Fork of the Skykomish River.

Life is simple for Brian Sweeney — camping at Gold Bar's hilltop parking.
Photo: Brian Sweeney

FOOD

The Gold Bar Family Grocer, on Rt. 2, is a standard supermarket where you'll find most everything needed for camping. In addition to the standard espresso huts, Gold Bar is also home to Prospector's Steak & Ale, where you'll find good local grub right off the highway. In these parts, the prized reward for a long day of climbing is the scrumptious cheeseburgers of Zeke's Drive-In, 1.0 miles east of Reiter on Rt. 2. Try a milkshake, as well. Just to the west of Gold Bar, the town of Sultan has a few more options, but for a real night on the town you'll have to keep going to Monroe, or cross the mountains to Leavenworth.

ACCESS: SPECIAL CONSIDERATIONS

Current situation: Most of the bouldering in Gold Bar is owned by Manke Timber Company, creators of the clearcut and the dirt road used to access the majority of the bouldering. The company has a rather hands-off approach to the land these days, as evident from the masses of dirt bikers enjoying the network of rutted-out logging roads in the area. Manke Timber has specifically granted climbers permission to use the area, partially due to the liability protection provided to private landowners under Washington's recreational use statute RCW 4.24.200. This bill, which specifically mentions rock climbing as an outdoor recreational activity, limits landowner liability for unintentional injuries incurred by public land users. What does this mean? Your get-rich-quick scheme of falling off a boulder and suing the company isn't worth a dime. Better to send instead.

Future: While Manke currently allows climbers to use the area unrestricted, the company plans to resume logging activity in the forest below Zeke's Wall in the next few years. While this would mean the re-grading of the notorious dirt road, it will also come with heavy costs to boulderers. Both the Forest and Sanctuary areas will eventually see some clear-cutting, and the entire hillside will be closed for at least several months.

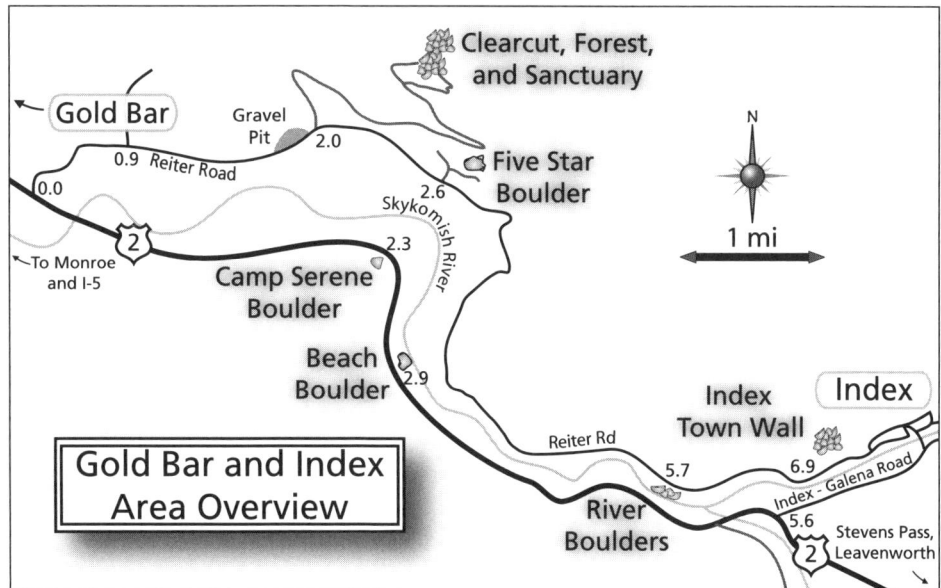

GOLD BAR : Introduction

However, continued logging activity below Zeke's Wall won't be a death-blow to Gold Bar bouldering; the climbing is good enough to shine through another environmental change. Many of the Clearcut's boulders were climbed before the recent logging, and they are still badass today. The ambience of the Forest and Sanctuary areas will be fractured, but the promise of new development further uphill should offer solace to the tree-hugger in all of us. Imagine how much more exploration will take place if you can drive your rig all the way to Lighten Up. And fortunately, the Snoqualmie National Forest boundary zigzags through the woods several hundred yards below Zeke's Wall, ensuring that there will always be some forest left in Gold Bar.

Yes, these are just silver linings in a big cloud, but it is imperative that climbers continue to respect the landowner's rights in the area, and be polite and respectful in any interactions with Manke Timber employees visiting the property. Our privilege to use the boulders of Gold Bar is contingent upon our cooperation and willingness to compromise. Want to make a difference? Contact the WCC and coordinate your efforts with those of other climbers across the state. It is largely due to the WCC that we have unrestricted access to these fantastic boulders, and through this organization that the future of bouldering in Gold Bar will be secured.

OTHER CONSIDERATIONS: BREAK-INS AND BLACK BEARS
Besides rednecks illegally firing handguns from the hilltop parking areas, another thing worth worrying about when bouldering in Gold Bar is the potential of a vehicle break-in. The majority of ORV users you'll encounter in Gold Bar are friendly and law-abiding, but the bad apples are also there. Random vandalism and theft do occur, however infrequently. Lock your vehicle, don't leave any valuables inside, and avoid parking around Reiter Road overnight. If you want to carpool up the hill, leave the extra vehicle at the Family Grocer and it should still be there when you return.

Black bears and cougars have also been seen in the forest below Zeke's Wall. While the thought of a large cat stalking you and your buddies might have you shakin' in your boots, the actual likelihood of spotting one is extremely low, and it is quite safe to boulder alone in the forest. If you do encounter a large animal, don't run. Cougars make decisions about prey based mostly on visual stimuli, so wearing your crash pad is a good idea. Chances are, they're more scared of you than you are of them and all you'll see is their tail…

Camp Serene : **GOLD BAR**

THE CAMP SERENE BOULDER

A.K.A. Zeke's Boulder. Gold Bar's Camp Serene Boulder lurks alone in the woods on the south side of Rt. 2 just east of town. Originally 'discovered' by Bob Buckley in the late 1990s, the Camp Serene Boulder gets its name from the well-done but unfortunate graffito on the west face. Though there are only a few problems here, the beautiful highballs of **Serenity Now** (V4) and **Ryan's Problem** (V6) are well worth the visit, being among the best in this guide for their respective grades. Though the Camp Serene Boulder was initially power-washed to a sparkling white, nature is quickly reclaiming her lost property so bring a wire brush along. Both the boulder's topouts and the somewhat technical downclimb are getting especially overgrown; make sure you have a look before you find yourself stranded in the summit jungle. The Camp Serene Boulder is well-shielded by the surrounding trees and stays shady most of the time, although on a busy summer weekend the heat and the black-throated wind of nearby traffic might interfere with the ambience.

Approach: From the west, drive 2.3 miles east of Gold Bar's Reiter Road on Rt. 2 and park in the righthand pullout at the start of a wide righthand curve. Just before the pullout, a yellow road sign indicates the righthand curve. When approaching the Camp Serene Boulder from the east, find the pullout on the left 3.1 miles west of the turn for the town of Index. It may be easiest to keep going, turn around at the famous Zeke's drive-in, and head 1.0 miles back east to the pullout as described above. From the pullout, walk roughly 40 yards west along the south side of the road and follow the faint trail into the woods to the visible boulder.

___1. **Chemical Imbalance** V8 ★★★
Climb the tall, blunt arête from head-high jugs. Harder than it looks and very cool.

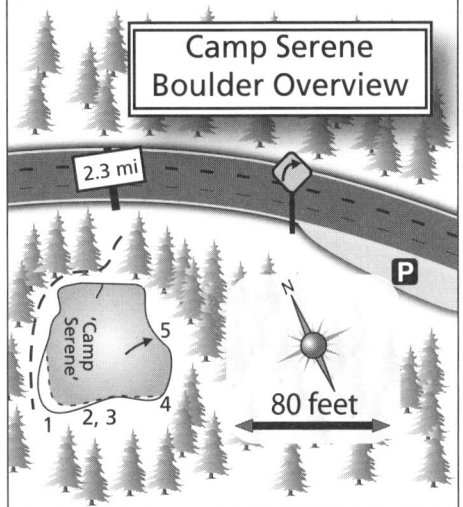

___2. **Serenity Now** V4 ★★★
From two decent head-high pinches near the left end of the face, climb up through slopers and work into the shallow dihedral. Reach high for the obvious square-cut pinch and make a committing reach for the jug high in the notch. Awesome!

___3. **Ryan's Problem** V6 ★★★
Start on the good holds as for **Serenity Now**, but move right from the sloper onto sweet edges and ledges. Make a cruxy lunge to the high crimp, then finish straight up with a nice mantel among the foliage. A beautiful, high line on perfect rock. F.A. Ryan Paulsness.
Variation (VH): Jumpstart to the edges of **Ryan's Problem** off the small stump. Ridiculously hard. F.A. Joel Campbell

173

GOLD BAR : Camp Serene

___4. **Insanity Later** V2 ★★

Climb the arête right of the previous two problems from a stand start with small edges around the corner. Follow crimps up the seam on the slabby right face, finishing straight up via a sloper on the lip. For more of a challenge, stay on the left face, finishing via a small gaston below the lip (V5).

___5. **Inserene** V0-

Climb the super-mossy corner on the boulder's east face. This is also the downclimb; you may want to give it some attention before topping out your proj.

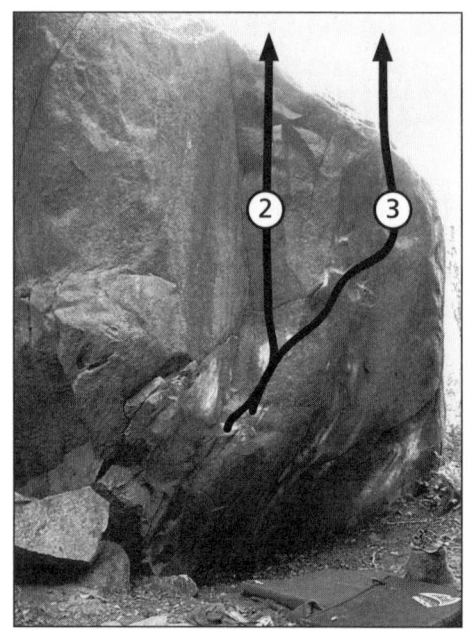

Joel Campbell on J-High (V7), Beach Boulder Photo: Brian Sweeney

THE BEACH BOULDER

Lying on the south bank of the Skykomish River some three miles east of Gold Bar, The Beach Boulder is a pleasant piece of river-polished granite within a stone's throw of Rt. 2. While the offerings may be rather scant at this lone boulder, the rock quality is the same as Index's River Boulders a few miles upstream: superb. A few difficult problems can be found on this sandy beach, with the striking jumpstart **J-High** (V7) being the area classic. A few more erratics are scattered along the banks of the Skykomish; the big cave across the river is a great place to start exploring. The Beach Boulder stays sunny all day, but the river's there to alleviate any excessive heat. Several different user groups visit this and other spots along this section of river, so please keep a low profile and avoid the private property upstream.

Approach: The Beach Boulder is located directly across from the 33-mile marker on Rt. 2. From the west, drive 2.9 miles east from the Reiter Road turn and park in either of the two righthand pullouts flanking the 33-mile marker. Approaching these pullouts from the west, watch for two yellow signs indicating that the right lane ends. From the east, drive 2.6 miles west from the Index turn to park in either of the lefthand pullouts by the 33-mile marker. Once you've parked, cross the road and walk along the wide drainage to the telephone pole between the pullouts. Turn into the woods on the well-worn trail just west of the mile marker. The Beach Boulder lies roughly 100 yards northeast at the water's edge.

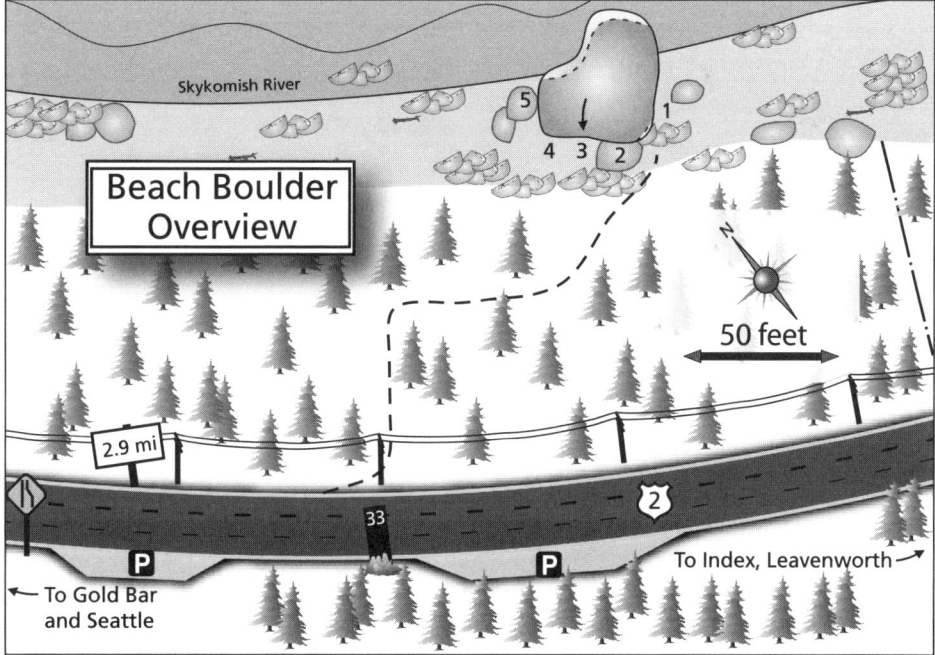

GOLD BAR : Beach Boulder

___1. **J-High** V7 ★★★

Start on the high incut jug above the built-up landing by either jumpstarting or hopping up from a head-high crimp in the seam. Grab the small crimp above, slap to the bad Karma-style sloper, and press it out after a cruxy hand-foot match. A beautiful line with just enough features to go. The static stand start (**J-Low**) is still a project.

___2. **Buquah** V6 ★

Starting from the smaller boulder, jump to the sloping lefthand sidepull and the lip, then mantel. Scary!

___3. **The Slip 'N' Slide** V2 ★

Press onto the blank slab using the small, slopey right-facing corner and smear to the top. This is also the boulder's downclimb, really an exercise in controlled sliding—and aim.

___4. **The Bathtub** V1 ★

Mantel into the scoop a few feet left of the previous problem, then traverse right and climb the slab to top out.

___5. **The Leap of Faith** V4 ★★★

Beginning from the smaller boulder on the downstream corner, jump out to the flat jug at the 10-foot level. The landing varies seasonally from flat sand to the full dunk. Too easy for you? Try the run-and-jump version!

Beach Boulder : **GOLD BAR**

Joel Campbell losing faith on the Leap of Faith (V4) Sequence: Brian Sweeney

GOLD BAR : Five Star Boulder

THE FIVE STAR BOULDER

Gold Bar's Five Star boulder is one of the best boulders in America, hands down. The Five Star sits alone like a remote fortress, its summit guarded by 25 feet of steep, striated granite on nearly all sides. The problems on the Five Star are generally both hard and high, every one a classic. From the striking, intimidating lines of **Ground Zero** (V8) and **Kambucha** (V7) to the immaculate movement of **Ross Bongo** (V9) and **Ebriosity** (V11), there isn't a bad climb on this boulder… Nor an easy one, for that matter. The Five Star offers only two moderate options for the less-burly among us. Though the 4x4 traffic on summer weekends brings a certain 'Return to Thunderdome' ambience, the boulder's atmosphere is improving annually as the area's re-vegetation progresses. The Five Star gets pretty steady sun during warmer months, but it's possible to find a shady side any time of day, provided you bring some power. The huge gymnastic mat formerly installed at the base of the boulder is long gone, so bring several friends and plenty of pads as well.

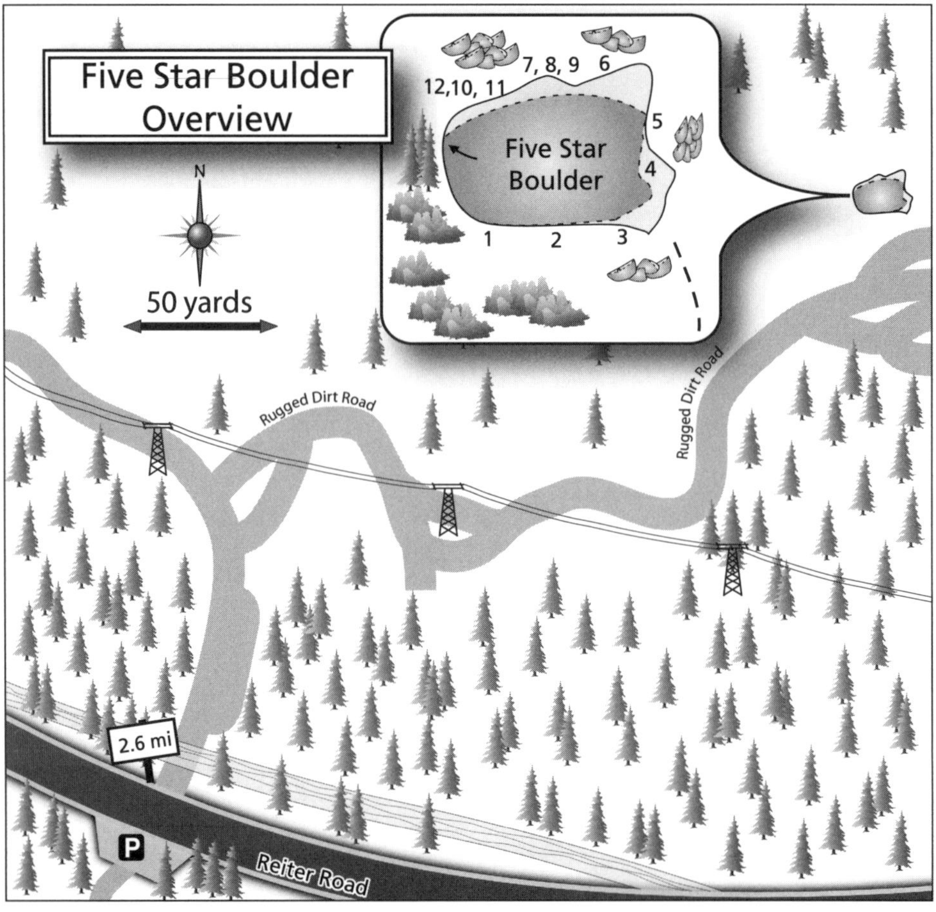

Five Star Boulder : **GOLD BAR**

Approach: The Five Star boulder lies at the base of the hillside below Zeke's Wall. The bouldering in Gold Bar is accessed via Reiter Road, which intersects Rt. 2 near the 30 miles marker, 1.5 miles east of the Gold Bar Family Grocer and 5.6 miles west of the turn to Index. Follow Reiter up a short hill, then stay right at the intersection with May Creek Road at 0.9 miles. After passing the large gravel pit at 1.8 miles, continue on Reiter up a short hill and park in the small pullout on the right 2.6 miles from Rt. 2. Cross the stream across the road and walk through the shady clearing. Turn right in the open area, heading up the hill towards a power line tower. Continue past the tower and keep left when the road divides into several rutted tracks. The Five Star will become obvious on the left within 10 minutes of the parking.

____1. **The Five Star Lip** V2 ★★★
On the left end of the tall vertical face, start on large blocks and follow the arête up and right to work through committing slopers before pressing it out. One of the boulder's easier lines, this climb is still quite proud!

____2. **Project**
The thin vertical face on the boulder's south side remains unclimbed, an invitation to future honemasters…

____3. **Ground Zero** V8 ★★★
Ground Zero climbs the left arête of the overhanging face visible upon first reaching the boulder. Start matched on a low rail over the pointed rock, moving through two horizontal rails on the left face before reaching right to a flat gaston under the roof. Slap left to the obvious fin, finishing up and right on better holds. Challenging, high, and beautiful.

____4. **Ross Bongo** V9 ★★★
Start sitting in a low corner on the right end of the overhang with two angular crimps in a seam. Climb up and left on the angled arête to a hard toss for a square-cut jug in the steep face. Finish up and left on the heady slab above the lip. Classic! F.A. Cole Allen.

____5. **The Five Star Arête** V6 ★★★
Start crouched a few feet right of **Ross Bongo** with a good righthand sidepull and a low left hand on the arête. Cross up and right to a jug on the left side of the overhung prow, climbing straight out the arête on opposing crimps to throw for the jug on the lip. Finish up and right on jugs. The boulder's first classic line to fall, and one of the best climbs around. F.A. Bob Buckley.

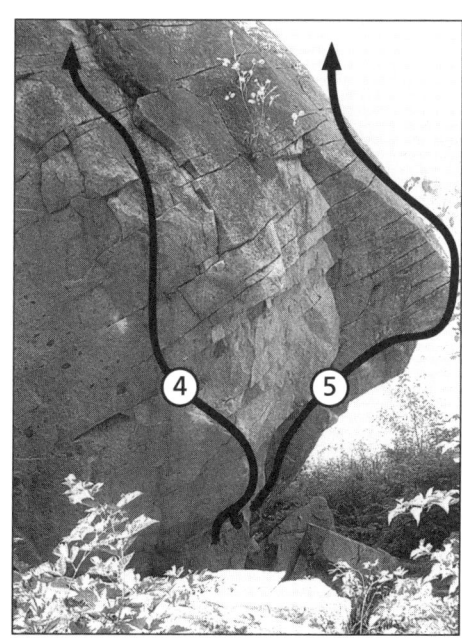

179

GOLD BAR : Five Star Boulder

___6. **Kombucha** V7 ★★★

Climb the center of the vertical face right of the arête from a left-facing crimp just overhead. Stab left to a big gaston and finesse up on small edges to the lunge. Hit the hidden jug in the bulge and air it out to the top on big holds. F.A. Josh Carroll.
Variations (V7): Both **Kombucha** and the **Five Star Arête** can be crisscrossed, climbing from the start of one to the finish of the other. Climbing both problems and both variations in a day earns you the Five Star merit badge.

___7. **Kombucha Sit** V9 ★

Start with a sharp low incut on the left end of the steep overhang. Move to cup the shelf above, then endure the pain of traversing left on small crimps to the start of **Kombucha** and on to the top. Great movement, though it's a bit marred by the butt-slicing landing. F.A. Cole Allen.

___8. **The Five Star Warmup** V2 ★★

Start as for **#7** and climb straight up on shelves. Follow the jugs up the tall corner just left of the steep face to small crimpers, finish either left or right when the boulder begins to slab out. Watch for loose holds on the Five Star's version of a warm-up climb.

___9. **Green Padded Ass** V6 ★★

Begin as for **#7**, following the line of sloping shelves in the overhang up and right from the start. For full value, avoid exiting onto the easier ground of the warm-up and finish straight up from the notch. More committing than it looks, this clean line would be a stand-out climb in different company…

___10. **Ebriosity** V11 ★★★

Climb the center of the steep overhang from two sidepulls on the lowest shelf. Technical climbing and some extreme drop-knees link the nebulous array of sloping rails before a big move for the top; exit to the lip either straight up or out right (cruxy either way), and finish on seams over the lip. Fantastic! F.A. Cole Allen.

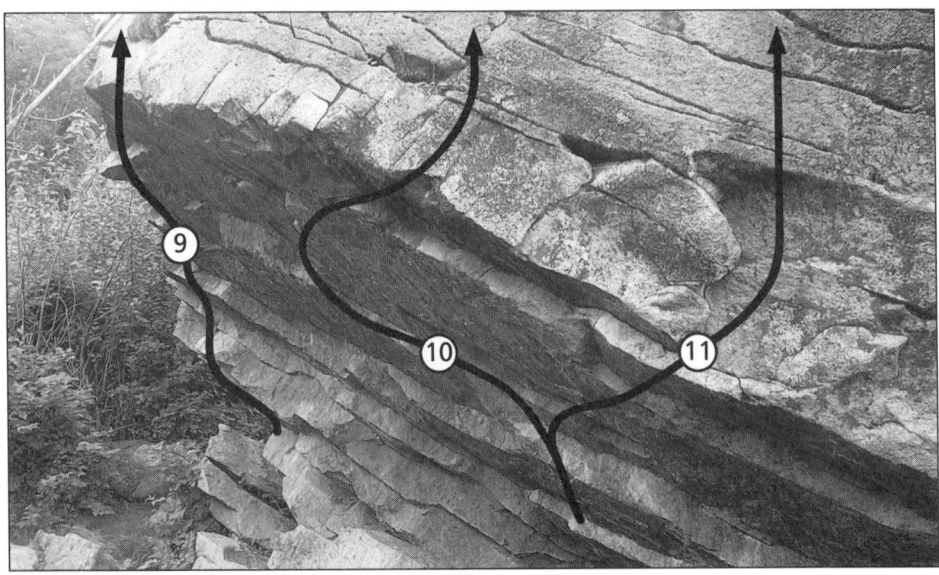

Five Star Boulder : **GOLD BAR**

___11. **Sobriosity** V6 ★★
Start as for #**10** and climb up and right through the steepest part of the roof on crimps and underclings. Make a tough move up and right to a sidepull jug and pull the lip on buckets. Steep and fun, this little gem is the Five Star's best lowball.

___12. **Red Rover** V7 ★
Start in the far right end of the roof on the footholds of #**11**. Move to a sloping rail, match, and work over the lip to finish as above. Not bad, and even lower than #**11**!

"The boulderer is concerned with **form** almost as much as success and will not feel that he has truly **mastered** a problem until he can do it gracefully."

- John Gill, The Art of Bouldering

Kelly Sheridan on Ground Zero (V8)
Photo: Todd Mannherz

Joel Zerr at the crux of Ross Bongo (V9)

THE CLEARCUT

A.K.A. The War Zone. The large clearcut below Gold Bar's Zeke's Wall is home to some of the biggest and best boulders in this guide. Though climbers have been visiting the area even before logging activity devastated this steep hillside, most boulderers will first encounter the boulders of The Clearcut in its lush, revegetated state. Visible from Rt. 2, these huge white boulders sport some of the Northwest's proudest lines. While most of the areas in this guide offer something for everyone, Gold Bar's Clearcut is the ideal realm of the expert boulderer. Difficult testpieces such as **The Equinox** (V10), **Twisted** (V10), and **The Rubik's Cube** (V9) are mingled amongst gorgeous challenges like **Obesity** (V7), **Que Luna** (V6), and **Water** (V6). Boulderers with less desire for hard off-the-deck cranking will find solace in the Forest area just above these exposed giants. The Clearcut dries quickly after wet weather, but receives a good deal of summer sun and can feel quite warm on a clear day; beware the "Gold Bar Effect," a sluggish mix of fatigue and dehydration that besets many Clearcut visitors!

Approach: To reach the Clearcut boulders from Rt 2, turn onto the well-signed Reiter Road by mile marker 30, just east of the town of Gold Bar. Stay right at the intersection with May Creek Road at 0.9 miles, then turn left at 2.0 miles onto a gnarly dirt road just past the large gravel pit. Follow this dirt road under the power lines and through a sharp right turn, the first of several switchbacks. Pass a gate, a large lefthand switchback, and another righthand switchback as you head up the hill.

The road is notoriously rocky and uneven. Those with lower-clearance vehicles may want to park in the narrow pullout on the right 2.6 miles from Reiter Road. From this parking, walk another 100 yards up the road to catch the well-worn trail heading uphill across from a small round boulder. Fraggle Rock is the first large boulder on the left; the trail continues uphill past the Que Luna cluster, eventually reaching the hilltop parking area and more established trails.

Most vehicles ought to be able to continue over several large ruts and another small switchback to reach the hilltop parking area on the left 3.0 miles from Reiter Road. This parking is the best way to access the Forest and Sanctuary areas, and an ideal way to catch a quick warm-up before entering the surreal arena of the Clearcut. The condition of the road varies from year to year, however, and inexperienced off-road drivers may find themselves looking for a way to turn around. Alternatively, high-clearance vehicles may turn left at the switchback 2.3 miles from Reiter Road, heading through several smaller zigzags to park within a stone's throw of the Equinox boulder, 2.9 miles from Reiter. This is the best option for those afraid of hiking, though it is the most rugged and seems to be the most popular turnaround for dirt-bikers, increasing the odds of random vandalism (however unlikely they may be). You make the call.

The Clearcut : **GOLD BAR**

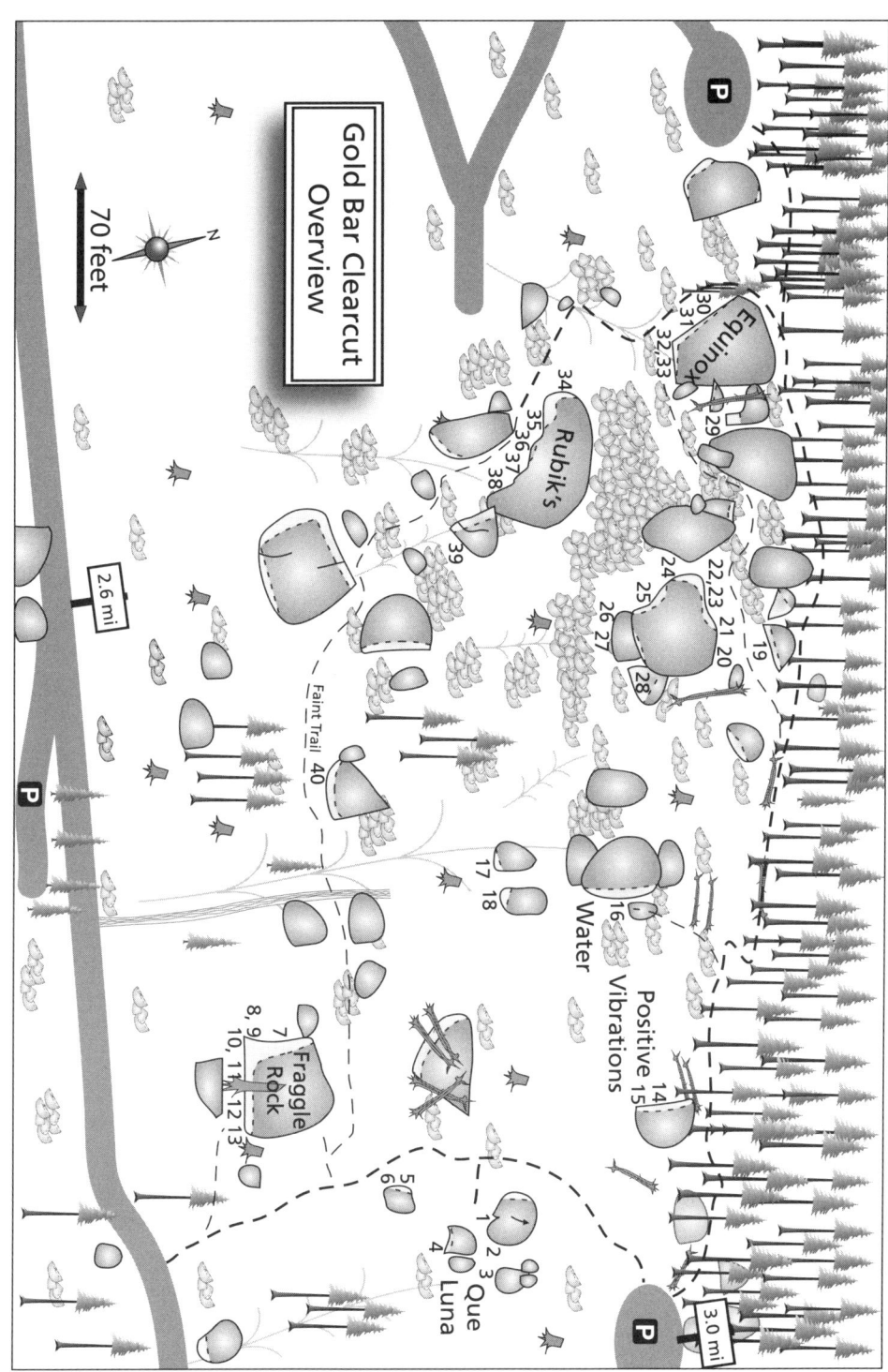

GOLD BAR : The Clearcut

The first tall boulder of the **Que Luna** cluster sports several highballs and toprope bolt anchors.

___1. **The Layback** V1 ★★

Climb the thick right-facing flake on the downhill side, working up the secure crack to an airy finish.

___2. **Tall Cool White One** V2 ★★

The tall face. Use the left arête and tenuous face holds to gain secure finger jams high above.

___3. **Tectonic Slab** V0 ★★

The striated slab with cool sloping edges. Perfect!

___4. **Que Luna** V6 ★★

This hidden climb can be found on the downhill side of the small cluster's lowest boulder. Begin crouched with a good right-facing edge, climbing up beautifully sculpted holds on both sides off the arete to make a delicate 'perch' to reach the lip. F.A. Kyle O'Meara.

___5. **Offa' My Cloud** V0 ★

Climb the left arête of this trailside boulder on incut jugs and sidepulls.

___6. **Moonlight Mile** V2 ★★

The right side of the tall face. Good holds to a cruxy fingerlock, finishing on jugs above.

___7. **Obesity Direct** V8 ★★

Find this reachy number on the steeply overhung west side of Fraggle Rock. Start sitting with a good incut on the far left end of the lower rail, slap way up and right to neat-o pinches on the higher rail, and finish up and left on better holds. Shorter climbers, prepare to feel stymied... F.A. Cole Allen.

___8. **Obesity** V7 ★★★

Start on the right side of the steep face with jugs on the lower rail. Climb straight up to the higher rail, traversing left through the pinches to slap for better holds at the apex of the rail. Finish straight up with an easy mantel. Classic!

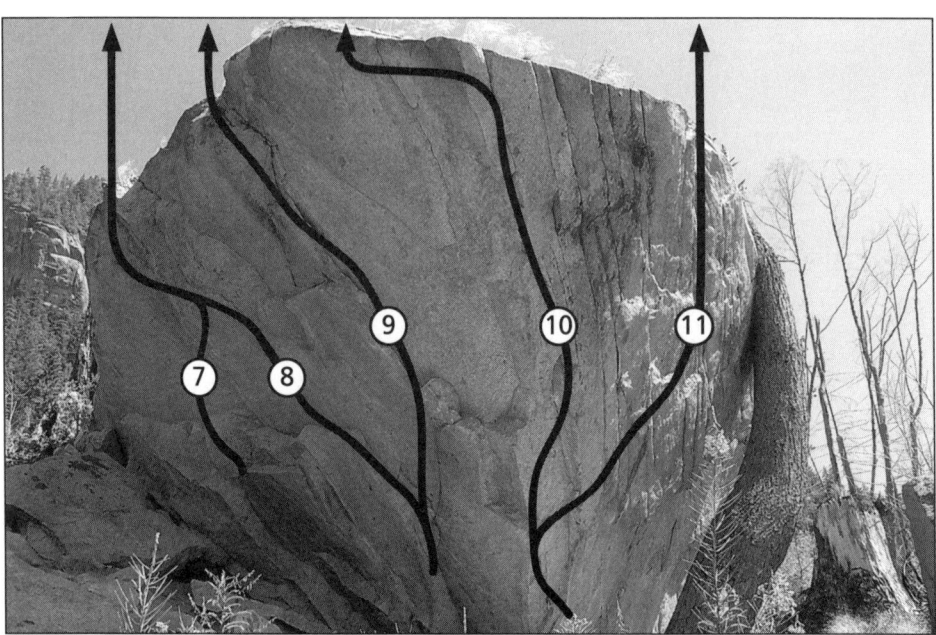

The Clearcut : **GOLD BAR**

Kelly Sheridan on The Equinox (V10). Photo: Brian Sweeney

___9. **Bob's Balls** V2 ★★★

Begin on a low jug as for **Obesity**, climbing up and slightly right on incut holds to a solid but heady top-out high above the talus. Careful now...

___10. **Glen's Problem** V6 ★★★

Start sitting on a low jug on the downhill corner. Climb straight out the right side of the steep arête on mail-slot jams in the seam. Once you're swinging from the sharp corner on the lip, traverse left a bit and mantel as for **Bob's Balls**.

___11. **Joel's Problem** V7 ★★★

 Begin on the low jug as for **#10**, moving up and right through all right-facing sidepulls in the gentle overhang. Thrutch up the shallow scoop at the lip to finish.

___12. **Bambi** V9 ★★

Start just right of the decapitated tree with two low opposing 'slimpers.' Make a hard move to the triangular crimp, match it, then climb up and right to top out in the corner.

___13. **Flower** V2

Climb the short right side of the face from a high left crimp and a low right undercling. Move to the lip and top out.

___14. **Positive Vibrations** (project)

This west-facing boulder can be found alongside the trail that traverses the forest's edge. The right-facing rail to the right of the large tree may seem pretty simple, until you actually try it...

___15. **Danny Devito** V7 ★★

A few feet right of **Positive Vibrations**, climb the shorter right-facing rail to better holds... basically a twin of the above problem, but just a little bit shorter. Grade unconfirmed.

The Clearcut : **GOLD BAR**

GOLD BAR : The Clearcut

Joel Campbell on Que Luna (V6)   Photo: Brian Sweeney

___16. **Water** V6 ★★★
Water is visible a few dozen yards below treeline, just down from where the trail makes a small switchback. Start off the jumble of rocks with chest-high sidepulls, moving through sloping edges to a shallow slot, then the lip. Named for a subterranean creek audible from the starting position during the spring.

___17. **Snack Attack** V0 ★
Climb up and left on the arête downhill from **Water.**

___18. **Wonka** V0+ ★
Climb the short overhang below **Water** on flat, blocky holds.

___19. **The Container** V1 ★
This short problem is the trailside landmark for the Aries boulder, visible just below. Climb up and right on shelves in the short overhang, topping out at the apex of the boulder.

___20. **The Hopeful** V7 ★★
On the tall face several feet left of the shady overhang, climb up and right on sloping shelves to a high undercling and top out. F.A. Joel Campbell

The Clearcut : GOLD BAR

___21. **Unholy** V5 ★★★

Start at the bottom of the slanting hole with a low jug on the left side of the overhang. Climb straight up on decent holds to the crux lunge right to a good crimp. Committing!

___22. **War of God** V8 ★★★

Start matched with the double-jug on the right arête, climbing straight up through the square pinch to a left-leaning crimp. Move left from here to finish as for **Unholy**. Good beta-intensive climbing.

___23. **Aries: God of War** V8 ★★★

From the double-jug start of **#22**, tick-tack up and right through poor crimpers on either side of the arête. From a good righthand incut, slap up to jugs above and an easy finish. Technical and solid for the grade.

___24. **Sagittarius** V4 ★

Start off of rocks in the corridor with a sloping righthand rail and high left crimp. Move up to better holds and top out.

___25. **Dave's Problem** V10 ★★

Start sitting in the overhung scoop with two left-facing edges, climing up and right to the lip to top out. Grade unconfirmed. F.A. Dave Thompson

___26. **The Stinker** V2 ★★

Start standing on the low, sharp arête with a high left crimp and a low righthand sidepull. Slap to the lip, then work your feet up to a challenging finish on sloping edges.

___27. **Bottlecap Banshee** V5 ★

Start crouched on the short face right of **#26** with crimps in the left-leaning seam. Climb up through the odd pocket to finish with a good right-facing sidepull on the slab.

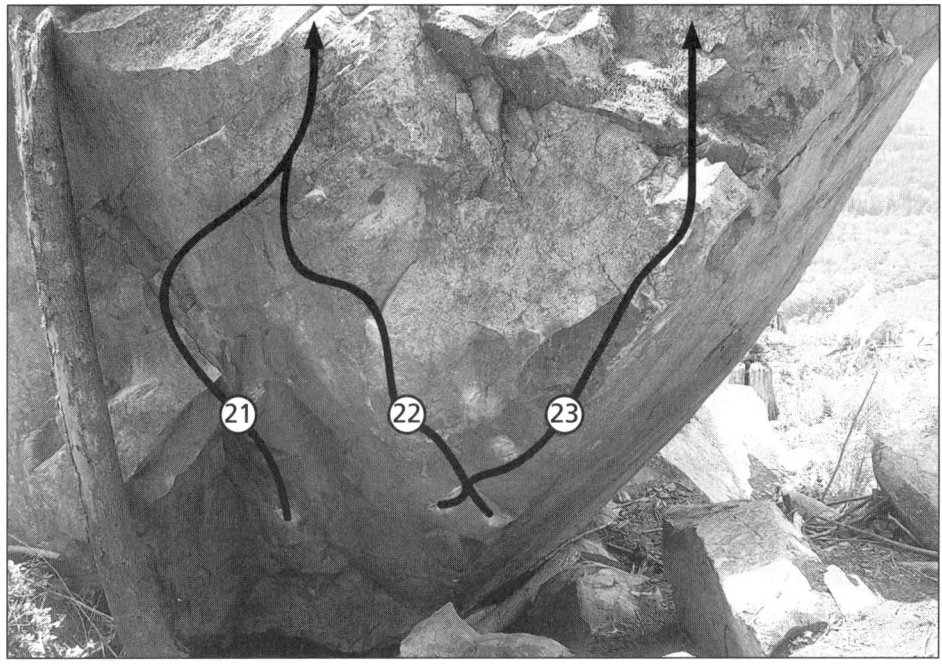

GOLD BAR : The Clearcut

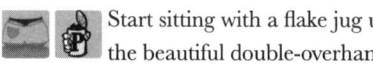

___28. **Project**
Crimps in the roof to the blank face. V13?

___29. **The Fin Within** V6 ★★
Climb the narrow fin set between the two boulders to an awkward finish in the corner. Great fun.

___30. **Summer Solstice** V3 ★★
Start sitting on the uphill side of the west-facing Equinox wall with low incut left of the sloping rail. Climb up and right to incuts and top out straddling the tree.

___31. **The Equinox** V10 ★★★
The classic line. Start with a rounded edge in the steepest part of the overhang. Climb to the sloping crimp and tiny pinch above, then chuck for the bucket up and left. Traverse left on jugs to finish straddling the tree as for **#30**. F.A. Cole Allen.

___32. **Twisted** V10 ★★★
Start on the downhill side of the steep arête with a low incut sidepull. Climb straight up the arête with opposing crimps on both sides, finishing on the tall face left of the arête. Savage!

___33. **No Chaser** V5 ★★
Begin with a low incut sidepull as for **#32**, but move up and right to decent holds in the crack. Follow the seam up and left to the lip and top out.

___34. **Devil Sticks** V6 ★
Start standing on the short uphill end of the broken overhang with a flat undercling shelf. Move right along the sloping shelf to a big move for the upper lip and a delicate top-out.

___35. **The Rubik's Cube** V9 ★★★
Start sitting with a flake jug under the beautiful double-overhang. Climb left along the steep belly to pinch the arête, moving desperately around the corner to a hard campus move for the fin on the upper lip. Finish straight up.

___36. **Sinistricity** V5 ★★★
Begin matched in the low incut slot right of the big flake jug. From crimps in the shallow corner above, work through a shouldery gaston on the dark xenolith to better holds above. Finish with a tenuous rockover onto the slab right of the scoop. Fantastic!

___37. **Wildberry Blast** V0 ★
Climb the low-angle corner right of **#36** to finish on dirty jugs.

___38. **Screaming Barfies** V3 ★
Start underclinging the short bulge on the right end of the low wall. Traverse left, hugging between the low undercling rail and the sloping lip to finish as for **#37**.

___39. **Clef Crack** V0 ★★
Climb up and left in the beautifully-shaped crack on sloping jugs. Mantel and top out on the lower-angle left face.

___40. **The 'Shroom** V4 ★★
This stout boulder lies most of the way down the overgrown trail from the **Rubik's Cube** to **Fraggle Rock**. A short but fun problem climbs the overhanging downhill side from a sit start on opposing slopers.

The Clearcut : **GOLD BAR**

Jessica Campbell considers her options on Sinistricity (V5)   Photo: Brian Sweeney

THE FOREST

The open, Squamish-like forest above the Clearcut is home to a pleasant variety of boulder problems on wonderfully textured white granite. Scattered pockets of problems dot the area just above the treeline, while regions further uphill remains largely undeveloped. The landings in The Forest area are generally not too bad, and classic testpieces like **The Doja** (V7) and **Lighten Up** (V9) are cheerfully placed among top-quality enjoyables like the **Warm-Up Slab** (V0), **Beam Me Up** (V2), and **Silver Slippers** (V3). The problems in the Forest tend to be a little shorter than those of the Clearcut, though the beginning boulderer will be happiest in the neighboring Sanctuary area. Along with the Sanctuary, The Forest area stays remarkably cool when the Clearcut is baking in summer sun. On the other side of the coin, be prepared for lingering moisture in winter. In any season, you're bound to find some solitude in the peaceful quiet of the Forest; please do your part to help keep this magical area un-trampled and litter-free.

Approach: As for the Clearcut. Turn left off of Reiter Road after 2.0 miles and follow the switchbacks up the hill, parking after 3.0 miles of dirt road. If you've got to park at 2.6 miles and hike up, head up the trail past Que Luna to the upper parking and take it from there. Alternatively, high-clearance vehicles can drive to the Equinox parking area and enter the forest from the west. All of the Forest bouldering is more or less visible from the trail traversing the treeline, which passes the modest uphill side of the Warm-Up Slab just past the parking area. Lighten Up lies directly above the Aries boulder, with the nebulous Green Goblin area (no topo) another five minutes uphill. As with many areas in this book, some of the trails are a bit rough, but if you keep your eyes open you'll find your way. Who knows what you might find if you get lost in the uncharted folds below Zeke's Wall?

Corrine Messer attacks Fern Crack (V3)
Photo: Brian Sweeney

The Forest : **GOLD BAR**

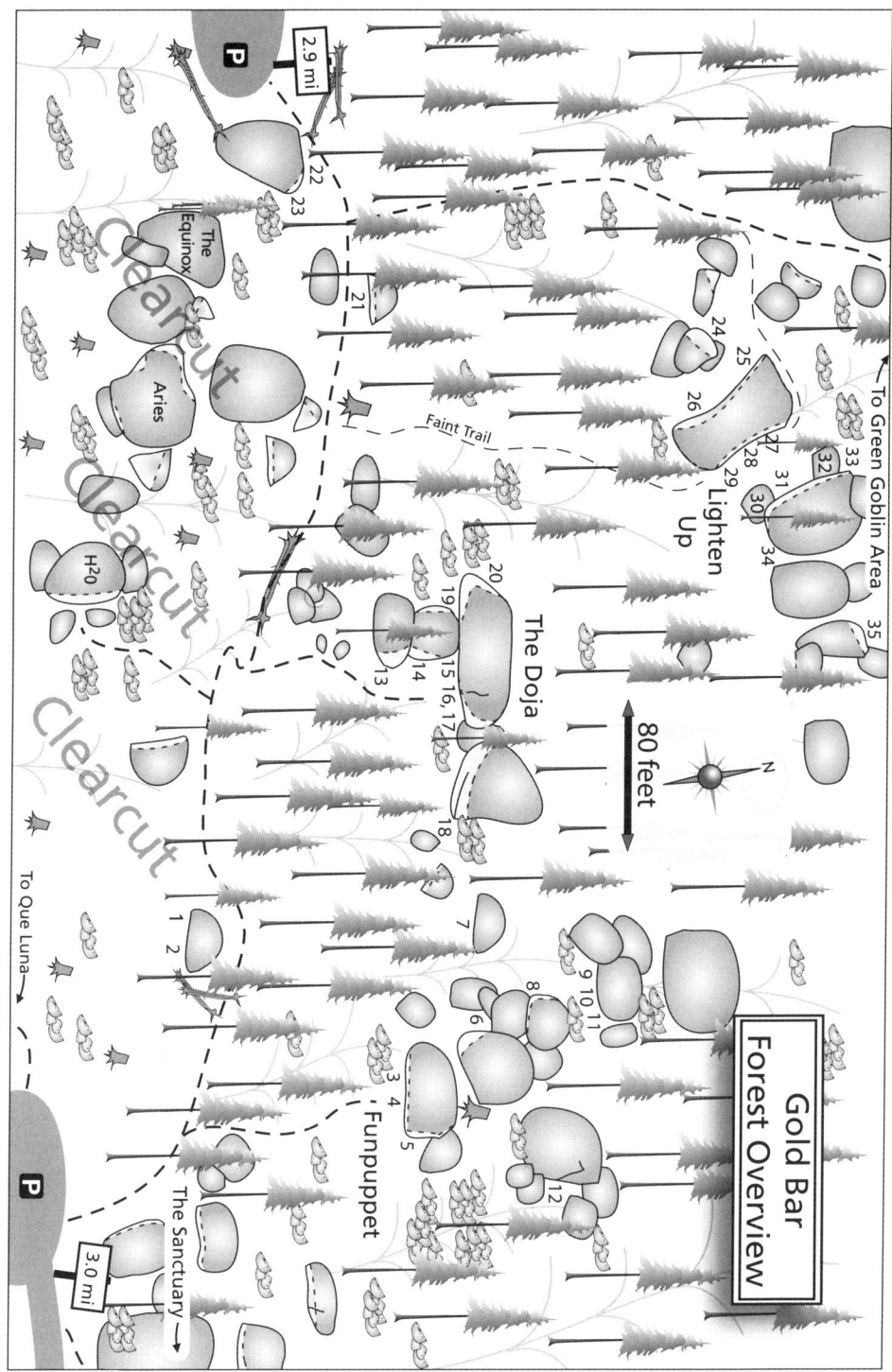

GOLD BAR : The Forest

___1. **Rocksteadeasy** V3 ★

Climb the left side of the slab from two slopey edges just right of the tree. A tough rockover right off the ground leads to the dark knob and an easy topout.

___2. **The Warm-Up Slab** V0 ★★★

Climb the center of the white slab on nicely-spaced edges. Repeat as necessary. Feeling saucy? Start on the right with the mono pocket, or sit start as low as you can.

___3. **The Wheel of Dharma** V9 ★★

Find this imposing overhang a short ways up and left from the warm-ups above the hilltop parking area. From a high righthand pod and a good triangular foothold, climb straight up via crimps and monos in the seam. Tough! F.A. Joel Campbell.

___4. **Funpuppet** V9 ★★★

Starting with your left hand on the high pod in the middle of the face, move up to a crimp and throw for the flat bucket above. Pure, hard moves. F.A. Joel Campbell.

___5. **Dookie's Pinchfest** V8 ★★

Start crouched in the steep overhang right of **Funpuppet** with a good left pinch and the low triangle in the roof. Work up and right through a pinch and an undercling, finishing straight up in the notch.

___6. **Float On** V2 ★

Start on two crimps on the right side of this small, dark corner. Move up and left on nice incuts to top out at the apex.

___7. **Them Antles** V1 ★

Start on the flat rounded sloper in the middle of the face, mantel and reach for the top. Trickier than it looks!

___8. **Chemicals** V4 ★★

On the uphill side of the taller cluster, start hugging the two sloping arêtes of the wide sliver from the top of a lower boulder. Climb up and right on slopers to rock onto the right face and top out.

___9. **Resonation** V6 ★★

Start on two low crimps on the left side of the tall striated face, climbing up and right on tiny sloping edges. Finish straight up, high above the disconcerting landing.

___10. **Brass Balls** V5 ★

Begin on the flat platform with side-by-side sloping edges, climbing up and left to finish as for **Resonation**.

___11. **The Argument** V8 ★

From the low sloping edge next to the smaller boulder, climb left to a tiny nipple and two-finger sidepull. Move right to edges, then chuck for the lip and top out. The grade is a point of contention, ranging from V3 to V9. F.A. Joel Campbell.

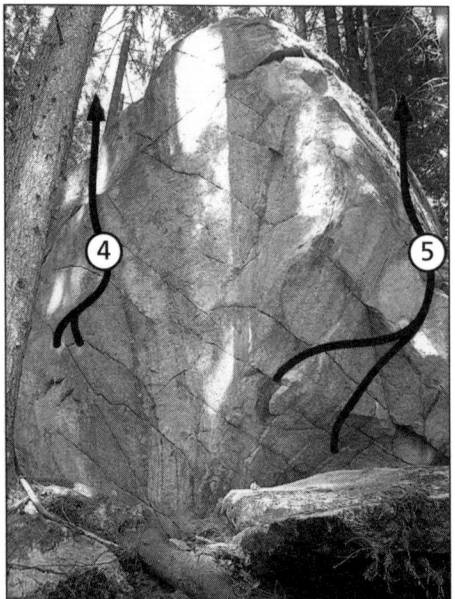

Joel Campbell poised for launch on the five-foot dyno of Lighten Up (V9) Photo: Brian Sweeney

GOLD BAR : The Forest

___12. **El Navigante** aka Breakfast at Sunrise V3 ★★★

Killer! Find this huge fingercrack up and right from **Funpuppet** on the east side of a tall green boulder. Follow the thin fingers-to-hands crack above the stepped landing to finish around the left corner of the juggy horn. Gold Bar's crack response to Hueco's **Ghetto Simulator**.

___13. **Devastation** V2 ★

On the lowest boulder of the Doja cluster, start matched on a jug in the low roof. Slap to the lip and move right to top out.

___14. **Frequent Fryer** V2

Start sitting on a sloping edge in the low overhang, hit the lip, and traverse right to top out.

___15. **Feelin' Irie** V4 ★★

Start in the corner just right of the flat boulder with a head-high jug. Climb straight up on decent edges to a crux lunge for a crimp below the lip. Fun climbing to a committing crux.

___16. **Fern Crack** V3 ★★

Start in the middle of the face with sloping crimps at head height, work to the detached jug, then finish on dirty ledges up and slightly right. Classic. **Variation** (V6) Start on slopers on the right corner of the lip and slap left to the start of **Fern Crack**.

___17. **Tom Fern** V7 ★

Begin matched on a big undercling below the roof with cramped feet, slapping to crimps on the lip and finishing up **Fern Crack**. Grade unconfirmed.

___18. **Crackulation** V1 ★

Start with blocky holds to the right of the corner. Follow the incut crack up and left. Drop from the black knob around the corner.

___19. **The Doja** V7 ★★★

Start on an incut crimp just right of the overhanging prow and a good right foot at nearly the same level. Move left to a flat edge and huge jug on the arête. Finish straight up on the corner. A proud, independent line with great movement. **Variation** (V8): Start on the sidepull foothold out right and climb left into the **Doja**. The straight-up is an obvious project...

___20. **Bulldozer** V2 ★

Climb the low overhang on incut holds to a mantel finish on the lip.

___21. **The Wrestler** V0+ ★

Climb the short face mingled amongst the trees and low boulders, using either the crack or flat ledges to the right.

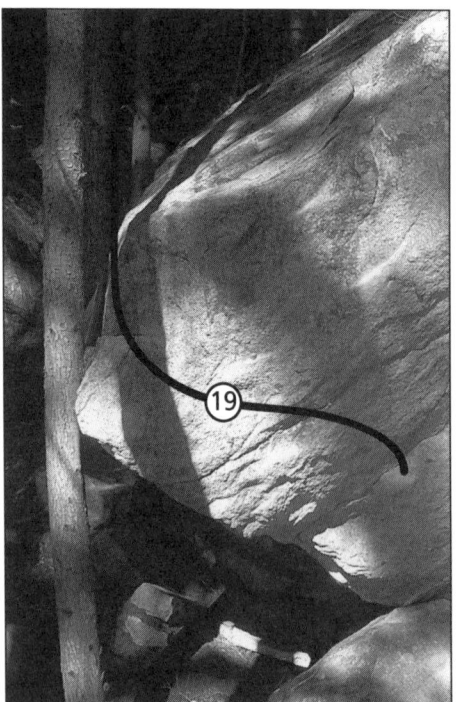

The Forest : **GOLD BAR**

___22. **Beam Me Up** V2 ★★★ ●

 Climb the overhung corner on opposing crimps from the low block. Awesome moves, but beware the semi-attached block!

___23. **Scotty** V0 ★

From strange jugs on the left end of the short face, climb up and right on cool edges to finish as for **Beam Me Up**.

___24. **Hamburger Train** V5 ★★

Start on a low, flat jug in the tube/cave. Climb straight out the roof via a tiny seam crimp, finishing atop this short boulder.

___25. **Who Nose** V7 ★

Start matched on edges under the roof, slap to the nose and thrutch over the low bulge to finish. Inventive footwork (read: cheating) will pay off on this one.

___26. **The Ta-Ta Box** V10 ★★

Start crouched in the steep overhang underclinging a low left-facing crimp. One savage move leads to a few tenuous edges at the lip; starting with the second hold is a fun V6 in itself. F.A. Dave Thompson

197

GOLD BAR : The Forest

___27. **The Trapeze** V4 ★★

Pull on to a sloping crimp in the shadows right of the tree. Stab to another crimp, then go big for jugs above. Tough!

___28. **Silver Slippers** V3 ★★

Start matched on two side-by-side crimps just left of the tree and make campusy moves up and left on the smooth rails. Bust to the jug on the lip and top out straight up. **Variation** (V7): Start on the two small edges but climb right, in between the tree and the wall, to link into the start of **The Trapeze**, finishing that problem.

___29. **Bearded Lady** V0 ★

Climb the left arête of the dark face, romping up and right to a few traverse moves over the rocks below. A fun direct line can be done from tiny underclings on the face six feet to the right at V3 or so.

___30. **Lighten Up** aka The Esssence V9 ★★★

This powerful climb starts matched on a low jug on the right arête just uphill from problems **#18**–**#20**. Grapple straight up on underclings and pinches to a huge throw for the square edge on the face above. Fat-boy climbing at its best, this one's got big moves on big holds. F.A. Jason Duckowitz

___31. **Kama Sutra** V7 ★★

Begin standing on the face left of **Lighten Up** with a decent righthand sidepull and a tiny left crimp. Slap up to the prominent sloping rail, then work up and left on square-cut edges to top out on jugs. F.A. Joel Campbell.

___32. **Crimpterbator** V7

 Start crouched, matched on two small crimps in front of the little-boulder. Climb straight up to the flat lip and top out.

___33. **Golden Girls** V2 ★

Start on the flexing jug on the far left side of the overhanging face, slap to the lip, and press it out.

___34. **Dukkha** V3 ★★

Climb the left side of the tall chimney on small edges. Head up and right to finish, and just put your foot back if you get scared! F.A. Joel Campbell

___35. **Scumsucker** V6 ★★

 This short overhang is on the uphill side of a small boulder adjacent to **Lighten Up**. Start sitting on the right side of the featured face and climb up and left through miserable holds via some really awful knee-scumming. Awesome and terrible at the same time. F.A. Brian Sweeney.

Brian Sweeney cranks the first ascent of Scumsucker (V6). Photo: Joe Treftz

The Sanctuary : **GOLD BAR**

They call it murder... Joel Zerr working the campus-off-the-pinch crux of Jamrock (V10)   Photograph by Brian Sweeney

THE SANCTUARY

The Sanctuary area in the forest at Gold Bar is one of the coolest spots in this guide. Scattered through the open, gently angled forest above the hilltop parking, the boulders of the Sanctuary are home to more moderates than the War Zone or Forest areas, with a distinctly different feel. The rock quality is superb, the landings near perfect, and the climbs inviting. The lower Sanctuary offers many nice warm-up options, while the upper reaches offer more opportunities for those looking to fall over and over again. Mutant boulderers will enjoy throwing themselves at the opposing crimpers of **Hagakure** (V8) or the pebble-pinching savagery of **Jamrock** (V10). The thirty-foot overhanging traverse of the **Road to Zion** (V5) is also not to be missed; if that was too easy, the full traverse (V9) adds another 20 feet of masochistic gratification. While the blocks of the lower Sanctuary have been climbed on since before the area was logged, the area above the Samurai boulder did not see extensive development until the summer of 2006. Even more so than other Gold Bar areas, the bouldering development in the Sanctuary area has remained close to the trails, and there is much untapped potential here. Be sure to bring a brush if you're the explorative type—you won't be disappointed!

Approach: The Sanctuary is the eastern part of the forest at Gold Bar. Access is the same as the Clearcut or Forest: park 3.0 miles from Reiter Road in the hilltop parking area (again, low-clearance vehicles should be left at the Fraggle Rock parking area, 2.6 miles from Reiter). The Warm-Up boulders are directly adjacent to the hilltop parking, and can be accessed from the start of the Forest area trail. The well-worn trail to the Sanctuary proper begins just east of the big boulder next to the road. Head up the steady incline, and stay left at the fork about two minutes in. Passing the trailside landmarks of the Tetris boulder and the obvious lightning-bolt hold of Midnight Lichen, one should reach the Samurai boulder in less than 10 minutes. The trail to the upper Sanctuary departs left from the main trail just past the Samurai boulder.

____1. **Shortstop** V1+ ★
Start matched on a low sloping edge, climbing straight up to the short layback above. Finish up and left on the sloping lip.

____2. **The Catcher** V0
Start sitting on the left end of the face with a triangular jug and climb the shallow crack to finish up and right on slopers.

____3. **Box Seats** V0- ★
Climb the double arêtes from a stand start, topping out straight up.

____4. **Stepping Razor** V2 ★★
Start crouched with the left arête and a low righthand sidepull. Climb straight up the arête to a crux move for a small righthand edge below the lip. Alternatively, layback the entire way up the arête.

____5. **The Button** V3 ★
Start on the left arête as for above, but stay low as you move right to a small pocket in the seam, finishing straight up from there on better holds. Footwork helps…

The Sanctuary : **GOLD BAR**

201

GOLD BAR : The Sanctuary

___6. **BMOC** V2 ★★
Start on the left side of the short face, matched on two sloping crimps at head height. Make campusy moves up cool slopers to slap for the lip above. Short, but very good.

___7. **Regatta de Blanc** V0 ★
Begin sitting, matched on the incut rail in the middle of the face. Climb up and left on decent holds to a balancey rockover. Finish straight up.

___8. **Shrimpers** V3
Climb the right arête from a crouched start with little crimps on the right face. A sitdown start can be done by those looking for more punishment.

___9. **Streambed Mantel** V0+ ★★
From two head-high jugs in the middle of the face, work your feet onto the shelf and rock up to incut holds and an easy finish. This one may be a bit dirty, but the movement is just so good…

___10. **Hot Stepper** V1 ★★
Start matched on the low sloping shelf on the left end of the face. Make a tough move to the lip, then romp up and left to finish at the apex of the boulder. **Variation** (V6): Start as for **#10**, but traverse left along the sloping shelf into the mantel of **#9**. Shouldery and slippery; you'll have to work for this one.

___11. **Big Baby** V2 ★★
Start on a good flat edge on the right side of the short, steep overhang. Make a big move left, then slap and rock straight up to a wide finish. Though it doesn't look like much, this super-fun oddity shouldn't be missed.

___12. **Air Boredom** V0- ★
Climb the short, juggy flake on the backside of this huge boulder. Fun in sneakers. The side facing the road also sports a highball V2.

___13. **Pillow Talk** V0+
Climb the left side of the short face from two low sidepulls.

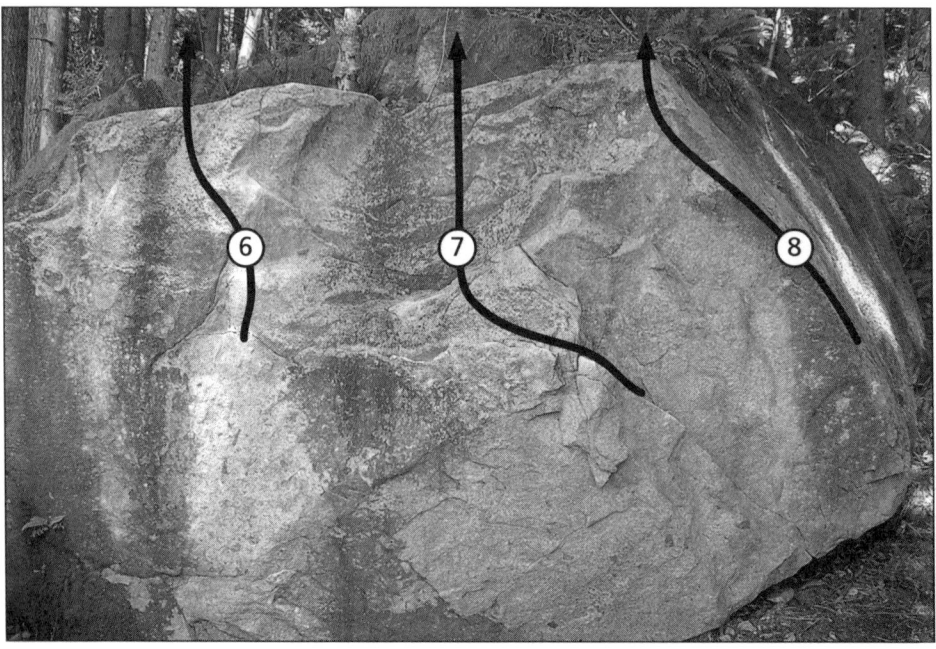

The Sanctuary : **GOLD BAR**

___14. **Chocolate** V3 ★★

 The short, obvious crack in the center of the face. At least the pain is short-lived…

___15. **It's Doo-Doo, Baby** V3 ★

Start on the right of the short face with a good undercling and a righthand crimper. Move to the juggy fingerlock straight above and top out.

___16. **Dr. Mario** V8 ★

On the trailside Tetris boulder, climb the short bulge behind the tree. Start sitting with opposing pulls, making some tough moves up and left to a jug near the seam. Great movement, if not a bit cramped.

___17. **Tetris** V1 ★★

 Climb the short trailside face on small, incut edges in the quartz intrusion. A fun challenge on unique stone.

___18. **So it Seams** V2 ★

Start sitting on the trailside arête with a good right pinch in the bottom of the angular seam and a high left heel hook. Slap up to the jug and top out. The sit-start out left is a silly V4, finishing as above.

___19. **Treeverse** V3 ★

Start matched on a good edge just in front of the small tree. Climb right to gastons with your best Frenchie footwork, then finish straight up the slab above. May need some brushwork.

___20. **Midnight Lichen** V4 ★★

 From a sit start on the blunt arête with two low opposing sidepulls, slap up and left to the lightning bolt hold, then follow the angled block up and right to top out. Pretty strenuous and very fun!

___21. **Lichen' It** V3

Climb the right arête from a crouched start, finishing as for **#20**.

___22. **Hagakuri** V8 ★★

 This overhung mini-prow is the first climb reached at the Samurai boulder. Begin crouching with a sharp lefthand crimp and a neat righthand pinch. Climb through a few hard moves between opposing crimps to chuck for an incut on the lip. Mantel onto the dirty slab, then traverse down and right to descend.

___23. **The Samurai** V4 ★★

 Start sitting, cupping the low nose, and climb up through pinchy slopers to a perfect edge on the lip. This striking scoop has some of the coolest holds around, but might feel like a bit of a sandbag—like one's strapped to your waist, in fact!

___24. **Unorthodox, But Effective** V2 ★

 A few feet right of **The Samurai**, the sloping ledges that serve as the downclimb for problems **#22**–**#25** also make for a fun climb with a tough first move.

___25. **The Sutra** V4 ★

Around the corner from The Samurai, find this neat climb nestled against the big tree. Start with an incut edge about a foot from the tree, put a foot on, and hop to the gorgeous sloper rail above. Slap up to a crimp and rock over, sans tree. **Variation** (V9): The static start. Pull on with the good lefthand edge and a tiny righthand in the seam, using an arm-bar in the tree to establish. Then, take your weight off the tree and slap up, finishing as above. F.A. Joel Campbell.

___26. **Chopsticks** V2

Climb the steeper of the two low bulges on the trail side of the Samurai boulder from a flexing flake and small edge. Finish up and right on blocks with an awkward mantel, then drop.

203

GOLD BAR : The Sanctuary

Todd Mannherz enjoys the layback of Stepping Razor (V2)

The Sanctuary : **GOLD BAR**

___27. **Rice Bowl** V1+ ★★
Climb the low bulge adjacent to the trail from a sit-start with two jugs. Climb to widely-spaced crimpers above, then rock onto the low-angle face. Feel free to drop off when you can stand comfortably.

___28. **Metroid Prime** V7 ★★
This is the first climb reached by following the side-trail uphill and left from the Samurai boulder. Climb the left side of the overhung downhill face from a stand start on the left arête. Hit the deceivingly bad incut on the arête above, then make a cruxy slap up and right to finish straight up the apex. F.A. Brian Sweeney.

___29. **Eight Bit Slab** V2 ★★★
The obvious grooved slab around the corner from #28. Work your way up the tricky vertical seams, smears and sidepulls giving way to a nice crimp just below the lip. The more time you have to put into this one, the more you'll get out of it.

___30. **Duck Hunt** V0 ★
Climb the right arête of the short uphill face, passing pleasant slopers on the arête to a nice mantel finish.

___31. **Contra** V3 ★★★
Climb the creased boulder from slopers on the lower lip. Slap up onto the slab, then rock up and reach out to the lip, mantling with a good hold on the left side of the slab. Fun, delicate climbing on a strange boulder.

___32. **Mario Kart** V0- ★★
Climb the juggy shelves on the uphill face of the Contra boulder. A good sneaker climb, this one doesn't have to be very clean to be enjoyable…

___33. **Luigi** V1
Climb the short uphill face of this low boulder from a sit start with a flexing jug.

GOLD BAR : The Sanctuary

___34. **Bowser Crack** V1 ★★
Climb the tall, dirty seam up the left side of the high slab.

___35. **Jamrock** V10 ★★★
Start in the middle of the face with a decent sloping edge on the lip. Climb right through a tiny pebble and a heinous pinch to throw for the gaston crack out right. Continue right to the corner and a somewhat pumpy finish on slopers.

___36. **Link** V0- ★
Thought it's a bit pointless, this thin little flake can be climbed on either side.

___37. **Slickfoot Sanctuary** V0- ★★★
Climb the tall, narrow fin of rock, slapping your way up the juggy opposing arêtes. At the top, mantel and step across the gap to the other boulder. Highly recommended.

___38. **Sanctuary Crack** V0 ★★
Climb the crack just left of **#37** to a high finish with giant holds.

___39. **Appeasing The Gods** V9 ★★
Start with two high pod crimps in the roof left of **#38**. Campus and slap straight up to finish in the juggy crack above. Grade unconfirmed. F.A. Joel Campbell.

___40. **Sore Thumb** V4 ★
On top of the Jamrock boulder, climb the steep, blocky face of this little boulder from a crouch start with a sloper and an undercling. A few tensiony moves right lead to a high jug on the corner and a nice top-out.

___41. **Four Eyes** V2 ★
Around the corner from **#40**, climb the tallish scoop on slopers, finishing up and left on better holds.

Brian Sweeney burls down on Road to Zion Low (V9)

The Sanctuary : **GOLD BAR**

Josh Carroll floats up the perfect stone of Chemicals (V4)   Photograph by Brian Sweeney

GOLD BAR : The Sanctuary

___42. **Track and Field** V1+ ★

A few feet right of **#41**, rock onto the flat shelf with crimps on the face, making a blind reach back and left for a big jug. Finish up and right on mossy jugs.

___43. **Road To Zion** V5 ★★★

Traverse the up and right along the huge overhanging face from two flat head-high jugs halfway across the wall. Powerful moves on big holds lead to a highball finish in the crack on the far right of the wall. F.A. Joel Zerr.

___44. **Road to Zion Low** V9 ★★★

Start low on the left side of the huge wall, traversing right on crimpers to a huge move for an incut pocket roughly one third of the way across the wall. Continue right into the start of **#43** and fight the heinous pump to finish the traverse and top out. A beautiful, striking line. F.A. Josh Carroll.

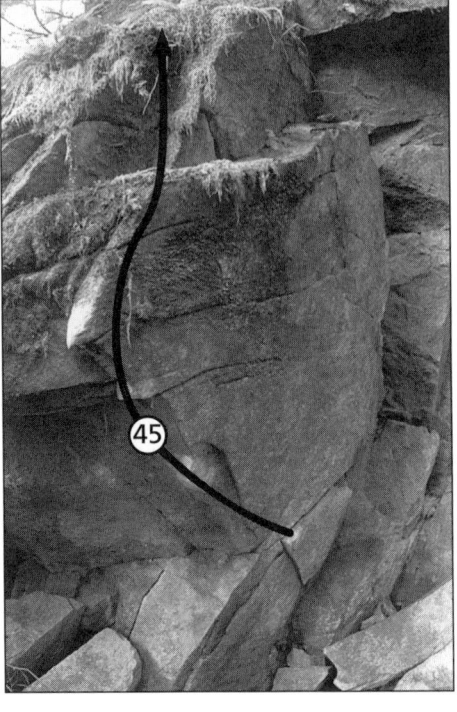

___45. **Vexation of Spirit** V5 ★★

Head uphill from **Contra** to find this rocky alcove on the left side of **Road to Zion**'s looming face. Start on a low jug in the horizontal seam, making big moves up and left on fat pinches to a tough barndoor move for a big horn on the left corner. Finish straight up with a really dirty mantel over the talus and mossy trees. F.A. Joe Treftz.

Joel Zerr is staring at the Road to Zion Photo: Brian Sweeney

Kyle O'Meara climbing at the River Boulders, Index

3 · Index

INDEX BOULDERS : Introduction

INDEX

Just five miles east of Gold Bar is the trad climbing Mecca of Index. Along with the long, steep climbs on the Upper and Lower Town Walls, Index is home to a small amount of developed bouldering, included here as an addendum to the Gold Bar chapter. The small collection of bullet-hard blocks below the Lower Town Wall is home to a few stellar climbs and well worth a quick visit, especially if you're in the area. The River Boulders are the only other area described in this section, and no specific problem names or descriptions are provided for this beautiful, secluded spot. This small section is really just a teaser, an example of the fact that the Cascades region of Central Washington is home to many more areas like these. All you have to do is poke around…

Getting There: Index can be reached easily from Gold Bar via either Rt. 2 or Reiter Road. Check out the Gold Bar overview map to get an idea of the area around the North Fork of the Skykomish. Good, free campsites can be found along the river across from the Town Wall parking, though you'll be competing with the traddies for a spot. More camping can be found past the town bridge on Index-Galena road. Water can be procured easily from the small park in town. Hit up the Index Town Store for chalk, snacks, and terrible coffee, or drive to Rt. 2 for a filling breakfast at the Index Café.

Index

INDEX LOWER TOWN WALL

Visible from Rt. 2, the Index Town Walls loom over the adjoining forest and the North Fork of the Skykomish River with over 500 feet of vertical granite. As you could probably guess from mere glances at the smooth, compact cliffs of Index, what few boulders have tumbled to the forest below offer some high-quality problems on bullet-hard stone. Interestingly, the silent giants found belaw the Lower Town Wall are all relatively *new*, having fallen from the wall since the area was clear-cut and quarried in the early 20th century. The intimidating **Boxcar Arête** (V8) alone is well worth the stop, a must-do for visiting boulderers looking to test themselves against Washington's proudest. Like Gold Bar, the forest at Index is typically a cooler option on hot summer days, though here you'll be sharing it with lots of 'real' climbers.

Approach: To reach the Index Town Wall parking from Rt. 2, take the well-signed turn for Index, some 5.6 miles east of Reiter Road. Continue 1.0 miles on Index-Galena Road to turn left at the Index bridge. Go straight past the town store and turn left after the school, crossing the tracks and making a forced dog-leg left onto 'Avenue A,' which soon becomes Reiter Road. The Town Wall parking lot is on the right, 1.0 miles from the store. The campsites along the left side of Reiter Road are free, for now, if you can find an unoccupied one. The Index Town Wall parking can also be reached from the town of Gold Bar by turning onto Reiter Road from Rt. 2 and winding a perilous 6.9 miles, passing the access road for much of Gold Bar's bouldering on the way. Naturally, the Town Wall parking will be on the left when approached from the west. Follow the trail up a short hill, cross the tracks, and enter the forest to find the boulders described here.

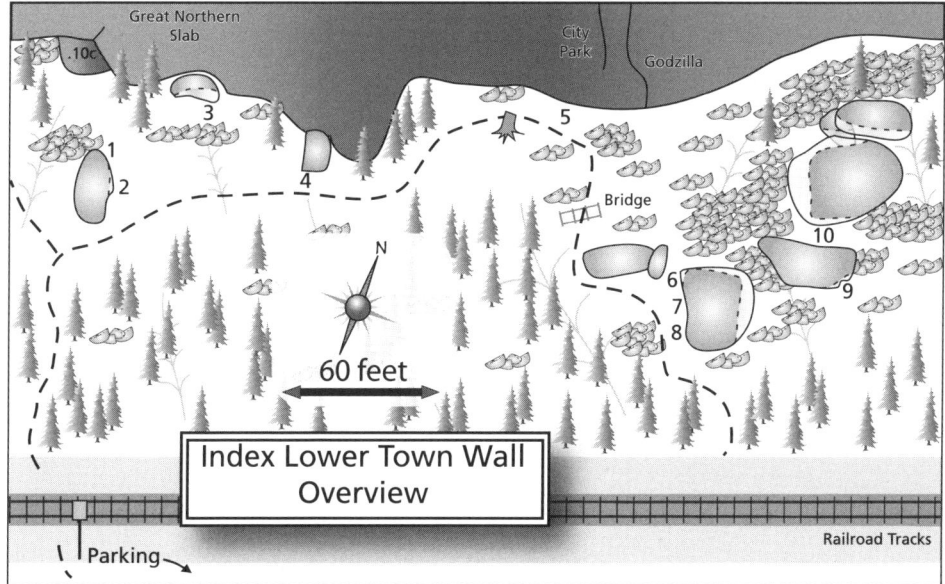

INDEX BOULDERS : Index Lower Town Wall

___1. V0 ★

Traverse right to left along the juggy lip of the short boulder.

___2. V0 ★★

Grab the two jugs in the middle of the face and climb straight to the lip. Good fun.

___3. V7 ★★★

Scramble to the base of the wall up and right from the previous boulder to find this clean, detached flake. From a wide start with the right arête and a lefthand crimp on the face, slap up the arête and huck for a high face edge. Proud and independent; a spot prevents you from falling off the landing of this one.

___4. V1 ★★★

The obvious clean arête next to the trail. Climb either side of the arête, laybacking on the slab or traversing up and left with feet on the vertical wall. Both ways are fun, and make for good footwork challenges. **Variation** (V3): For a real lesson in Index friction, the slab can be climbed with the arête 'off.' This stupid eliminate has been touted as the best boulder problem in Index—you decide.

___5. V1 ★★

Much of the Lower Town Wall can be linked together as a traverse. Try climbing from left to right, starting near the base of **Japanese Gardens** and finishing around the popular crack **Godzilla**. Several different variations can also be done to add difficulty to this pumpy traverse. On busy days, a helmet may be in order…

___6. **Boxcar Arête** V8 ★★★

 Follow the trail down from the crag and across a defunct bridge to the base of this big, square boulder. Start sitting with low sidepulls near the uphill corner, stabbing up edges on the arête to a committing slab move high above the talus. Scary, but a gimme for the grade; those who drop from jugs on the lip have done the business, but not the problem.

___7. V? ★

Climb the short, steep face right of the arête from high crimps in the seam, finishing straight above the dirty lip.

___8. V3 ★

Climb the shallow scoop on the right side of the steep face.

___9. V0 ★

Climb the undercut arête from a high jug on the corner. A low start down and left on edges can be done as well.

___10. V3 ★★★

This somewhat hidden highball climbs the tall face behind the previous problem from two opposing sidepulls around chest height. A few strenuous moves on good edges lead to better holds an a high finish. Classic!

This is only a small selection of Index's bouldering; more problems can be found on the other side of the steep gully to the north. If the bouldering below the Lower Town Wall has only whet your appetite, turn right at the railroad track and walk for roughly fifteen minutes to the start of the Upper Wall trail, a crude bridge across a small stream. The Zelda Boulders are vaguely visible to the left of the trail roughly halfway to the Upper Wall, at the top of a small rise. And who knows what other wonders may lurk in these woods???

IMAGINE ALL YOUR FAVORITE VIDEOS ON ONE CHANNEL... THAT'S MY CHANNEL!
1 GO TO WWW.UCMAG.TV
2 LOG IN
3 SELECT A VIDEO
4 CLICK ADD TO MY CHANNEL

URBANCLIMBER.TV
MAGAZINE

www.urbanclimbermag.tv IS THE NEW FREE
CLIMBING FILM AND VIDEO NETWORK

- SICKEST FOOTAGE
- UPLOAD YOUR OWN VIDEOS
- REVOLUTIONARY WEBSITE
- GLOBAL REACH. LOCAL BETA

POWERED BY:

THE NORTH FACE
NEVER STOP EXPLORING

INDEX BOULDERS : River Boulders

THE RIVER BOULDERS

Just over a mile from Index Town Walls, a nice collection of polished granite boulders can be found along the bank of the Skykomish River. The River Boulders are home to roughly two dozen established problems, primarily in the intermediate range. The river-polished stone here is exceptionally smooth, and while the frictionless holds are easy on the skin, the thrutchy movement makes for a tough arm workout. More importantly, the River Boulders are a great place to hang out, have a swim, and heckle passing kayakers on a warm summer afternoon. I haven't included a map or problem descriptions for this low-key spot, so enjoy picking around the jumble of rocks in search of your own classics. The stone is generally very clean, and doesn't require much brushing, but bring along several pads as many of the landings are rocky.

Approach: To find the River Boulders, drive west on Reiter Road 1.1 miles past the Index Town Wall parking to a small lefthand pullout, an overgrown access road easily identified by two large concrete blocks placed to impede vehicle entry. Park well off the road and follow the steep trail down to the railroad tracks. Walk west along the tracks for roughly ten minutes until the boulders become apparent on the left. Several trails lead downhill from this point on; pick one and begin your explorations! Alternatively, park another 100 yards west in front of the white gate signed as "Forks of the Sky State Park." Follow the old road down to the tracks and walk several more minutes until the boulders can be seen at water's edge.

Shrine at Index Camp 5
Photo: Brian Sweeney

4 · Other Areas

Cole Allen climbs The Token (V7) beside the blue waters of Lake Serene

OTHER AREAS

The title of this book is somewhat of a misnomer—Central Washington is in fact home to many more amazing bouldering areas than mentioned, and probably many more than we'll ever even find. Here are a few tips to get you started on some 'extended explorations.'

LAKE SERENE

Across the Skykomish Valley from the town of Index, the clear blue waters of Lake Serene lie below the steep 1,000 foot east face of Mt. Index. This picturesque but popular lake boasts fantastic bouldering on unique stone, which seems to be some blend of basalt. The hike is rough, but not nearly as long as those to the lower Alpine Lakes, and the boulders offer a good deal of steep, featured faces. As an added plus, camping is permitted outside of a quarter-mile radius of the lake, meaning the hike can be split between two days without the hard-to-procure wilderness permits required in the Alpine Lakes.

Lake Serene is reached from the Bridalveil Falls trailhead on Mt. Index Road. From Rt. 2, turn right onto Mt. Index Rd. just west of the narrow Skykomish bridge, roughly a mile west of the turn to Index. Turn immediately right into the trailhead parking lot, where parking requires a Northwest Forest Pass. The trail follows old logging roads before beginning the steep climb past the falls to the lake, a total trip of three or so steep miles. Information for this popular hike can be found via the internet and in several hiking guidebooks.

STEVEN'S PASS

The steep mountainside across from the west side of Stevens' Pass summit is Skyline Ridge, home to a large talus field housing much bouldering potential. The arduous hike is a bit of a deterrent, however, and the area hasn't seen many visits. To reach Skyline Ridge, follow the Ramone Rock trail from the north side of the summit to the top of the ridge, traversing to the west to reach the wide, gentle basin of bluish boulders. Don't get suckered in by the direct approach visible from Rt. 2—I've hiked to these boulders from the Old Cascade Highway, and I won't ever make that mistake again.

A bit of other bouldering can be found on the east side of Steven's Pass, in the low-lying jumble of rocks just east of Yodelin Place, as well as FS 6700. The latter road, signed as Smithbrook, eventually circumvents Rock Mountain and follows Rainy Creek to the western end of Lake Wenatchee. A small cluster of boulders can be found 1.1 miles from Rt. 2, but the real bounty lies hidden somewhere along Rainy Creek.

ALPINE LAKES

For many climbers and non-climbers alike, Leavenworth's Icicle Canyon is one thing: the gateway to the beautiful Alpine Lakes Wilderness. Comparable in feel to the granite wonderland of California's High Sierras, the Alpine Lakes are home to a mind-boggling amount of beautiful white granite. Though many of the higher lakes and peaks are best reserved for a hike or ambitious climbing outing, several of the lower lakes are worth hauling a crash pad to. Nada Lake, Lake Colchuck, and to a smaller extent, Lake Stewart are all surrounded by pristine granite boulders within a few hours

OTHER AREAS

and several thousand vertical feet of your vehicle. But be warned, this is definitely "off the beaten path" bouldering (though the hoards of backpackers sort of betray this description). You'll be doing some hiking for your climbing, and it's definitely not the Happy Boulders; the features are sparse and the emphasis lies more on the scenery and remote atmosphere. This is true alpine bouldering—talus landings, great big boulders, and perfect stone are all the norm.

For Nada Lake, park at the Snow Creek Trailhead 4.1 miles from Icicle Junction, fill out a day pass, and hike roughly six miles up many switchbacks and pleasant straightaways to the lake. For Lakes Colchuck and Stewart, turn left off of Icicle Road onto Eightmile Road, 8.3 miles from Icicle Junction, and follow it to the Colchuck/Stewart Trailhead at the end. After filling out your Forest Service day pass, hike roughly two miles to the trail junction. Lake Stewart lies several mellow miles ahead, while the trail to Lake Colchuck departs to the left, climbing several steep miles to this deep blue lake below the granite spires of the Dragontail Formation. Stop by the Forest Service Ranger Station in Leavenworth for maps and information, or check out Ira Spring and Harvey Manning's classic *100 Hikes in Washington's Alpine Lakes Wilderness* for quirky choose-your-own-adventure style directions and a dose of old-school environmental ethics.

Boulders in the talus above Nada Lake

OTHER AREAS

ABOUT THE AUTHOR

Kelly Sheridan began climbing on the schist cliffs of Rumney, New Hampshire as a student at Dartmouth College. A Washington resident for the last few years, Kelly found himself instantly drawn to the rocky hillsides and beautiful granite boulders of Leavenworth's mountains. ***Central Washington Bouldering*** is Kelly's first guide. It is the product of his desire to share the joys of his climbing experience here in Washington, and to further the pursuit of this mad game by providing accurate route information alongside fun descriptions and inspiring images. You'll find Kelly climbing in any of the fine areas covered in this guide, or developing new spots in the Cascade Range during frequent excursions from his new home in Seattle.

OUR ADVERTISERS ROCK!

Five.Ten	Back Cover
La Sportiva	11
Urban Climber	213
Der Sportsman	49
The Gingerbread Factory	37
Stealth Rubber	113
Metolius	4
Feathered Friends	15
Revolution	187
Access Fund	114

INDEX OF AREAS, BOULDERS AND PROBLEMS

INDEX

Symbols

14 Years V7 146
1999 V2 68
2001 V4 68
420 Slab V0 94

A

Abandon Ship (Project) 164
Abstraction V0 58
Ace V4 107
Against The Wall V1+ 85
Aggressive Reject V9 129
Air Boredom V0- 202
Air Is Air V0 161
Alcove Center V4 57
Alcove Left V3 57
Alcove Right V3 56
Alfalfa or Spanky? V5 57
Alpine Cow V0- 130
Alpine Feel V0 41
ALPINE LAKES 216
The Ampitheater V4 46
Andy's Arête V5 161
Angelina Jolie (Project) 94
Anorexia V4 141
ANSWER MAN 74
Answer Man V6 74
Appeasing The Gods V9 206
The Argument V8 194
Aries: God of War V8 189
Arrested Development V3 60
Atomic Energy V9 71
Atomic Hole V4 71

B

Backdoor Ass Attack V7 60
The Backscratcher V6 151
The Backstroke V2 130
Bad Moon Rising V2 64
Balance Slap V4 152
Ballet V3 123
Bambi V9 186
Bam V2 149
Bananas V8 64
Band of Gypsies V0+ 97
Bangladore Torpedo V8 150
The Barista V1 149
Barnacles V1 41
The Barn Door V4 161
The Bathtub V1 176
BATMAN 77

Batman V8 77
THE BEACH 128, 132
Beached Whale V2 132
BEACH AREA 132
Beach Arête V2 134
THE BEACH BOULDER 175
BEACH PARKING 126
Beach Slab V1 132
Beam Me Up V2 197
Bearded Lady V0 198
Bearly V0 74
Bear Hug V4 74
Beckey's Problem V7 122
Bedroom Bully V8/9 61
Ben Carney's Bowling Balls V5 94
Bertha V0 108
Between The Legs V6 136
Big Baby V1+ 202
Big Booty Bitch Slap V10 151
Blurred Vision V5 163
BMOC V2 202
Bob's Balls V2 186
Bofunk V2 130
Bole Weevil V2 53
Bombs Away V7 68
The Bone Collector V6 122
Bottlecap Banshee V5 189
Bowled Over V3 101
Bowser Crack V1 206
Bowser V3 83
Boxcar Arête V8 212
Boxers V0 101
Box Seats V0- 200
Brass Balls V5 194
The Brawl V1 87
Breadline V0+ 60
Breakfast at Sunrise V3 196
Brickwork V0 131
Briefs V3 101
BSE V3 160
Bubbleslab V4 138
Bubbles V0- 149
Buddy Miles V3 97
Bulldozer V2 196
Bullwinkle V0 129
Buquah V6 176
Bushmen V4 42
Busted V3/4 110
Busted V8 62
The Button V3 200
Butt Surfing V1 85

C

The Campus Problem V0+ 85
THE CAMP SERENE BOULDER 173

Carlisle V2+ 107
THE CARNIVAL BOULDERS 84
Castle Run (In 12 Parsecs) V0 158
The Catcher V0 200
The Cattleguard Arête V8 161
Cattleguard Dyno V8 161
Cattle Terrace V1 160
Caught Red-Handed V4 67
Caveman Cole V9 148
Cellar Door V3 32
Chalksucker V10 118
Chemicals V4 194
Chicken Man V8 149
China Cat V2 108
Chocolate V3 203
Chopsticks V2 203
Chunky V4 56
Cinderella Boy V4 123
Claim Jumper V4 137
CLAMSHELL CAVE 50
The Classic V2 102
Claustrophobia V4 74
THE CLEARCUT 182
Cleaver Crack V1 53
Clef Crack V0 190
Clipped Wings V0 138
Clod-Hopper V2 64
The Coffee Cup V10 64
Cole's Campus V8 71
Cole's Corner V8/9 102
Cole's Dyno V8 55
Cole's Jump V7 63
Concavity V0 60
The Container V1 188
Contra V3 205
Cool Down V0- 32
The Corner V2 68
Cornucopia V2 52
THE COTTON PONY 76
The Cotton Pony Low V12 77
The Cotton Pony V11 77
Cowardly Lion V0 62
Cow Jumped Over The Moon V1 161
Cracked Out V1 91
Crackulation V1 196
The Crack V0- 101
The Crack V2 42
Cramps V2 146
Crank V1 46
Crimp, Crimp, Slap, Throw V4 53
Crimpsqueak V8 48
Crimpterbator V7 198
The Crimp V5 42
Crispy Duck V7 85
The Cro-Magnon V6 64
Cruise Control V6 62

219

INDEX OF AREAS, BOULDERS AND PROBLEMS

The Crystal Method V3 131
Cube Crack V2 52
Cube Traverse V0 53
The Cube V1+ 52
Cubicle Gangster V0 102
Cud Crack V0+ 160
Curtis Suave V5 64

D

The Dagger V3 103
Damian's Thoughts V7 143
Dangle V7 63
Danny Devito V7 186
Dan Akroyd V0 87
Dark Days V2 151
Dark Hollow V6 107
Darth Maul V4 157
Darth Vader V10 158
Dave's Problem V9 189
David Bowie V3 121
Deal V2 108
Death to Rednecks V2 64
The Desert Of The Real (project) 165
Devastation V2 196
Deviled V2 93
Devil Sticks V5 190
The Devonian Fish V0 148
The Dildo V3 94
Dingleberry Junction V0 101
Dirty Dude V10 66
Dirty Harry V1+ 97
The Dish V1 42
Divided Sky V3 113
Dog Log V2 48
Dog Named Rehab V4 76
The Doja V7 196
Donkey Kong V4 83
Dookie's Pinchfest V8 194
Double Vision V4 164
Dr. Doom V2 42
Dr. Mario V8 203
Dredge V1 62
THE DRIFTWOOD BOULDER 138
Driftwood V2 139
The Drill Sargeant V8 61
Droppin' the Kirschbaum 67
Drugstore Cowboy V4 41
Duck Hunt V0 205
Dukkha V3 198
Dutty Rock V1 87
Dyno 101 V3 134

E

Easy One V0 67
Easy Two V0 67
Ebriosity V11 180
EGG ROCK 106
Eight Bit Slab V2 205
Elfen Magic V1 53
El Navigante V3 196
Emperor's Lightning V7 158
Epoxy Flake V10 110
The Equinox V10 190
Etna Mantel V3 94
Evil Petting Zoo V4 129
Ex-Pat Scotsman V0 83
The Executioner V5 127

F

F*ck The Crystal V3 131
Faht V0 113
Fairly Desperate V4 161
Fat Lip V2 56
Fat Lip V3 74
Fedge V2 62
Feelin' Irie V4 196
Feelin' Sappy V2 86
Feel the Pinch V4 62
Fen Fin V0+ 86
Fern Crack V3 196
The Ferret V3 86
Fiend it Like Crack V3+ 62
Finished Product V9 141
The Fin Within V6 190
The Fin V2 130
The Fin V7 57
Firebelly V7 56
The Firefly V1 48
The Five Star Arête V6 179
THE FIVE STAR BOULDER 178
The Five Star Lip V2 179
The Five Star Warmup V2 180
The Flake V4 44
Flex V1 131
Float On V2 194
Flotsam V1 132
Flounder V2 41
Flower V2 186
The Footless Traverse V5 152
THE FOREST 192
FORESTLAND 58
Fountain Blues V0 130
Four Eyes V2 206
Frequent Fryer V2 196
THE FRIDGE BOULDER 32
Fridge Center V4 33
Fridge Door V2 33

Fridge Left V8 33
Fridge Right V4 33
Fridge Slab V0 33
Full Metal Hairbrush V3 164
Funiculi Funicula V0- 107
Funny and Cheap V4 64
Funpuppet V9 194
Fun House Stairway V1+ 55
FUZZ WALL 109

G

Gandalf V2 53
Gatorade Bowling Balls V4 94
Gaze of the Grasshopper V4 127
German Acres V0+ 80
Get Shorty V0- 130
Get Up, Stand Up V5 131
Giant Man V4 86
Girlfunk V8 123
Glen's Problem V6 186
Goat Boy V7 149
Goicoechea V9 131
Golden Girls V2 198
Gold Bar 167
Goodnight Moon V8 160
The Goods V4 53
Gooseneck V1 138
Go Baby! V6 103
Gradisfaction V2 80
Grain Brain V3 86
Greed V2 53
Green Eggs and Ham V0 122
Green Lung (project) 83
Green Padded Ass V6 180
Green Tea V4 122
Ground Zero V8 179
Guano Slap V2 82
GZA V6 121

H

Hagakuri V8 203
Hairy Spotter V5 41
Hamburger Train V5 197
Hanta Man V9 44
Han Solo's Lightsaber Tournament V5 127
Han Solo V3 157
Hara-Kiri V5 108
Hate Monger V3 146
Haunted Shack V2 110
Head and Shoulders V4 141
Hearthstone V0 62
Heeler V2 85
Heel Hook Center V2 148
Heel Hook Left V1+ 148

220

INDEX OF AREAS, BOULDERS AND PROBLEMS

Heel Hook Right V2+ 148
Heir Apparent V0 42
Hemp V3 76
The Hesitatator V2 55
The Hobbit V2 53
The Hobo V0 127
The Hole V6 44
Hoofin' It V0 160
THE HOOK CREEK BOULDER 70
The Hopeful V7 188
Hormonal Monkey V8 150
Hot Stepper V1 202
The Hourglass V7 102
THE HUECO CRIMPER 137
The Hueco Crimper V6 137
The Hueco Route V1 41

I

THE ICEHOUSE 72
The Icehouse V4 72
Ice Age V6 74
Ice Grip V4 74
Icicle Canyon 29
The Icicle V3 74
IHOP V1 136
INDEX 209
INDEX LOWER TOWN WALL 211
Insanity Later V2 174
Inserene V0- 174
IS V7 76
It's Doo-Doo, Baby V3 203
I ♥ Jerry Garcia (project) 107
I ♥ Jugs V2 102
I Know, Dyno! V9 76

J

J-High V7 176
Jabba The Slab V0 158
Jack of Spades V6 150
Jamrock V10 206
Jazz Arete (Project) 121
Jennifer Connoloy V3 121
JENNY CRAIG 140
Jenny Craig VBlahblahblah 141
Jetsam V0 132
The Jib V8 42
Joe's Nose V5 113
Joel's Jump Start V8 57
Joel's Problem V7 186
Joel's Traverse V6 149
Jolly Roger V2 164
Jumper V3 130
Jumping Spiders V4 33

K

Kama Sutra V9 198
The Kiddie Pool V1 46
Kim + Randy (Project) 140
King Kong V6 83
The Kiwi V5/6 137
Kobe Tai V8 63
Kombucha Sit V9 180
Kombucha V7 180

L

The Labyrinth 120
The Ladder Project 76
LAKE SERENE 216
The Lamb V3 41
The Layback V1 184
The Layman V5 136
Lead Pants V3 150
The Leap of Faith V4 176
Leavenworth 21
Ledges V0 129
The Lefty V7 96
Lichen' It V3 203
Lighten Up V9 198
Link V0- 206
Lip Gloss V2 148
Little Bear V5 74
LITTLE BRIDGE CREEK WALL 96
Little One V2 93
The Lizard V5 33
The Lobster V4 118
Lock and Load V4 58
Lock and Pop V3 58
The Logmonster V5 141
THE LONELY FISH 66
The Lonely Fish V9 66
Long John Silver V1 165
Lovage V3 63
Lowe Rider V1 149
Lowpers V3 57
Luigi V1 205

M

THE MACHINE GUN 97
Machine Gun Funk V2 97
Madvillian V2 42
Mad Max V7 82
MAD MEADOWS 40
Marathon Man V1 58
Mario Kart V0- 205
Max Attacks V3 80
Maybe V4 74
Metroid Prime V7 205
Mickey V0 148

Midnight Lichen V4 203
Millennium Mantel V1 68
The Millennium Traverse V8 68
Mine V2/3 85
Minnie V1 148
Missin' Nugget V2 137
The Mole V4 125
Moondog V0 64
Moonlight Mile V2 184
Moon of Endor V2 158
Mossline V1 129
MOUNTAIN HOME ROAD BOULDERS 153
Mr. Joel's Wild Ride V8/9 86
Mr. Leftist V6 93
Ms. Pac-Man V3 90
Musashi V9 108
Musk V9 57

N

Neanderthal V1 163
Nice Men V2 157
Nobody's Watching V5 37
Nosebleed V7 80
Nosy V1 130
No Chaser V5 190
No Pain No Gain V5 44
No Pitons Here V0 148
Nuthin' V4 93

O

Obesity Direct V8 184
Obesity V7 184
Obi-Wan V9 157
Occum's Razor V5 41
Oceanfront V1 149
The Octopus V3 44
The Octopus V7 50
Oditee V2 91
Off-Kilter V0 130
Offa' My Cloud V0 184
Off The Couch V7 102
One-Mover V2 80
One Stupid Problem V6 127
One Summer V5 60
Ouchies V7 56
Over Easy V0 93
Over Myself V1 87

P

Pac-Man V3 90
Padmi Trainer V1 157
Pair of Deuces V1 164
Palm Down V9 163

221

INDEX OF AREAS, BOULDERS AND PROBLEMS

THE PASTURE 159
Peach Fuzz V0 110
The Peephole V10 41
The Pee Problem V1 39
Pentaphobia V5 50
Percolator V1 149
The Phatness V2 56
The Physical V4 63
Piano Trainer V2 163
The Pickle V3 87
Pillow Talk V0+ 202
PIMPSQUEAK AREA 46
Pimpsqueak V9 48
THE PITLESS AVOCADO 135
The Pitless Avocado V5 136
Pizzaface V1+ 90
Playback V1 52
Played Like A Poop Butt V0+ 102
Pocket Rocket V3 41
The Pocket V4 42
Pod Racer V1 150
Pod Racer V1+ 110
Pokin' The Pope V0 125
Polish Bob's Slab V0 163
The Pony Ride V4 77
Positive Vibrations (project) 186
The Practitioner V12 64
Premium Coffee V7 149
Presto Change-O V3 130
THE PRETTY BOULDERS 88
Pretty Boy V7 90
Pretty Burly V4 91
Pretty Easy V0- 90
Pretty Girl V3 90
Pretty Hard (Project) 90
Pretty Hate Machine V8 91
Pretty Sweet V1+ 91
Pretty Woman V5 90
The Prey V0 148
The Prism V9 102
Private Pile V2 82
Probletunity V2 163
Pruning Shears V1 42
The Pumphouse V2 37
Punk Ass Kid V6 165

Q

Que Luna V6 184

R

Raging Bull V7 151
Raging Cow V1 150
The Rail V0 55
The Rail V3 42
Rainbow V1 57

The Ram V11/12 42
THE RANGE BOULDERS 124
Raptorman V3 94
THE RAT CREEK BOULDERS 78
Raven V9 146
The Real Thing V4 60
Red Rover V8 181
Regatta de Blanc V0+ 202
Resonation V6 194
Resurrection V8 103
Rex Flex V3 76
The Rib V4 87
Rice Bowl V1+ 205
Rich's Non-Star-Wars-Named Climb V3 158
Rick Moranis V0- 87
Rider V0 108
Right Angles V8 82
The Ripple Effect V1 149
THE RIVER BOULDERS 214
Road to Zion Low V9 208
Road To Zion V5 208
Rocksteadeasy V3 194
Rocks For Jocks V1 134
Rocky V2/3 129
Ross Bongo V9 179
Royal Flush V2 151
Rubick's Arête V0 52
The Rubik's Cube V9 190
Flex The Matrix V6 42
The Rudder V1 42
Rudy V4 57
The Ruminator V6 63
Runner V0 58
Ryan's Other Problem V7 173
The RZA V6 124

S

Sagittarius V4 189
The Sail V9 41
Salem Slab V0 136
The Samurai V4 203
THE SANCTUARY 200
Sanctuary Crack V0 206
Sassy Chipmunk V3 80
The Savage Act V5 130
The Scarecrow V1 62
Schisthead V2 148
The Scoop V2 44
The Scorpion V2 125
Scotty V0 197
Scrambled Eggs V8 93
Scram V2 53
Screaming Barfies V3 190
Scumsucker V6 198
Seams Dangerous V6 112

Seam of Pain V5 103
Sega V3 83
The Segment V0 52
Serenity Now V5 173
Seussology V3 122
Shallow V1 52
The Sheath V4 104
The Shield V7 60
Ship of Fools V1 164
Shiver Me Timbers V1 164
Shock and Awe V3+ 146
Shoeless Joe V0 165
Shortstop V1+ 200
Shrimpers V3 202
The 'Shroom V4 190
Silly with an S V0 62
Silver Slippers V3 198
Sine of the Times V5 123
Sinistricity V5 190
Sitting Bull V3 150
Size Wise V5 48
Skittles V3 136
The Skuke V3 142
Slab Cow V1 160
Slap and Dangle V3 146
Slaughterhouse V5 160
THE SLEEPING LADY 38
Sleeping Lady Extension V2 39
The Sleeping Lady V2 39
Sleeve Ace V3 151
Slice of Cake V3 55
Slice of Pie V2 57
Slice of Tea V3 52
Slickfoot Holiday V1 62
Slickfoot Sanctuary V0- 206
Slingblade V6 136
The Slip 'N' Slide V2 176
The Slot Problem V4 112
Smokestack Lightnin' V2 108
Snack Attack V0 188
Snake Eyes (project) 146
The Soap Dish V1 124
Sobriosity V6 181
Sofa King V0 102
Solar Arête V4 136
Sore Thumb V4 206
Sound Asleep V1+ 39
THE SOUTH SEAS 162
South Seas Arête V0+ 165
So it Seams V2 203
Spanish Traverse V2/3 112
SPAN MAN 111
Span Man V10 111
Spongebob Squarepad V3 44
Spooner V0 130
Squarepusher V3 41

INDEX OF AREAS, BOULDERS AND PROBLEMS

The Squatter V3 149
Squeezer V3 58
The Stairway V0+ 102
STARFOX 34
Starfox V6 34
THE STAR WARS BOULDER 156
The Stem V0 86
Stepping Razor V2 200
STEVEN'S PASS 216
Stinger V2 124
The Stinker V2 189
Stinkfoot V2 122
STRAIGHTAWAY BOULDERS 72
Straight Shot V0+ 93
Streambed Mantel V0+ 202
Summer Solstice V3 190
Sumthin' V0 93
Sunny and Steep V2 64
Sunshine Daydream V4 107
The Sutra V4 203
Swamp Thing V0+ 129
Sweenis V3 71
SWIFTWATER 144
Swordfish V4 41
THE SWORD BOULDERS 100
The Sword Toprope 5.13 104
The Sword V3 103

T

The Ta-Ta Box V10 197
Tahitian Moon V0 64
The Taint V0- 101
Taller V5 74
Tall Boy V5 74
Tall Cool White One V2 184
Tall People Suck V4 163
Tampax Arête V4 77
Tap V1+ 123
Tectonic Slab V0 184
Television V4 163
Tentacles V0 150
Terminal Traverse V2 52
Terrapin Station V0+ 108
The Terrible V7 130
Tetris V1 203
THAT DEMON 142
That Demon V5 142
Them Antles V1 194
Therête V0 57
The Africa Project (Project) 123
The Hardest Problem In The Universe
         V0- 130
Thirty Seconds V4 46
Three-Armed Baby V4 127
Throwin' The Hoolihan V4 77
Thumper V3 165

TIN MAN 112
Tin Man V6 112
Tom Fern V7 196
Tonya Harding V5 112
Top Foot on the Good Foot V1 131
THE TORTURE CHAMBER 118
Toto V4 62
Track and Field V1+ 208
The Transverse V1 148
The Trapeze V4 198
Treeverse V3 203
Tree Crack V1 55
The Tree Problem V8 104
Tron V0 52
The Tube V0 123
TUMWATER CANYON 115
Tweaker V4 129
Tweedle Dee V0- 46
Tweedle Dum V0 46
Twisted Stone V3 94
TWISTED TREE 92
Twisted V10 190

U

U2 V3 131
Ugly Boy V1 91
The Undercling V5 44
Under the Bleachers V5 53
Unholy V5 189
Unobvious V2/3 149
Unorthodox, But Effective V2 203

V

V13s Don't Have Kneebars V1 48
Vaseline V4 125
Veltex V6 129
Vexation of Spirit V5 208
The Virgin V8/9 143
The Vision V2 163

W

Walk The Line V3 129
Walk The Plank V2 164
Wario V0 83
The Warm-Up Slab V0 194
War of God V8 189
WAS 74
Washed Up V0+ 124
WAS V8 76
Water Torture V4 118
Water V6 188
The Wave V1 132
Weather Report V3 107
Weird One V1 91

The Wheel of Dharma V9 194
The Whirlpool V9 141
The White Arête V5 82
White Fang V3 141
White Sands V2 102
The White Traverse V7 80
Who Nose V7 197
Why? V2 56
Wildberry Blast V0 190
Winterbottom Arête V3 46
With A Twist V1 93
The Wizard V2/3 102
Wonka V0+ 188
Wookie Crack V1 158
Wooly Mammoth V0 42
The Wrestler V0+ 196

X

XI V0 102
X2 V2 102

Y

Yeti V6 127
Yoda V9 157
The Yosemite Highball V3 82
YOUR FRIENDS ARE WATCH-
         ING 36

Z

The Zebra V4 123
Zorro V8 103

Sharp End Book Titles

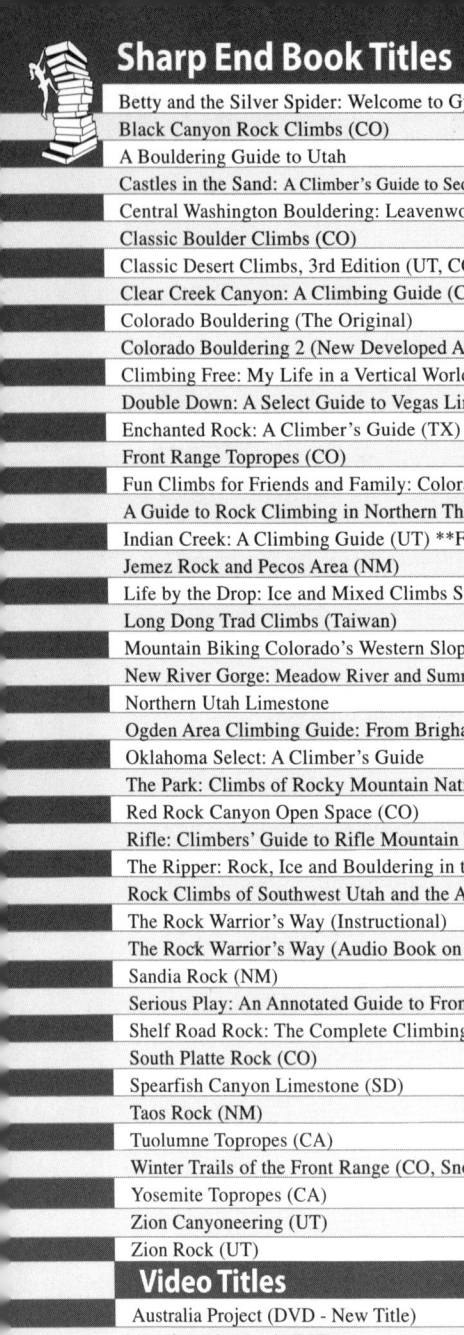

Title	Price
Betty and the Silver Spider: Welcome to Gym Climbing (Instructional)	$12.95
Black Canyon Rock Climbs (CO)	$28.00
A Bouldering Guide to Utah	$34.95
Castles in the Sand: A Climber's Guide to Sedona and Oak Creek Canyon (AZ)	$24.95
Central Washington Bouldering: Leavenworth and Gold Bar (WA)	$25.00
Classic Boulder Climbs (CO)	$9.95
Classic Desert Climbs, 3rd Edition (UT, CO)	$15.95
Clear Creek Canyon: A Climbing Guide (CO)	TBA
Colorado Bouldering (The Original)	$29.95
Colorado Bouldering 2 (New Developed Areas and Problems)	$28.00
Climbing Free: My Life in a Vertical World Lynn Hill (Hard/Soft Cover-Autographed!)	$24.95/$15.95
Double Down: A Select Guide to Vegas Limestone and Sandstone (NV)	$14.00
Enchanted Rock: A Climber's Guide (TX)	$16.95
Front Range Topropes (CO)	$25.00
Fun Climbs for Friends and Family: Colorado Edition	$16.95
A Guide to Rock Climbing in Northern Thailand	$24.95
Indian Creek: A Climbing Guide (UT) **Full Color**	$32.95
Jemez Rock and Pecos Area (NM)	$28.00
Life by the Drop: Ice and Mixed Climbs Surrounding CO's San Luis Valley	$14.00
Long Dong Trad Climbs (Taiwan)	$28.00
Mountain Biking Colorado's Western Slope (CO)	$9.95
New River Gorge: Meadow River and Summersville Lake Climbing Guide (WV)	$29.95
Northern Utah Limestone	$16.95
Ogden Area Climbing Guide: From Brigham City to Echo Canyon (UT)	$19.95
Oklahoma Select: A Climber's Guide	$16.95
The Park: Climbs of Rocky Mountain National Park (CO)	$9.95
Red Rock Canyon Open Space (CO)	$9.95
Rifle: Climbers' Guide to Rifle Mountain Park (CO)	$7.95
The Ripper: Rock, Ice and Bouldering in the Wet Mountains near Pueblo, CO	$14.00
Rock Climbs of Southwest Utah and the Arizona Strip, 2nd Edition **Full Color**	$32.95
The Rock Warrior's Way (Instructional)	$18.95
The Rock Warrior's Way (Audio Book on CD)	$29.95
Sandia Rock (NM)	$14.95
Serious Play: An Annotated Guide to Front Range Trad Classics 5.2-5.9 (CO)	$18.00
Shelf Road Rock: The Complete Climbing Reference (CO)	$28.00
South Platte Rock (CO)	$12.95
Spearfish Canyon Limestone (SD)	$14.95
Taos Rock (NM)	$19.95
Tuolumne Topropes (CA)	$10.95
Winter Trails of the Front Range (CO, Snowshoe and XC Ski)	$7.95
Yosemite Topropes (CA)	$8.95
Zion Canyoneering (UT)	$19.95
Zion Rock (UT)	$14.00

Video Titles

Title	Price
Australia Project (DVD - New Title)	$30.00
Comfortably Numb (DVD)	$29.95
A Day in the Life: 5 Women Who Climb (DVD)	$24.95
First Ascent (New Title, You Will LOVE it.)	$30.00
Fitlife Pilates (VHS)	$15.00
Friction Addiction (VHS and DVD)	$30.00
Free Climbing the Nose (Lynn Hill, VHS)	$14.95
Front Range Freaks (VHS and DVD)	$30.00
Inertia 1 & 2 (DVD)	$24.95
Just Tie It (Instructional, DVD)	$12.95
Karma (DVD)	$30.00
Red River Ruckus (DVD)	$29.95
Return2Sender (DVD)	$30.00
Soul Cal (DVD)	$29.98
Yoga for Climbers (DVD)	$22.95